The Cultural Work

Corinna Campbell

THE CULTURAL WORK

Maroon Performance in

Paramaribo, Suriname

Wesleyan University Press   Middletown, Connecticut

Wesleyan University Press
Middletown CT 06459
www.wesleyan.edu/wespress
© 2020 Corinna Campbell
Manufactured in the United States of America
Typeset in Minion Pro by Nord Compo

Audio tracks are available at
https://www.wesleyan.edu/wespress/cultural-work.

Library of Congress Cataloging-in-Publication Data
available upon request

Hardcover ISBN: 978-0-8195-7954-6
Paperback ISBN: 978-0-8195-7955-3
Ebook ISBN: 978-0-8195-7956-0

5   4   3   2   1

CONTENTS

ACKNOWLEDGMENTS

This book was made possible, first and foremost, by the cultural groups whose members have allowed me to witness and participate in their rehearsals and performances over the years. In particular, I am indebted to the cultural groups Kifoko, Saisa, and Fiamba for allowing me to be a part of their communities during the most intensive stage of my research, during 2008–9. I could not have done this research without the support and patience of the leaders of each group—Eddy Lante and Saiwini "Maria" Dewinie from Kifoko, Eduard Fonkel and Dansi Waterberg from Saisa, and Clifton Asongo from Fiamba. Founding members and veteran performers whose input and assistance was crucial to the success of this project include André Mosis, Georgio Mosis, José Tojo, Louise Wondel, and Erwin Tolin Alexander.

Membership in each group fluctuated during my research, but the following regularly participating members contributed profoundly to my understanding of these groups and the broader social and expressive conversations in which they were involved, both in rehearsals and outside of them: from Kifoko, Lucia Alankoi, Lucia Pinas, Carmen Ajerie, Vera Pansa, Irma Dabenta, Graciella Dewinie, Herman Tojo, Minio Tojo, Liento Day, Marguerite Deel, Martha Adraai, and John Binta; from Saisa, Delia Waterberg, Jill Trisie, Mariska Emanuels, Jolisa Fonkel, Debora Fonkel, Nicholas Banjo, Carlos Pinas, Silvana Pinas, Benny Fonkel, Cheke Pinas, and Clyde Pinas; from Fiamba, Mano Deel, Errel van Dijk, Ita Saint-Elle, Sandrine Akombe, Sheryl Tesa, Faizel Pinas, Sizwe "Borsu" Amoinie, Hugo "Man" Abani, Charly Abisoina, Abby, Sayenne, and Berto. I also want to acknowledge the work of other Maroon cultural groups in and beyond Paramaribo—the groups that existed prior to my arrival, including Denku and Maswa, as well as Tangiba, Oséle, and Wenoeza, each of which contributed to the thriving performance scene I encountered during my research in 2006–17.

In particular, my thanks to Clyde Pinas and Bernice Kantenberg for acting as liaisons between me and Oséle, and Dyaga Plein for acting as a liaison between me and Tangiba.

Since my earliest visits to Suriname and French Guiana, Max Bree has been a valued teacher, confidant, and companion. It was with his help that I made my biggest strides in learning the Okanisi language and through him that I met innumerable contacts who helped this research take shape. Additional thanks are owed to his family and the members of the *aleke* band Fondering, who showed me kindness and compassion at every turn. Guno "Boike" Hooglied, Ine Apapoe, and Alida Neslo have inspired me through their educational efforts and scholarly work, and at the same time they have become trusted confidants and treasured friends.

During my first visit to French Guiana as a graduate student, Diane Vernon helped me with crucial introductions and offered support as I got my bearings. My humble thanks go to Kenneth Bilby, who has been so generous with his re-sources, conversation, and expertise over the many years that this research has taken shape. Additional thanks go to the many individuals who shared with me their expertise and insight. The following people have been especially influential: Salomon Emanuels, Cyriel Eersteling, Hillary de Bruin, Marlene Lie A Ling, Paul Tjon Sie Fat, Sharda Ganga, Kries Ramkhelawan, Joekoe "Nano" Delano, Wilgo Baarn, Henk Tjon, Ernie Wolf, Percy Oliviera, André Pakosie, Raymond Williams, Ifna Vrede, Thomas Polimé, Paul Abena, and Herman Snijders.

I had the tremendous good fortune to have Ingrid Monson and Kay Kaufman Shelemay as mentors from graduate school through the present. Both offered valued perspectives, crucial guidance, and willing counsel as I completed my dis-sertation and as that research continued to grow into the present book. This work is shaped by their scholarship and the confidence they have in me. My thanks to Gini Gorlinski and Steven Cornelius, who advised me at the undergraduate and graduate levels, respectively. Each of them has shaped me profoundly as a researcher and a person. I have benefited from an overwhelming wealth of sup-port and guidance from teachers and mentors over the years. Of these, David Harnish, Jeremy Wallach, Michael Herzfeld, Tomie Hahn, Paul Berliner, and Deborah Foster have all been formative to my growth as a scholar.

Thanks to my scholar friends for their own intellectual pursuits that have offered such inspiration and their fantastically vibrant and varied personalities that I so treasure: my "G" cohort—Katherine In-Young Lee, Anna Zayaruznaya, and Ryan Bañagale—who saw me through the overwhelming early stages of this research; and to Cherie Ndaliko, David Kaminsky, Michael Heller, Meredith Schweig, Natalie Kirschstein, Patricia Tang, Sarah Morelli, Justin Patch, Marië Abe, Grete Viddal, Sheryl Kaskowitz, Marc Gidal, Munjuli Rahman, and Sharon Kivenko. Christina Simko's incisive editorial eye and willing conversation have seen this book to fruition. Further thanks go to Anicia Timberlake, Sharan Leventhal, Betsy Grossman, Stephen Pruitt, Tiffany Coolidge, Kat Jara, and (of course) Rocky and Lola for their enduring friendship.

Thank you to Wesleyan University Press for supporting and helping shape this book—in particular Suzanna Tamminen; series editors Deborah Wong, Jeremy Wallach, and Sherrie Tucker; my copy editor, Jeanne Ferris; and my external readers. Joanna Dee Das, Rashida Braggs, and Michelle Apatsos offered valued advice as the book was in its organizational stages. Kenneth Bilby, Sally Price, Richard Price, and Gregory Mitchell gave influential feedback on an earlier draft of this manuscript. Additional thanks go to my colleagues at Williams College—in particular the members of the Music Department and Krista Birch at the Oakley Center—for their support and assistance.

Portions of my research were funded by Harvard University's Graduate School of Arts and Sciences, as well as grants from the William Mitch Foundation (Harvard University), the Fulbright Council for International Exchange of Scholars, the David Rockefeller Center for Latin American Studies, Mellon Postdoctoral Dance Scholars, and the Oakley Center for the Humanities at Williams College. I am grateful to the following organizations in Suriname for their assistance and/ or access to resources: the Suriname Conservatory, Suriname's Directorate of Culture Studies, the Ministry of Culture, NAKS, ArtLab, Anton de Kom University, Peace Corps Suriname, and the US Embassy in Suriname.

My heartfelt thanks to the communities and individuals—too many to name— that have kept me afloat in more indirect ways: students; dance communities in Boston, Massachusetts, and Albany, New York; friends I've known for decades and newer networks and acquaintances.

Finally, I would like to thank my family for being there through it all. Above all to Mom and Dad, Bob and Yvette, Megan and Dickson, and Plover and Ira, thank you for your love and brilliance.

The Cultural Work

CHAPTER 1

Introduction

As the cultural group Kifoko's rehearsal neared its end, Max Bree showed up unexpectedly to watch. Some of the group members knew him personally, but everyone recognized him—he was a lead singer in the group Fondering, among the best-known bands in the locally popular *aleke* genre. Excited by this local celebrity's impromptu visit, the group took a short break to greet him. They invited him to join in what was left of the rehearsal—perhaps he could sing a song for them to dance to. Bree was dressed to go out, wearing a crisp white long-sleeved shirt (even though it was a warm day), sporting clothes with designer brand names and carefully chosen accessories. He respectfully declined their invitation, promising he would come back and join them some other day. One of the two group leaders, Saiwinie "Maria" Dewinie (who was indirectly related to Bree through marriage), approached him, giving him a hard look. The room quieted. Slowly, she reached for the cloth she had been using during rehearsal to mop the sweat from her body and held it out in front of her. In one controlled movement, eyes still locked on him, she wrung out the cloth. A thin but continuous stream of sweat formed a small puddle between them. Her defiant expression cracking into a grin, Dewinie responded in Pamaka, her native language, "Na wroko u wroko dja [it's work that we're doing here]."[1]

The room erupted in laughter, Dewinie's friends clapping her on the back as she sauntered away from Bree. It was a brilliant dramatic moment—playful, but with an unmistakable air of defiance and validation. Bree had opted out of the rehearsal, and Dewinie's gesture didn't change his mind, but in her actions she had a hand in defining what it was that he had declined. The puddle of sweat on the floor between them served as a physical testament to Dewinie's efforts, what had transpired in rehearsal, and what Bree had refused to engage in. She defined it in relationship to *wroko*—work.

In this context, work could have many meanings. Certainly, Dewinie drew attention to the fact that she had worked hard. In addition, she could have meant to imply that, just as Bree considered music his work and profession, the core members of Kifoko described their activities as more than a hobby or pastime. As a group leader, Dewinie was also giving younger members the benefit of her expertise and guidance—she was working as a member of Kifoko but also for Kifoko. Her gesture and reference to work played up the difference between her expended energy and Bree's choice to remain on the sidelines as a passive observer, apart from the group. But for all the ways in which her response established a challenge and a division, Dewinie's actions also indicated a connection. Bree was more than a guest; he was part of her family network and a known and admired musical personality, a performer in a popular genre that was also deeply tied to the expressive culture of the Maroons (descendents of self-emancipated slaves). To jibe and chastise him in this manner indicated a degree of intimacy and playful camaraderie. Kifoko members' cheers, chuckles, and friendly embraces left no doubt that Dewinie's response had found resonance, but as with so many other performative utterances, the moment passed without prompting (or demanding) any verbal clarification. The nature of the work may have been ambiguous, but Dewinie's affirmation of her own efforts and those of her fellow group members was abundantly clear.

This book is about the work of culture-representational performance—as labor, effort invested to achieve a given objective, a poetic practice, and an aesthetic object. It was work that Kifoko was doing before Bree's arrival—group members training their bodies to produce the right sounds and movements, aligning their actions in relationship to those of the other members, fine-tuning choreographic "works" that narrated stories and demonstrated technical skill. It is work they were doing for themselves and on themselves in preparation for paying gigs and for their communities. Cultural continuity is achieved through the deliberate efforts of individuals, and urban migrants (like the members of Kifoko) often work particularly hard to sustain cultural practices. The situation for Maroons in Paramaribo mirrors what Thomas Turino observed among migrants from the rural Peruvian highlands to Lima: "The maintenance of tradition may not be automatic or simply the result of unconscious habit in the rural district. Yet in Lima, community, identity, and 'traditional' practices must be even more actively and self-consciously *created*—a task made difficult by the size, diffuseness, dissonance, and varied nature of the social space" (1993, 194).

Culture-representational performance is also a vehicle through which performers and audiences can "work out" ideas and tensions that they face in the course of their lives, utilizing "a physical rhetoric or corporeal argumentation that attempts to activate audiences to attend to the complexities of daily life in terms of race, gender, spirituality, social relations, political power, aesthetics, and community life when we are often reluctant to do so" (George-Graves 2010, 3). I suggest that ambivalence—fundamental to the folkloric enterprise and magnified in this case by social circumstances particular to urban Maroons—enhances possibilities for social criticism for performers and audiences alike. Put differently, culture-representational performance emerges amid shifting priorities and anxieties concerning cultural transmission, commodification, and authorization. Performances that occur under these circumstances can engage discomfort or uncertainty (whether foregrounding these feelings or ameliorating them) as performers and audiences interact across various kinds of difference. As Bree and Dewinie demonstrated, this "working out" is not exclusive to formal performance: rehearsals likewise offer opportunities for articulations of individual and group identities in relation to various social pressures or objectives. Taken together, these many dimensions of work (the creation of composed "works," the ways in which rehearsal and performance constitute labor, a manner of working on the self, working to create and sustain communities, and "working out" points of social or ideological tension or ambiguity) stress dynamism and multivalence. In essence, to reckon with the full range of "cultural work" involved in culture-representational performance is to consider how abstract notions of "tradition" and "culture" can impact people's immediate circumstances, identifications, and relationships.

At the heart of this book are Kifoko, Saisa, and Fiamba—three collectives specializing in the music and dance traditions of the Maroons of Suriname and neighboring French Guiana. These groups are known by various names—cultural groups, dance groups, social-cultural associations, or *awasa* groups (awasa is the eastern Maroon dance genre that was a mainstay of their various repertoires), but here I refer to them as cultural groups, as this name is the broadest in scope and was among the most commonly used.[2] Beneath these groups' surface similarities lie disparate interpretations and applications of Maroon performance culture, motivated by an equally varied array of interests and aspirations. Though the groups may have performed many of the same genres, variations in the practice and interpretation of these genres created opportunities for their members to engage differently with one another and their broader networks. An in-depth consideration of their rehearsals and performances demonstrates the wide array of functions and meanings that culture-representational performance can have, while also highlighting interweaving pressures and interests that feature prominently in the lives of Maroons living in Paramaribo.

ABOUT THE MAROONS

The social, expressive, and economic work that Maroon cultural groups undertake in the twenty-first century is essentially linked to the forced labor of their ancestors, who were among the nearly 341,000 Africans shipped to Suriname as slaves from 1650 to 1825.[3] "Maroon" is a word used throughout the African Diaspora to refer to people who escaped from slavery and their descendants.[4] Derived from the Spanish word *cimarròn*, the term initially referred to domesticated cattle that had wandered off, and it was later applied to runaway slaves. Richard Price notes, "By the end of the 1530s, the word had taken on strong connotations of being 'fierce,' 'wild,' and 'unbroken,' and was used primarily to refer to African-American runaways" (1992). Under first British and subsequently Dutch jurisdiction,[5] Suriname's colonial economy was primarily invested in sugar and coffee. Historical records depict a colony distinctive in the high number of slaves per planter, the low life expectancy of slaves, and the barbarity of the punishments inflicted upon them.

In his *Narrative, of a Five-years' Expedition, Against the Revolted Negroes of Surinam . . . from the year 1772, to 1777* (1796), John Gabriel Stedman detailed the brutal punishments he witnessed being meted out to slaves and free Africans alike in Suriname (see figures 1.1 and 1.2). His *Narrative* is described by Richard Price and Sally Price as "one of the most detailed 'outsider's' descriptions ever written of life in an eighteenth-century slave plantation society" (Stedman 1992, xix). The accompanying engravings by William Blake, Francesco Bartolozzi, and others are among the most widely known and influential depictions of slavery conditions from this time.

Nonetheless, owing in large part to the dense and abundant rain forest south of the plantations, in Suriname escape efforts were uncommonly successful, resulting in the eventual formation of six distinct Maroon groups: the Saamaka, Matawai, and Kwinti in central Suriname and the Ndyuka (or Okanisi), Pamaka, and Aluku (or Boni) along Suriname's eastern border with French Guiana.[6] These initial runaways displayed uncompromising resolve, first in leaving the plantations knowing that brutal punishment awaited them should their escape prove

FIGURE 1.1 (left) Francesco Bartolozzi, "A Female Negro Slave, with a Weight chained to her Ancle [*sic*]." In punishment for not being able to complete her daily labor, ("to which she was by appearance unable," according to Stedman), the slave depicted here was sentenced to "200 lashes and for months to drag a chain of several yards in length, one end of which was locked to her ankle and at the other end of which was a weight of three score pounds or upward" (Stedman 1992, 15). Courtesy of Chapin Library, Williams College.

FIGURE 1.2 (right) William Blake, "The Execution of Breaking on the Rack." This image accompanies the story of Neptune, a free black who was condemned to death for murder. Stedman recounts: "He then begged that his head might be chopped off, but to no purpose. At last, seeing no end to his misery, he declared that though he had deserved death, he had not expected to die so many deaths." Stedman comments further, "Even so late as 1789, on October 30 and 31 (at Demerara), thirty-two wretches were executed, sixteen of whom in the above shocking manner" (Stedman, 1992, 285–86). Courtesy of Chapin Library, Williams College.

unsuccessful, and subsequently in traversing long distances in the unfamiliar and inhospitable rain forest where they sought refuge. Newly escaped slaves were aided by Amerindians they encountered in the rain forest, who proved instrumental in teaching them how to survive in these unfamiliar surroundings.

The magnitude of these Maroons' accomplishments and the force of will that brought their societies into existence are difficult to grasp fully. I experience this

FIGURE 1.3 Courtesy of Nations Online Project, https://www.nationsonline.org
/oneworld/map/suriname-political-map.htm.

Map of Suriname.

most acutely when traveling to Maroon settlements along the Lawa, Tapana-
honi, and Suriname Rivers—journeys for which the motorized canoe remains
the most common mode of transportation. On such journeys, watching miles
of dense rain forest vegetation slide past for hours and sometimes days at a

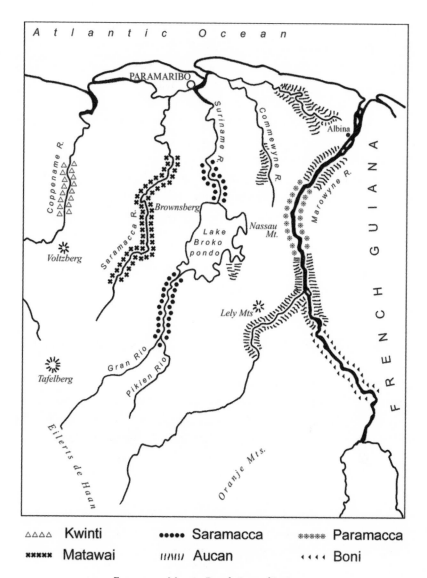

△△△△ Kwinti	••••• Saramacca	⁕⁕⁕⁕⁕ Paramacca
⁎⁎⁎⁎⁎ Matawai	⊔⊔⊔⊔ Aucan	◄◄◄◄ Boni

FIGURE 1.4 Maroon Populations of Suriname.
Illustration by H. Rypkema, Naturalis Biodiversity Center.

time, aided by robust outboard motors and experienced boatmen who have memorized the rivers' rapids and contours, it is hard not to be overwhelmed by the thought of the obstacles the first generations of Maroons faced in their escape, setting out into a vast and largely unfamiliar rain forest with hardly any resources to aid them, while trying to elude colonial campaigns committed to their death or recapture.

After their escape, the first generations of Maroons waged war on the Dutch colonists and plantation owners who pursued them, succeeding despite being outnumbered and dramatically outresourced. By the mid-eighteenth century, slaves were escaping in greater numbers, and their plantation raids posed a mounting threat to planters' profits. As colonists' costly expeditions to attack, recapture, and kill Maroons met with limited success, the colonial government began to sue for peace.[7] The first enduring peace treaty was signed between the Dutch and the Ndyuka Maroons in 1760, over a century before slavery was abolished in Suriname.[8] This treaty and subsequent settlements with the Saamaka (1762) and the Matawai (1767) recognized these Maroons' freedom and established their rights to land and self-governance. In exchange, these Maroon groups agreed to a number of stipulations, including restrictions on their movement to Paramaribo and the coastal region (see figure 1.3) and their surrendering any new runaways to colonial authorities. The latter point was part of a larger strategy to pit Suriname's African populations against one another, preventing them from joining forces against their common colonial adversaries. Although the terms of these agreements were seldom strictly observed by either party, through them a tentative peace was established and maintained.

Between the time when the peace treaties took effect and the abolition of slavery in 1863, slaves continued to escape and settle in the forest interior. Some attempted to join existing Maroon communities, despite the written mandate that they be turned over to the Dutch officials. Others established new societies (see figure 1.4). The Pamaka and Aluku (Boni) Maroons formed in this later period, independently of (and sometimes in opposition to) the three "pacified" Maroon groups. The Kwinti—the smallest of the six Maroon populations—claim descendants who escaped at various points in the colonial period, from as early as the 1650s to 1793, when a group fled westward from Ndyuka territory (van der Elst 2004, 12).

Away from the plantations and the city, Maroons were better able to pool their knowledge, drawing on their African roots in establishing their communities and new ways of life. As a result of these circumstances, cultural connections between the Suriname Maroons and African societies have often been depicted as being particularly strong; some have gone so far as to call the Suriname Maroons among the "most African" populations in the African Diaspora.[9] Taken together, these six distinct Maroon populations constitute the largest extant Maroon community. Their extraordinary history and cultural legacy serve as a source of pride and a potent symbol of black resistance and resilience in the New World.

Maroons refer to this chapter of their history—their escape, fight for freedom, and founding of the initial settlements—as First-Time (*fési-tén* in Saamakan; *fositen* or *loweten* [runaway or escape time] among the eastern Maroon groups).[10] First-Time functions as far more than a distant historical context and referent: it plays a vital role in Maroons' contemporary circumstances, constituting a resource on which they draw when facing their own challenges. On a general level, the concept of freedom and the Maroons' pursuit of it is infused into everyday discourse. Examples abound, including the self-identifications *fiiman* (free man), *fiimanpikin* (free man's child), and *loweman* (runaway); declarations of collective freedom, as in "u komoto katibo, u á de a keti moo [we've come out of slavery, we're not in chains any more]"; and reflections on social and political injustice or workplace mistreatment as proof that "saafuten de ete [slavery is still here]."[11] In these and many other common expressions, the notion of freedom constitutes a framework through which Maroons interpret the events and experiences in their day-to-day lives.[12] The parallels they draw between then and now serve as reminders to remain vigilant in the face of domination, while also framing the right to self-determination as fundamental to Maroon collective identity.

Information about First-Time is considered to be inherently powerful—not in the sense of profundity alone, but in its capacity to exert influence on people and circumstances. Accordingly, it is carefully guarded. Améiká, a Saamaka elder, explained its power in a conversation with Richard Price: "First-Time kills people. That's why it should never be taught to youths. . . . That's why, when you pour a libation at the ancestor shrine, you must be careful about speaking in proverbs [because you may not be aware of all their hidden implications]. There are certain [people's] names that, if you call them, you're dead right on the spot! There are names that can't be uttered twice in the course of a whole year!" (R. Price 1983, 7). Améiká's comment conveys the serious and potent nature of this kind of knowledge, while also illustrating the extent to which, in Maroon spiritual practice, human affairs are in constant dialogue with the realm of the spirits.[13] As with spoken allusions to First-Time, drummers must take care when using rhythms associated with the spirits or using the *apinti* drum language. Eddy Lante, one of the Kifoko leaders and the group's artistic director, explained: "Sometimes you're just playing one little thing [on the drums], then someone will tell you [to stop. If you don't know what you're doing], you can make a spirit come without your wanting it" (pers. comm., 11 October 2009).

Suriname's civil war (1986–92, discussed in chapter 2) provided a clear illustration of the degree to which historical, spiritual, and martial knowledges from First-Time are intertwined and are seen to have continuing relevance. In the conflict, which pitted the government (controlled by the military) against the Jungle Commando (an insurgent group composed primarily of Maroons), knowledge of their early ancestors' wartime strategies and the use of spiritual protections (*obiya*) were seen as powerful military aids by fighters on both sides of the conflict (Thoden van Velzen and van Wetering 2004, 239–62; R. Price 1995).[14]

The continued viability of the peace treaties signed in the late eighteenth century are tremendously important to contemporary Maroon populations, as it is through them that Maroons have been able to defend their territories and communities against the state-sanctioned large-scale mining and lumber operations that threaten their ways of life and the rain forest ecosystem on which they depend. Since Suriname's independence from the Dutch in 1975, the government has tried to dissolve the rights that Maroons were granted under the auspices of a unified nation of undifferentiated citizenship. Such a dissolution would allow resource extraction on Maroon territories to occur without impediment, effectively closing the few channels of legal recourse that are available to Maroons (see chapter 2).

On a broader scale, Suriname Maroons' remarkable accomplishments during First-Time and the strong African foundations of their social and cultural practices have made a considerable impact on African Diaspora studies. They have crucially informed such canonical works as Melville Herskovits's *The Myth of the Negro Past* (1941) and Robert Farris Thompson's *Flash of the Spirit: African and Afro-American Art and Philosophy* (1983), both of which cite Maroon traditions in proposing cultural continuities between Africa and the African Diaspora.[15] Richard Price and Sally Price have made numerous and lasting contributions to multiple fields of study (including anthropology, history, and art history and criticism), while demonstrating an ongoing commitment to ethical representation and political advocacy. Scholarly attention to Maroon and Afro-Surinamese music has tended to focus on providing a broad overview and general description (Agerkop 2000; Wetalk 1990; Gilbert 1940; Manuel, Bilby, and Largey 1995; S. Price and R. Price 1999; Campbell 2012a)[16] or addressing the popular music activities of young men in urban metropolitan areas (Bilby 1999, 2000, 2001a, and 2001b; Pakosie 1999; Jaffe and Sanderse 2009). Beyond my own writings (Campbell 2012b and 2018), research on dance consists of a fascinating cross-cultural study of the dance genre *banya* by Trudi

Martinus-Guda and Hillary de Bruin (2005) and brief mentions elsewhere (S. Price and R. Price 1999; Daniel 2011).

This book shares with existing works an interest in Maroons' cultural and expressive practices amid social change, while addressing un- or underrepresented issues including dance, folkloric presentation, intersections with nationalism and the tourist economy, and the contributions of women as well as men in performance art.[17] I do not aim to give a definitive account of Maroon performance practice, nor do I undertake the task of providing a comprehensive ethnography of Maroon culture and customs, whether in Paramaribo or in general. Rather, I am concerned with the ways that Maroon musicians and dancers living in the city come together to engage with cultural practices—how these performers who are occasionally charged with representing Maroon culture approach that task, and what ideas and processes their performances activate. Such an approach foregrounds processes of meaning making through Maroon music and dance genres in various rehearsal and performance contexts, while promoting on a more general level further exploration of the character and expressive potential of culture-representational performance as a distinctive aesthetic framework.

GEOPOLITICAL CONTEXT: SURINAME

Like all things "folkloric" or "cultural," Maroon cultural groups articulate identity in relation to various "others." While they may practice and represent Maroon traditions, these organizations are very much a product of their circumstances, fashioned by members of a disenfranchised population within a multiethnic city in a newly independent nation. A brief consideration of their broader social, geographical, and political contexts will help put their activities and performances into perspective.

Covering 163,820 square kilometers (roughly the size of Wisconsin), Suriname is South America's smallest independent country. The majority of this land area is composed of rain forest. Amerindian and Maroon villages dot Suriname's riverbanks, but vast stretches of virtually uninhabited land lie beyond and between these settlements.[18] A narrow strip of savannah separates the rain forest from the country's more populous northern coast, but by and large spatial divisions are drawn between the coast (occupying a strip roughly 50–100 kilometers wide) and the interior—the rain forest area to the south.[19] The 2012 census estimated that only 13.4 percent of the country's population (then totaling 541,638 people) inhabited districts south of the coast, which account for over 80 percent of Suriname's land area. Well over half of the country's population resides in or around Paramaribo, the capital city.[20]

Suriname's ethnic diversity—emphatically touted as the cornerstone of the nation's identity—is largely the by-product of a colonial economy that depended on slave and indentured labor. In the mid-nineteenth century, as emancipation appeared imminent, Dutch colonists began to reckon with the fact that the African populations could not be convinced to continue work on the plantations as free people. To maintain their workforce, indentured workers from India, Indonesia, and China were imported in 1853–74.[21] These historical circumstances have resulted in a present-day population in which East Indians (locally called Hindustani), Javanese, Creoles (the descendants of plantation slaves), and Maroons each make up 10–30 percent of the population (see table 1.1).[22]

TABLE 1.1. Major ethnic groups comprising Suriname's population, as listed in the 2004 and 2012 censuses

Census category	2004 census	2012 census
Hindustani (East Indian)	27.4%	27.4%
Maroon	14.7%	21.7%
Creole (Mixed African and European descent)[a]	17.7%	15.7%
Javanese	14.6%	13.7%
Mixed	12.5%	13.4%
Amerindian	3.7%	3.8%
Other (including European, Chinese, Afro-Surinamer, and undisclosed)	9.4%	4.3%
Total	492,829	541,638

Source: Menke and Sno (2016).
Note: Census categories are problematic indicators of racial and ethnic identity. As discussed further in chapter 5, under an *apanjaht* consociational political structure, ethnic identifications interact importantly with political party affiliation. When they are not hindered by the categorical framework of the census, many people who claim a single identity would likely choose different terminology or affiliate with multiple categories.
[a] Functionally, any Surinamer descended from Africans who are not Maroons.

While the multicultural, multiethnic nature of Surinamese society is well established, the character of the multicultural mix is constantly changing, reflecting immigration trends and the country's internal dynamism as social and cultural boundaries are constructed, maintained, and redrawn. Some of these changes are clearly illustrated in the national census. For instance, it was only in the twenty-first century that the census recognized a "mixed" category—before that time, the only category that acknowledged mixed ancestry was "Creole," which asserts African heritage as a primary identifier. Political efforts to synthesize the two Afro-Surinamese populations (Maroons and Creoles) are gaining slow but steady traction, as several thousand residents identified themselves as Afro-Surinamer in the 2012 census. With no clear majority population within the country, and given the primacy of ethnicity in the national political structure (see chapter 5), shifts in the demographic statistics can have dramatic implications for political power. Accordingly, Surinamers have followed the sharp increase in the percentage of Maroon-identified citizens with interest.[23]

Along with this ethnic diversity, the nation encompasses tremendous linguistic variety.[24] Dutch is officially recognized as the national language, predominantly used in education and in formal and public addresses. However, most of the nation's population can speak more than one of the roughly twenty languages commonly found in Suriname. Sranan Tongo ("Surinamese tongue"), an English-based creole language, functions as a lingua franca in Paramaribo; other common languages include Sarnami (a dialect of Bhojpuri, spoken among the Hindustani), and Surinamese Javanese. Among the Maroons, each of the six groups has its own creole language. However, the central Surinamese groups (the Saamaka, Matawai, and Kwinti) share more linguistic similarities among them, and likewise the eastern groups (the Ndyuka, Pamaka, and Aluku) can be seen as speaking dialects of a common language. Maroons in Paramaribo demonstrate a tremendous degree of linguistic flexibility, often drawing from various Maroon languages and dialects as well as Dutch, English, and Sranan Tongo in their expressions—at times to a point where it proved difficult during fieldwork to discern a single, primary language being spoken. Those individuals who intermixed Sranan Tongo and Maroon languages were often referred to as speaking "Nengee", whereas people whose vocabulary, phraseology, and interactive patterns demonstrated that they were well versed in a Maroon language were described as speaking the deep (*diipi*) language.

PARAMARIBO: A TOUR OF THE CITY

A ride through Paramaribo will inevitably take you past a number of Chinese corner stores with hand-painted illustrations of beer cans and brand-name staple foods depicted, larger than life, on their facades. Characteristic neighborhood businesses include taxi stands, restaurants and bars, beauty salons, and barbershops. Along the busiest roads, street vendors sell local produce from under tents; others roam between cars at major intersections, selling newspapers and trinkets.

Cultural centers and houses of worship for various ethnicities and faiths interrupt a landscape pervaded by cement storefronts and houses made of wooden slats. Notable among them are the Mosque Keizerstraat and Neveh Shalom Synagogue, situated next to each other in downtown Paramaribo—a much-celebrated example of Surinamers' capacity for peaceful coexistence regardless of religious faith and cultural background. While in the historic downtown area Dutch colonial buildings are carefully maintained and regularly repainted, beyond a limited radius many similar structures are considerably the worse for wear—graying houses are often held dubiously upright, with large gaps between their wooden slats. The trenches on either side of residential streets constitute an effort to control irrigation in the face of the country's persistent tropical showers, but streets inevitably flood during the height of the rainy season.

During the day, schoolchildren travel about town in their uniforms—green plaid shirts for those in primary school, light blue shirts for those in secondary. Women often travel with a parasol handy, useful both for shade from the intense glare of the sun and for the frequent showers that arrive and dissipate with astonishing speed. Minibuses provide an inexpensive and relatively efficient way of getting around the city. Most buses feature a variety of decals representing political or entertainment personalities, women striking a variety of seductive poses, or various braggadocious phrases in either English or Sranan Tongo.

But beyond these shared landmarks and characteristic sights, people's experience of the city—its places of significance and most familiar attributes—vary dramatically depending on an individual's age, class, and (perhaps most of all) ethnicity. Many places of primary importance in urban Maroon culture are virtually unknown to people of other ethnicities and vice versa, despite the fact that the groups often exist in close proximity to one another. Although there tends to be more interethnic interaction among younger generations, it remains common for people of different ethnic identifications to live alongside one another while maintaining clear social and cultural divisions between them (see chapters 5 and 6).

Paramaribo is a place where the social and political importance of ethnic identification is constantly being "worked out." This is a recurring theme, a point of focus and interest not only for the Maroons but also for people—Surinamese citizens and visitors alike—to whom the issue of how multiculturality is to "work" in an ethnically diverse country like Suriname is a compelling issue. Far beyond simply providing light entertainment, folkloric performance can act as a testing ground on which cultural and intercultural ideals can be envisioned, enacted, and measured against engrained social habits and people's everyday experiences.

FOLKLORIC PERFORMANCE

Though culture-representational ensembles in Paramaribo are known locally as cultural groups, functionally and aesthetically they are aligned with the more broadly recognized category of folkloric performance. I take folkloric performance to be any performance of music, dance, or theater that is self-consciously represented *as* cultural material. It is a metacultural undertaking in that, as Francis Mulhern says, it "is that in which culture, however defined, speaks of itself. More precisely, it is discourse in which culture addresses its own generality and conditions of existence" (2000, xiv)—or, to use Andriy Nahachewsky's terminology, the folkloric mode is distinctive in the degree of performers' "reflectiveness" (2000, 20).[25] Folkloric performance uses a cosmopolitan aesthetic vocabulary that varies but often includes an orientation toward a proscenium stage, the use of culturally emblematic performance apparel, the presentation of discrete pieces or "works" of relatively short duration, and intermittent pauses for applause or explanation or other formalized interactions between performers and onlookers. Ample use of this aesthetic palette signals to an audience that they are witnessing a showcase of cultural particularity, and the value of the performance rests (at least in part) on the "cultural" status of its contents. For example, when a Maroon cultural group performs awasa, audience members may or may not be able to identify awasa dance or know anything about the Maroons, but through folkloric modes of staging and aesthetic cues they would likely recognize that the dance in question was being presented as somehow representative of a particular cultural practice and population.

In this folkloric mode of presentation, performers act as culture brokers: they are involved in generating, reframing, and synthesizing cultural "content."[26]

In the process, they develop or affirm new formats (the "cultural show," workshop, and demonstration) and performance roles (professionals and semiprofessionals[27] and members of a folkloric performance group), while simultaneously satisfying and influencing the tastes and practices of consumers (tourists, national audiences, sponsors, and patrons). In this capacity, the folkloric idiom structures interactions along axes of cultural consumption and production, situating performance within the realm of cultural economy. This is a cosmopolitan endeavor in two ways: it is a local manifestation of "constellations of habits that are shared among widely dispersed groups in countries around the world" (Turino 2008, 118), and it also reinforces for its audiences a cosmopolitan civic ethic that places value and importance on increased cultural awareness—on being a more fully engaged citizen of the world (Appiah 2006).

In defining folkloric performance in this way, I try to emphasize aesthetics and performance strategies while steering clear of generalizations or assumptions concerning patronage, intended audience, or performers' motivations. In particular, while folkloric performance requires an awareness of an "other" (without which the concept of "the folk" would have no dimensions or meaning), I do not hold that the folkloric designation requires that the "other" is the primary or intended audience. Likewise, I disagree with characterizations that juxtapose folkloric performance with "authentic" cultural expressions that take place in "the field" as a matter of course.[28] In fact, this book posits that limited definitions of such categories can in turn limit our capacity to recognize and interpret cultural groups' full social and expressive impact, or even their main objectives.

Many of these assumptions can be related back to the nineteenth-century origins of the terms "folklore" and "folklorism," which had at their core the domination, racialization, and marginalization of designated populations as part of the nationalist and modernist enterprise.[29] As a representational form, folkloric performance is inherently involved with power, and there are abundant examples of contemporary nationalistic and touristic instantiations of cultural representation that continue unambiguously to affirm hegemonic structures. Yet recent scholarship (including Schauert 2015; Mendoza 1999 and 2008; and Feldman 2006) has drawn attention to ways that performers have claimed agency through this same format, at times problematizing the very power structures that folkloric performance is so often seen to affirm. For instance, Zoila Mendoza demonstrated that, while folkloric performances in Cuzco, Peru, have entrenched various ethnic stereotypes, they have also "creat[ed] a field in which *cusqueños* redefine their own ethnic/racial and social-class identities, in some cases reworking some of these stereotypes" (1999, 89). Through self-representation, she argues, performers can make strategic and meaningful changes in their public perception. In a similar vein, Paul Schauert found that members of the Ghana Dance Ensemble employed the notion of "managing" "not only as a way to denote the capacity to get by but also as an expression of personal agency; participants often employ[ed] it to articulate a sense of control over the situation at hand—the ability to 'run things' by navigating economic, political, and social challenges, turning the social order to their advantage" (2015, 5). In both cases, the power of cultural representation derives in part from its role as a technology whereby one's place in a given social order can be asserted (and, by extension, contested or problematized). My notion of folkloric ambivalence draws similar conclusions, but with the added consideration that the ways in which the ambivalent features inherent in the medium of performance help create the conditions whereby external discursive and political structures become more malleable or find their fullest expression. Walter Johnson (2003), Lila Abu-Lughod (1990), and others have made important observations about the limitations of scholarly arguments for agency, yet it becomes possible to consider how agentive actions interact with broader, dominating factors only under two conditions: we recognize that performers are capable of deliberate and potentially subversive action, and we make a practice of identifying both what those actions are and what they can do.

Of particular importance in the case of Maroon folkloric groups is the heterogeneity and multiplicity of groups' listening and viewing publics. Katherine Hagedorn provides a clear demonstration of how important an audience can be in determining what a performance might signify or establish. In describing her first experience of attending a weekly scheduled performance by the Havana-based Conjunto Folklórico de Cuba, Hagedorn takes care to convey in detail the audiences' reactions and interactions, alongside the performers' folkloric renderings of dances for the *orichás* (deities in the Santería religious tradition). She explains: "Because the audience at a Conjunto Folklórico event is typically composed of at least four distinct groups, what is communicated between the performers and the audience is by no means monolithic. Each sector of the audience—young foreign tourists (*extranjeros*), older Cuban religious practitioners (*creyentes*), young Cuban black marketers (*jinteros*), and the young dancers and singers hoping to perform with the troupe (*aficionados*)—lends its own particular dynamic to the performance" (Hagedorn 2001, 58).

The primacy of the audiences' roles as interpreters was borne out time and again in my own research. As Maroon groups performed at gigs ranging from backyard birthday parties to international cultural expos, their audiences spanned a similarly wide range of subject positions. A group's relatively fixed "set list" of prepared material did not in itself determine the nature, function, or significance of a given performance. Rather, the character of the event and what it accomplished socially was established collaboratively as group members and audiences interacted in real time. Audience members can have widely varying interpretive practices, and so too can a single performance be many things at once. Furthermore, just as Hagedorn describes "becoming" a tourist through her interpersonal negotiations as she paid her admission and was directed to a seat that was designated for tourists, the event of performance has the potential for all those in attendance to perform social roles and interrelationships. In addition to group members' roles (for instance, lead or supporting drummer, singer, or dancer), others come to occupy the roles of patron, audience member, honored guest, cultural critic, tourist, fellow Surinamer, or city resident.

CULTURAL GROUPS IN SURINAME

Before the emergence of cultural groups, according to Lante, when there was an occasion that required music, Maroons in Paramaribo would have to rely on word of mouth to find the musicians necessary for the performance: "When they wanted a Ndyuka *pee* [an event featuring Ndyuka music and dance], then they had to go to *awoyo* [Paramaribo's main Maroon market]. They'd ask someone, 'You don't know how to play music, do you?' 'No. . . .' [a person] says he doesn't know how to play music. [To another], 'You know someone who knows how to play music?'—he says yes—'Call him for me.' That's how people looked and looked for people" (pers. comm., 10 November 2009). Cultural groups streamlined this process significantly, providing a network of performers who could mobilize efficiently.

Established in 1983, Kifoko was among the earliest Maroon cultural groups in Paramaribo, but others preceded it. Denku, founded in the 1970s by the Saamaka drummer and ritual specialist Anike Awagi, is widely regarded as the first Maroon cultural group to rise to prominence. Beyond providing a consolidated network of performers (drummers in particular) for Maroon social and ritual events in Paramaribo, Awagi was also invested in representing Maroon culture and traditions to national and touristic audiences in a folkloric capacity. As an effective presenter and a knowledgeable *apintiman* (a drummer trained in the apinti drumming language), Awagi traveled internationally as a cultural representative throughout the late twentieth century, demonstrating to others that folkloric performances could bring benefits such as travel and a modest supplementary income. From their earliest iterations, then, cultural groups like Denku had aspects of their operation and performance agendas that were directed both inward (fulfilling the needs of Maroon communities in Paramaribo) and outward (demonstrating for, entertaining, and educating broader publics), setting a precedent for the cultural groups that have followed. As a growing number of Maroons have taken up permanent residence in the city, their needs have expanded. Subsequently, groups have placed increasing emphasis on education and social sustenance through rehearsals.

The appeal of cultural groups for their Maroon audiences in the twenty-first century is clearly aesthetic as well as pragmatic or social—a point made clear, for instance, as groups received occasional invitations to perform for events in the interior, where the provision of instruments and the availability of knowledgeable and willing performers was not an issue. Likewise, the fact that there are now cultural groups in interior villages and camps (not just in coastal cities like Paramaribo and Saint-Laurent-du-Maroni, French Guiana) indicates an enjoyment of this mode of rehearsal and performance, regardless of whether or not other community-wide opportunities for these styles of music and dance are readily available. During and after a performance, theatrical flourishes and carefully choreographed sequences drew praise and comment from Maroon audiences, who were better equipped to spot groups' innovations and theatrical play by virtue of their familiarity with the genres in their repertoires and their linguistic proficiencies. While composition and choreography are certainly features of Maroon performance practice outside of cultural groups' activities (especially on an individual level), cultural groups were able to explore a greater range of possibilities for collective composition through their regular rehearsals and by employing a wider array of presentational structures and modes of stagecraft.

Among the features that distinguish Maroon cultural groups in relation to the broader classification of "folkloric groups" is their lack of long-term sponsorship or patronage. None of the cultural groups were funded directly by the state or any other parent organization. Without state, corporate, or institutional patronage, groups had in common both a large degree of creative autonomy and a perpetual state of financial instability. Their expenses, which included instrument maintenance, "uniforms" (typically hand-sewn garments made out of the same pattern of cloth and fashioned in roughly the same style), and rental of rehearsal space (if it was not privately owned by a group member), were usually taken care of though money collected as the group's performance fee. Depending on the group and the amount of surplus money after expenses had been accounted for, individuals would receive either no compensation or a modest sum for their time and efforts.[30] In none of the three groups I studied with extensively (Kifoko, Saisa, and Fiamba) was performing a lucrative endeavor: at best it was a sporadic source of supplementary income. Members invested significant time in these groups, often taking lengthy, arduous bus rides across town to attend rehearsals once or twice weekly and arranging schedules that included work, school, and family obligations to attend both rehearsals and performances (referred to using the Dutch words *oefens* and *optredens*, respectively, rather than Maroon words such as *puubei* or pee in Okanisi). A performance engagement could occupy a whole evening if it was in the city, or days if it entailed travel into the interior or abroad. While performances may have been sources of personal and social satisfaction, they also required dedication and sacrifice.

In 2008–9, the primary Maroon cultural groups that were active within Paramaribo were Kifoko, Saisa, Fiamba, Tangiba, and Wenoeza. My choice to work with Kifoko, Saisa, and Fiamba was determined in part by chance: these groups (in that order) were the first three cultural groups in Paramaribo that I met. As I became more familiar with other groups active in the area, I began to realize that Kifoko, Saisa, and Fiamba happened to represent a particularly broad stylistic range. Kifoko was the longest-running group in Paramaribo, with well-established connections to people and institutions involved with promoting national culture. Saisa's strong connections to the nearby village of Santigron were well-known, and its membership and performance style both evidenced regional particularities. Fiamba was the youngest group—both in terms of the year of its founding and its general membership—which gave its rehearsals and performances a "youth group" feel, as members in their teens and early twenties of varying backgrounds and experiences pooled their knowledge and cheered each other on in their efforts. While these three groups were easy to distinguish from each other owing to features including their demographics, social network, and performance aesthetics (see chapter 3), there were other combinations of cultural groups in Paramaribo that demonstrated a clear overlap in all or many of these ways. Such overlaps were especially common as leading figures broke off from an existing group to start their own, much as the group Tangiba emerged from Saisa, and as Wenoeza did from Fiamba.

My ability to conduct comparative research with these groups in the intensive way that I did was made possible in part because the differences between Kifoko,

Fiamba, and Saisa were evident to their members: none posed an immediate threat to the operation or long-term success of the others, a testament to the size and diversity of the Maroon population residing in and around Paramaribo. Such would not have been the case if, for instance, I had endeavored to work with both Saisa and Tangiba, which were struggling to establish a peaceable coexistence while catering to the same communities and networks with aesthetically similar performances. While tensions between Wenoeza and Fiamba did not run as high, to involve myself intensively with both of those groups would have exacerbated these unnecessarily, as the groups were at a vulnerable time in their growth as independent entities.

PERFORMANCE EVENTS

I have already alluded to the diversity of cultural groups' audiences and the variety of engagements for which they were frequently hired to perform. A brief discussion follows of the particularities of Paramaribo's social and musical landscape and the performance opportunities available to cultural groups that should put their activities in perspective.

In contrast to the prominent role that tourism plays in other studies of folkloric performance—in Arcoverde, Brazil (Sharp 2014); Cuzco, Peru (Mendoza 1999 and 2008); and Havana, Cuba (Hagedorn 2001)—in Suriname, the tourist economy operates on a comparatively small scale, despite its steady growth throughout the twentieth century. There are a number of successful travel and tour agencies, focusing on ecotourism and catering primarily to English- and Dutch-speaking clientele, but there is not a sufficient volume of tourists to sustain weekly performance engagements (such as the Conjunto Folklórico's "Sabados de Rumba" to which Hagedorn referred) or to generate consistent income. These performances might be commissioned by a hotel or a restaurant (as in the case of the performance at Zus en Zo described in chapter 8), or by a tour organizer in anticipation of travel further inland.

Within this particular nationalist and citywide context, multiculturalism exercises perpetual influence. A public event calendar in Suriname is awash with officially recognized holidays, alongside a host of historical and religious observances aligned with each of the nation's main ethnic groups. Thus, opportunities to perform for the general public as a "piece" in a larger multicultural puzzle abound. Added to these are large-scale regional celebrations (examples in 2008–9 included Carifesta [the Caribbean Festival of Arts], the Rainforest Arts Festival, the Ethnic Food Festival, and the Parade du Littoral in Kourou,

Guyane), in which Maroon cultural groups have contributed to broader imaginings of regional variety and affiliation. Explorations of muticulturalism and the multicultural nation can take the form of formal, carefully constructed performances with targeted messages promoting cultural interaction and integration, as in Alakondre Dron (chapter 5), or in more improvisatory, vernacular contexts, as in the Avondvierdaagse parade (chapter 6). These performances of and/or for the general public take place on stages, on city streets, in parade processions, in hotel lobbies, and even on the plush carpet of a casino's main floor, surrounded by the tinny chimes of slot machines.

As the discursive categories "cultural," "traditional," and "popular" intertwine, cultural groups' opportunities for performance and exposure are constantly diversifying. Within Maroon communities, groups have provided entertainment interludes or accompaniment at various dance competitions and pageants; in all-night concerts (featuring local Maroon bands performing in styles including aleke and *kaseko*, as well as Jamaican reggae and dancehall) they occasionally serve as opening acts.[31] Since the mid-2010s an increasing number of these concerts have made more overt references to Maroon "culture" and "traditional" styles, leading to new collaborations and ever more opportunities in which performers interpreted as "popular" or "traditional" might change roles, fuse styles, or share the stage (Campbell 2018; Bilby and Jaffe 2018).

For their part, in their repertoires cultural groups created narratives about cultural identity that blurred these categorical divisions as well. Although Kifoko did not regularly play aleke in their performances in the 2000s and 2010s, this popular genre of Ndyuka origin had previously been part of their repertoire. In fact, the group continued to rehearse and perform using drum stands that had the dual function of eliminating the the drummers' need for chairs and allowing them to play with the same posture and bearing as though they were playing the longer aleke drums (Mosis 2012). Fiamba included aleke drumming and dance in its repertoire, as well as its own adaptation of *loketo*, a fast-paced, high-energy dance inspired by Congolese *soukous*.[32] Louise Wondel, Fiamba's founder, explained to me the logic for loketo's inclusion:

LW: Loketo [is an] African dance. And we are African people who were left here in Suriname. So we are doing . . . this thing—African dances also. Loketo is an African dance.
CC: But you have many African dances. Why do the people from Suriname care more for loketo?

LW: They care more for loketo because the loketo . . . let's say loketo is popular
    here. . . . But other dances haven't become popular in Suriname as has loketo.
CC: Do you think that [Suriname Maroons] think of it as their own culture?
LW: Yeah, man. Yeah. (pers. comm., 20 August 2009)

Fiamba's inclusion of loketo in its repertoire complicates a narrow reading of
Maroon "culture" and "traditions" through its popular status, and the fact that
its origins are both relatively recent (1960s) and attributed to Congolese musicians. Though the popular conception of these groups is that they are performing
primarily their *gaansamasani* (their traditions—literally, the "things" of their
elders) such choices in repertoire help performers avoid being pigeonholed. This
is all the better for the members of this group in particular, as all of them were
young people—in 2009, Clifton Asongo, then twenty-four, was the group's oldest
member. Fiamba's choices in repertoire and a general trend toward the melding
of "traditional" and "popular" categories at concerts combined in a fortuitous way
in 2016, when the group was invited to perform as an opening act for Dr. Sakis,
a locally popular Paris-based soukous singer. Ever since, a banner advertising
the concert (with Fiamba's name on it) has framed the group's rehearsal space.
    Cultural groups' recordings, too, achieved token status on the radio and in
record shops. DJs at Radio Koyeba, Paramaribo's only radio station that caters
explicitly to Maroons,[33] would slip the occasional awasa or Saamakan *sêkêti* song
into a musical lineup that favored genres including reggae, dancehall, soul, aleke,
kaseko, and gospel and an assortment of international hits. Alongside bootleg
copies of local and international popular music and DVDs of blockbuster hits
dubbed with dialogue in the Saamakan or Okanisi languages, most vendors had
on hand a few CDs of "traditional" music performed by cultural groups.
    For Saisa and Fiamba in particular, birthday parties (*fuuyali oso*) were among
their most frequent commissions. These events have their origins in city culture
and national politics. While the Creoles have a long-established tradition of
celebrating birthdays,[34] among the Maroons the date of one's birth began to be
formally noted and recorded only in the 1960s—as part of the politician Johan
Adolf Pengel's campaign to register Maroon voters in an effort to establish an Afro-
Surinamese political electorate big enough to defeat the dominant Hindustani
Party (Vooruitstrevende Hervormingspartij, or VHP). Birthday parties tended to
be modest neighborhood affairs featuring light entertainment and a simple meal.
They were most often organized to celebrate the birthdays of children or women,
but they were attended widely by friends, family members, and neighbors of

varying ages, attracting men as well as women. Party hosts were likely to employ performing groups with which they had some kind of personal connection, giving these events a lighthearted, familiar feel. A party's host might employ one or several groups, as finances allowed. Other ensembles that regularly performed for *fuuyali osos* included gospel-themed pop music groups, loketo groups, brass bands, and *kaskawi* (a mixture of the popular genres kaseko and kawina) bands. Landmark birthdays (*bigi yalis*) call for more elaborate arrangements (see chapter 8), typically involving renting a space for the celebration and requiring more (and more lavish) food and entertainment, as a person's family and network can afford.

Finally, funerary rites were among the events that cultural groups took most seriously, as important community-focused occasions in which music plays a vital role. These rites take place at designated increments between the death and the conclusion of the mourning period (*puu baka*), which can take place anywhere from six months to over a year later. Of special significance to cultural groups are the playing of *tuka* and the *booko dei*, what Kenneth Bilby characterizes as "a kind of first funeral" (2011, 4). Tuka is a percussion and dance genre that is played beginning a day or two after a person dies, typically repeated nightly until the burial occurs (ibid.). This is a particularly vulnerable time for the deceased person's community, for it is at this point that the spirit is entreated not to torment the souls of the living and instead to begin its transition to *dede kondee*, the realm of the dead. Eddy Lante and Maria Dewinie of Kifoko both insisted that tuka would never function as part of their group's repertoire, for to play it out of context is to invite death into one's community. In contrast, while members of the cultural group Saisa had the same general view of the power of this music and the precariousness of the situation in which it is played, several of them listed the genre as part of the group's repertoire. At funerary rites, they often provided the drums and contributed to dancing tuka, but whereas for Kifoko's coleaders this was considered separate from group activities, these Saisa members were making the statement that their attendance at a funeral constituted a collective appearance by the group, even when they were not performing pieces they had rehearsed separately as a collective. Thus, tuka illustrates how the idea of repertoire was itself a somewhat flexible concept. Booko deis are events of intense music making. They feature a standard series of genres that must be performed in their proper order (*mato, susa, songe,* and awasa). Kifoko used this order, called the *gaansamapee*, in structuring their rehearsals and other performances, regardless of the occasion. With groups that did not perform all of these genres or that performed many others as well, the gaansamapee did not function effectively as an organizational framework.

These were by no means all the kinds of events at which a Maroon cultural group might expect to perform, but even with this rough sketch it's possible to appreciate their dramatically different characters and objectives. Despite these differences among performance contexts, cultural groups tended not to make significant changes to their "set lists" or compositions from one performance event to the next. Some group members said that it was particularly gratifying to perform at certain kinds of events (for instance, at high-profile international festivals or for close friends and family members), but most people found value and enjoyment in the full range of a group's performance engagements. Saisa member Jill Triesie's reflections on these different performances are broadly representative:

> All of the [kinds of] performances we have, I love. No matter when you play ["pee"] . . . the thing is [to] bring enjoyment to the people. Right? So you go to a dede oso where people are full of sorrow, you pull a *little* bit of that sorrow from them. Parties, fuuyali osos, that's for enjoyment ["piisii"]. Maybe a reception or something for some organization, it's bringing some enjoyment to them too. Thus, I see it as all of them except for a few are bringing enjoyment to people when you perform. Then, I can't say that, 'oh it's a dede oso—I don't want to go, or a meeting. It doesn't matter where we go. Always, if I can, I'll go perform. (pers. comm., 28 October 2009, my translation from Okanisi)

WORK SITES

The notion of work can apply to culture-representational performance in countless ways, and it is precisely this polysemous nature that mirrors the dynamism of cultural groups' practices and metapractices. Therefore, in determining the frame and scope of the current project, I find it simpler and more expeditious to designate sites of work rather than kinds of work. In addition to culture-representational performances in the public sphere—by far the work for which cultural groups are best known—here I address two additional sites that receive far less notice, though they are no less crucial: the body and community.

The Body

Graciella Dewinie, Maria's younger sister and a fellow veteran member of the cultural group Kifoko, stands beside a novice dancer as she attempts *umanpikinfutu*, the foundational step of awasa dance. The young woman bends her legs slightly, moving her hands in a circular motion in front of her. Graciella motions for her to keep dancing as she molds her body into the correct posture. Placing her hands on the dancer's shoulders, she stills the side-to-side motion of her torso, directing her to deepen her squat by several inches. Placing one hand on the small of her back and the other on the front of her shoulders, she adjusts the dancer so her rib cage is vertical, creating a dramatic curve in her spine. Graciella lets go and steps away to take in the difference. "You see?" she says approvingly, "*That's how you dance awasa.*" The young woman dances for just a few more seconds, straining to maintain the position despite burning thighs and a strained back. As she stands upright, catching her breath and shaking out her legs, she exclaims, "Mi weli! [I'm tired!]" She has been dancing for less than a minute.[35]

When done correctly, awasa can be sinuous and graceful, with an undulating spine and torso and footwork that is both rhythmically precise and so fluid that it seems as though the dancer is floating. Performers impress audiences through their creative expressions and personalized touches in this malleable form, but also by virtue of the fact that its fundamental posture and footwork are so challenging to maintain—the result of accumulated time dancers have invested in creating kinesthetic fluency within the dance style. Even then it takes considerable work not to betray the body's physical strain during performance. Aspects of dancers' technique are audible as well as visible, their *kawai* ankle rattles sounding out missteps or shaky rhythms, even if one foot is favored over the other. Drummers, too, assert themselves as practitioners, communicating not only strength but an ongoing relationship to their instruments through the precision and stamina of their performing bodies. In these ways, the body in performance tells stories (and threatens to divulge secrets) about the history of its practice and the intimacies of its sensations.

Bodies are at once the tools of the physical labor of performance, the site of the work, and the product or manifestation of that work. "In dance, even more than in other disciplines," Priya Srinivasan writes, "the labor of dancing cannot be separated from its means of production, the dancing body. Dance is also unique in that labor is equivalent to the product in dance: the dancing body's very 'liveness' and the display of its labor in performance produces a dance product. Therefore, the dancing body as a laboring body disrupts traditional Marxist understandings of the act of labor, the means of production, and the product" (2012, 11–12). Srinivasan (along with Browning 1995; Hahn 2007, 155; and Kedhar 2014) details how the physical work of performance often finds resonance with dispositions and ideals that dancers are encouraged or pressured to assume within the social sphere, whether the work in question involves inversion, code-switching, flexibility, or something else. The performer's bodily labor creates habits of motility, but the work also fashions the very substance of the body, for instance through accumulating calluses and developing and sculpting muscle mass.

At the same time, the body is at work as an interpretive mechanism, a site of feeling, knowing, remembering, and acquaintance. As Stanley Fish (1980), Tomie Hahn (2007), and Kathryn Geurts (2002) have all demonstrated, it is through the sensing body that we "make sense" of the world around us (Fish 1980, 29). Performance has nearly limitless referential capacity—it can appear to institute various kinds of affiliation or copresence, even lessening or collapsing the distance between, for instance, city and rain forest interior locations or past and present. Maroon cultural groups offer many opportunities for this kind of interpretive work. In one of Fiamba's signature choreographies, dancers pantomime aspects of women's work in a village, from harvesting rice to grating cassava. Not all the dancers in Fiamba have done the domestic activities they imitate, but through dance they develop a physical acquaintance with those tasks, facilitating an awareness of different aspects of the sense and sensations that contain social and cultural meaning. Similarly, in the genre songe (performed regularly by Kifoko and Saisa), the fundamental movements recall the natural landscape and fishing practices of the interior. This dance is named after *agankoi* (*Geophagus harreri*, or Maroni eartheater), a freshwater fish that swims from side to side as it guards its eggs. The steps and postures that women use to dance songe replicate this side-to-side motion, and the men often make as though they are drawing a bow, as the agankoi is typically fished using a bow and arrow. One awasa song, canonical among cultural groups, describes Sa Asenowe, a woman of exceptional beauty and talent as a dancer. As a singer describes the woman's delicate feet and shapely figure and how she moved her waist and hips, dancers embody and refigure these feminine ideals, finding Sa Asenowe's form and gait in their own dancing bodies. The body also lends substance to concepts that might otherwise seem abstract. For instance, ideas of "unity" and "brotherhood"—so prevalent in Suriname's national discourse—gain immediacy and specificity as they are enacted by a group's coordinated performance.

Maroons often use the phrases "kiibi i kulturu" (keep or safeguard your culture),[36] "sabi i gaansamasani" (know the things belonging to your elders), and "teki leli" (take [your] lesson or learning) to describe the work of maintaining and perpetuating Maroon culture. Particularly for those living away from Maroon lands and villages, music and dance practice can be ways of maintaining a connection—doing the work of "keeping," "knowing," and "learning" in their muscle memory and interactive practices. These processes are all personal and personalizing (Campbell 2012b), and as such they become a technology of the self (Foucault 1988)—a way of "taking care of oneself" through cultivating social and cultural belonging.

Community

The communities I designate as the second "work site" for this book involve the Suriname Maroons, in particular those who reside in Paramaribo, and the discrete communities of the cultural groups themselves above all. Long-standing members of Kifoko, Saisa, and Fiamba all spoke passionately about how important these groups have been in their lives:

> "Mi de a Saisa, te mi meki dii pikin, mi de a Saisa ete. Dii. De feti anga mi, omen sowtu sani . . . toch mi de a Saisa ete [I was in Saisa, when I had three children, I'm still in Saisa. Three. They fight with me, all sorts of things—even so, I'm still in Saisa.]."
> Silvana Pinas, Saisa (pers. comm., 16 November 2009)

> "Mi lei a wroko pe fu komoto go pee [I lie at my place of work so I can leave and play (perform)]."
> Carlos Josimba Corason Pinas, Saisa (pers. comm., 16 November. 2009)

> "Baka mi famii, na Kifoko [After my family, it's Kifoko]."
> John Binta, Kifoko (pers. comm., 11 November 2008)

> "Mi group, eigenlijk san mi be lobi, be de Fiamba. Yah. Fiamba mi be lobi. Mi be gii mi ati in' a Fiamba. Dus, di mi go a Holland seefi, a eerste lesi . . . dus, te a oefen dei doo—Veedag—da mi be denki soso Saanan [My group, truly what I loved, was Fiamba. Yah. Fiamba I loved. I gave my heart to Fiamba. Then, when I went to Holland, the first time . . . when the rehearsal day arrived—Friday—then I thought only [of] Suriname.]."
> Louise Wondel, Fiamba (pers. comm., 30 August 2009)

These group members make clear that cultural groups were much more than simply a means to achieve the broadly valued ends of learning and practicing a part of their heritage. Cultural groups constituted communities that often inspired fierce dedication and affection. Both in rehearsals and through performance engagements within their social networks, group members grieve together, celebrate together, take notice of each other's developing proficiencies, and bear witness to the high and low points in each other's lives. They do the valuable work of providing spaces and regular opportunities for Maroons living in Paramaribo to congregate; express themselves artistically; and provide solidarity, support, and cultural affirmation in conditions that can at times be hostile or ostracizing. In this capacity, they serve a centering function, building spaces for community formation that otherwise wouldn't exist.

While the communities that take shape through cultural groups are the result of deliberate effort and experiences accumulated over time, there are some ways in which the very forms and structures of performance require a communal ethos. As detailed in chapter 4, the genres in their repertoires—including awasa, songe, mato, *bandámmba*, and susa—are fundamentally and essentially communal expressions.[37] They require interlocking percussive rhythms, a lead singer and a chorus, and dancers primed for communication and interaction. On those rehearsal days when fewer than eight people showed up, groups sometimes opted to work on targeted issues of technique or practice song texts, but seldom would they attempt a rehearsal with the requisite elements of song, dance, and percussion—a crowd is needed to sustain these forms, and the bigger the better. The community sentiment that groups cultivate in rehearsal provides a basis for gathering communities together through public performance. As people come together to perform these genres in any space, their physical configuration in relation to one another has the power to superimpose the spatial and interactive logic of the dance onto the physical site of performance, thereby remaking or repurposing a driveway or city street or casino lobby and claiming it as social and cultural space.

Yet while cultural groups' practices and performances can effectively refute narratives that link urban migration with uncritical assimilation, their roles in relationship to cultural preservation lead to an ambiguous and ambivalent social terrain. Graciella Dewinie's comments illustrate the issue. Responding to the recent departure of several longtime Kifoko members to the Christian group Gadoe Talentie, she explained:

> It carries two feelings. Kifoko is a school. You don't have to stay exclusively in this group. . . . You're a Busikondeesama [a Maroon (literally, a bush country person)], you can do your Busikondee [Maroon] things. But you must know

how it goes. That's important. If they come and they really take it on, we're happy. We're happy for that. You can join a church group, you can do what you want. . . .

But if everyone leaves, who will take over? One day it won't be here. When they leave, they water down the thing. They take one piece, one piece [of the tradition] they're not doing. But if everyone comes and takes a little something and takes it away, then nobody will continue with it. When it's finished, there won't be a place to take more.[38]

Graciella's words echo anxieties that are often expressed about Maroon culture in general. Whether regarding language, tracing family lineages, history, or various aspects of cultural practice, many feel that younger generations and urbanites are shirking those activities that set Maroons apart from other groups in the African Diaspora, passing them up in favor of other practices and pastimes. Here, participating in a cultural group is presented as one way of preserving and perpetuating Maroon music and dance.

Graciella described this knowledge as a birthright—it is there for people to engage with and apply as they see fit, but people can access it because others have taken pains to perpetuate it. She describes Kifoko as a school and archive, a resource that can be tapped. Yet in relation to others who practice and perform these genres without the folkloricizing touches of a cultural group, Kifoko could be framed much like Gadoe Talentie, itself more an adaptation and abridged version of the forms people encompass than what the group practices in rehearsal or demonstrates onstage. Depending on one's perspective, cultural groups might appear to function either as distortions of traditional genres or as community resources, engaging in the work of preservation.

FIELDWORK

I visited Suriname and French Guiana for the first time in the summer of 2006, propelled by curiosity about the tremendous cultural diversity that exists within such a small nation, and in particular about the Maroons and their remarkable cultural legacy.[39] Since then I have conducted roughly thirty-four months of fieldwork in the region. My involvement during my primary dissertation term (June 2008—December 2009) consisted of formal and informal interviews and conversations with group members and other individuals involved with cultural promotion and production.[40] I attended and participated regularly in the rehearsals of Kifoko, Saisa, and Fiamba and went to numerous performances in the capacity of a research affiliate, a "friend" of the group, or as a fellow performer and group member—in whatever capacity they preferred.[41] In rehearsal, I participated primarily as a dancer and a supporting singer in the *koor* (the choir or chorus).

I have spent the bulk of my time in Suriname in Paramaribo rather than in the villages and informal settlements in the rain forest interior—the places where these Maroon societies were founded initially and where the activities of daily life (including religious practice and social interactions) and work (including hunting and farming) are aligned more directly with notions of "traditional" Maroon practices. The majority of my visits to the interior have been to villages along Suriname's border with French Guiana, both during large-scale ceremonies and under more mundane circumstances when social life was following its expected daily and seasonal rhythms. These trips were of relatively short duration (usually between four days and two weeks at a time), but they provided a useful point of comparison to the life practices of Maroons in urban areas, with which I was more familiar. I began research in Saint-Laurent-du-Maroni, a town on French Guiana's border with Suriname, and my social ties, language proficiencies, and points of reference favor the eastern Maroon groups—the Ndyuka, Aluku, and Pamaka. The majority of the music and dance genres represented in cultural groups' repertoires came from these groups as well.

Finally, writing at a time when the privileges and performances of white womanhood were coming under increased and useful critical discussion,[42] it seems appropriate to comment on my role as a white woman researching Maroon music and dance. My presence and participation prompted a variety of reactions. Some group members insisted that I participate in rehearsals and expressed disappointment when I was not able to attend social or performance events, whereas others took a more guarded approach, questioning what degree of access I should be given. When I performed with groups, my difference was highly visible and immediately apparent. This had multiple effects. In some instances (in particular when a group was to perform for predominantly Maroon audiences), my performance was a matter of considerable curiosity and proved useful in securing gigs and a sizable audience. During 2008–9, the cultural group Saisa was undergoing upheaval relating to a group founded by its former members. These two groups became competitors, relying on similar networks and a similar performance aesthetic. My participation in Saisa at this juncture was one way in which one group could be distinguished easily from the other. In other cases (for instance, when performers were operating as cultural representatives), my evident foreignness tended to be less desirable. For tourists who were expecting to consume cultural authenticity ("real" Maroons performing their own traditions), my obvious outsider status could be distracting or off-putting. I performed on only those occasions when I was explicitly invited to do so.

Even to the degree in which it was welcomed, my presence (as, among other things, a foreigner, a white American, and an ethnographer) is bound to have altered cultural groups' activities and interactions beyond the extent of which I am already aware. Cultural groups offer their members a chance to be together and enjoy each other's company in their shared culture and traditions—a valued opportunity to express common sociality and solidarity in a city that demands their constant adaptation. Though I asked for and was granted permission to participate in their activities, these permissions do not obviate the fact that in many senses I was encroaching. Independently of my efforts to reciprocate,[43] the fact that my presence required accommodation and led to various inconveniences deserves to be acknowledged—my involvement in their activities required them to do extra work. It is cause for my gratitude, and it is also a debt that I owe.

By their very nature, cultural groups are doing representational work. While none of the three groups performed exclusively for outsiders, all had taken on, as part of their operation, the task of educating and performing for those who did not know much about Maroons or their traditions—like me, initially, and also like many readers of this book. In my own research, I was interested in using ethnography (another form of cultural brokerage, and one about which I have my own ambivalent feelings) to amplify this aspect of their own representational endeavors, and I took heart in the fact that I was not asking group members to engage in a project of no interest or relevance to them. My particular arguments and perspectives might be of greater or lesser interest to group members (the seventy or so regular members of these groups were hardly monolithic in this regard), but the core themes presented here—the technical and intercommunicative skill these dance genres demand, the power and particularities of groups as communities in their own right, the ways their activities generate meaning within the multiethnic frameworks of the city and nation, and the ways they composed "works" that affirmed their multidimensionality as performers and as human beings—were all aspects of consistent, widespread interest and importance.

I also chose to focus on cultural representation for the opportunity it afforded to interrogate the interests and interventions of various cultural consumers.

What kinds of social or political work is being done, and how or who does it benefit? While cultural groups are the central focus of this study, their audiences are consistently within the field of vision, a perpetual reminder that these performances occur within a shifting landscape of power and privilege. I include my own interests, ambivalences, and dilemmas in the mix—occasionally as performer, occasionally as spectator, but always with social options informed by the intersection of my race, age, class, citizenship, gender, and so forth.

Inherent in this book is the conviction that bodies talk—they contain and convey more than words alone can express.[44] As someone who is convinced of the utility of performance analysis, believes that bodily communication requires "thick description" (Geertz 1973, 6) that goes beyond a technical vocabulary, and is also aware of the ways in which descriptions of bodies and movements exercise considerable representational power, I suggest that these reflexive pauses to contemplate an author's positioning continue to serve a valuable purpose, even decades after ethnomusicology and anthropology underwent its "reflexive turn" (see Clifford and Marcus 1986; Barz and Cooley 2008).

OUTLINE OF CHAPTERS

After laying the conceptual and contextual groundwork in the opening chapters, this book addresses aspects of rehearsal and performance practice and then extends its scope to include issues the groups confronted as they operated within the public sphere. Chapters 3 and 4 address Kifoko, Saisa, and Fiamba collectively, first introducing them in a comparative context and subsequently using examples from all three groups in performance analysis. The next three chapters each highlight a single cultural group, focusing on an issue or practice of importance in that particular group, while also shedding light on a different aspect of Maroon cultural engagement in Paramaribo. Each of the featured cultural groups exhibits its own unique and discernable character. My aim is to give readers, as the book progresses, an increasingly rich understanding of the groups, their membership, and the social worlds in which they operate.

Specifically, chapter 2 situates Maroon cultural groups in Paramaribo in an ambivalent space, caught between social registers and discursive categories. I outline the stakes of performing identity as Surinamers, Maroons within Suriname, Maroons living in the city, and traditional practitioners performing in a folkloric idiom. At every level but in different ways, performers experience conditional belonging, facing a perceived lack of fit in relation to established categories.

By the very terms they use to identify themselves (most clearly as *Businengee*, or "Bush Negro", as opposed to the Creole who are known as *Fotonengee*, or "City Negro"), Maroons are defined in juxtaposition to the city. For Paramaribo-based cultural group members, who have varying degrees of experience living or traveling outside of the city, their location makes them susceptible to claims that their cultural practices are illegitimate or inauthentic (the city is simply not where the "real thing" takes place), while on the other hand they face discrimination in the city because they are perceived as people who came from (and belong in) the country's more remote regions. Amid this general social climate, cultural groups assume a role as cultural stewards and ambassadors, though their authority is undermined by virtue of the very aesthetic codes and presentational strategies through which they are identified as cultural representatives. Their performances reflect this position, at once seeking to contain and direct cultural discourse while also drawing attention to its inherent insufficiencies. I suggest that these features of conditional belonging and ambivalence resonate with Maroon communities' relationship to the Surinamese nation, and Surinamese national belonging within the region.

At first glance, the cultural groups Kifoko, Saisa, and Fiamba might appear nearly interchangeable: all are based in Paramaribo, performing similar repertories of Maroon music and dance, at roughly the same kinds of performance engagements. Yet by looking at specific features of each group's operation, it becomes clear that their articulations of Maroon culture and their relation to it are quite distinct. Each constitutes what Fish calls an interpretive community (1980), with different modes of making sense of an expressive work, based on the particularities of their experiences as a collective. In chapter 3 I demonstrate how the apparent minutiae involved in engaging with tradition is in fact the key to tradition's trajectory and transformation, as well as its practical application. I investigate the ways in which cultural groups' generic commonalities relate to aspects of practice that distinguish one group from another—not in appearance alone, but also in their fundamental operation. In producing the features by which a group becomes recognizable as a cultural group, Kifoko, Saisa, and Fiamba necessarily engage in what I call technologies of differentiation: by fulfilling the basic requisites through which cultural groups become identifiable as such, they cultivate the very characteristics that will distinguish them within the genre. I compare in detail three technologies of differentiation (groups' names, rehearsal spaces, and their public performance projects) and their impact on groups' operation and general character, suggesting that technologies of differentiation are one way in which interpretive communities come into being.

Without considering the specific ways in which social actors animate a performance form in space and time, it is easy to imagine a traditional performance form as something that simply plays itself and, therefore, as something over which individuals have little influence. Chapter 4 presents a structural analysis of the awasa genre to demonstrate the interactive properties and opportunities for individuation that are built into the genre's formal logic, and the networks of awareness through which performers build upon each other's creative input. In so doing, this chapter demonstrates that "newness" and cosmopolitan touches are not exclusively the result of "repackaging" traditional forms in folkloric staging conventions, but that innovation and variation are inextricable from traditional content.

Throughout chapter 4 I highlight the ways in which sound and movement inform one another in performance. While deep connections between music and dance in African and African Diasporic genres are frequently mentioned (even celebrated), seldom are these interconnections treated as fundamental in analysis. My integrated analysis takes this challenge to heart, resulting in a clear demonstration that an exclusive focus on either audible or kinesthetic elements of performance risks obscuring crucial logical, logistical, and creative aspects of performance that emerge through their combination.

Chapters 5 and 6 both contend with the ways that cultural groups engage with the nation as a multiethnic community, but in starkly different ways. Chapter 5 introduces Alakondre Dron, a nationalistic ensemble made up of select performers from preexisting cultural groups. Kifoko has represented the Maroons in this ensemble since the early 1980s. Through an analysis of Alakondre Dron's signature piece and various multiculturalist tropes that feature prominently in its performances, I contend that these performed representations of the nation lend specificity to a multiethnic discourse that would otherwise seem vague and generic. As Suriname enters its fifth decade as an independent nation, it faces shifting identifications among the population, but with ethnopolitical and representational models that have remained largely the same since independence. Alakondre Dron as an ensemble replicates some of the country's broader political tensions, facing the challenge of updating the country's cultural rhetoric while keeping intact a continuous and teleological national narrative.

Chapter 6 concerns the creation of a nationalist subjectivity through Suriname's largest annual event—a four-day walking event called the Avondvierdaagse

(AVD), or Wandelmars. Modeled after a Dutch colonial event, the AVD became seen as "uniquely Surinamese" through the addition of advertising and cultural performance objectives. These additions make the AVD somewhat difficult to categorize, having characteristics of a fitness event, a parade, and a business and industry fair. In contrast to Alakondre Dron's staged and painstakingly rehearsed routines by the "specialist" representatives, the AVD is thoroughly popular in character. It closes down Paramaribo's streets and leaves its residents to improvise their own encounters, determining for themselves what is most significant amid an array of social, political, and economic objectives, all clearly advertised and vying for their attention. I examine the role of ethnic performativity (Tjon Sie Fat 2009) in the social poetic processes by which people use this ambiguous, large-scale event to demonstrate and formulate ideas about their place in the world. Drawing from my own experiences as a participant with the cultural group Fiamba in 2009 as well as interviews with and observations from Fiamba members, I argue that communal and national sentiment is enforced by the physical experiences of participation and the ambiguous and contingent nature of the event as a whole.

Chapter 7 explores the creative means through which performers are able to change the relational dynamics between themselves and their audiences. Specifically, I examine instances in which the cultural group Saisa uses a combination of traditional and cosmopolitan referents in their choreographies to make their marginality within Maroon cultural discourse a point of interest rather than a liability. I analyze three choreographies from the group's standard repertoire, highlighting the ways group members seize opportunities to complicate stereotypes, reshape the politics of inclusion, and present tradition as it is personally experienced rather than as collectively imagined.

In Chapter 8 I close the book with a discussion of a gesture used so often to bring a folkloric performance to its conclusion—an invitation for audience members to join group members in dance. Using examples from my fieldwork, I compare how this common social and performative device operates in disparate circumstances: at a founding group member's birthday party, at a "cultural show" for an audience of tourists and expatriates, and at a political rally for a party representing a Maroon constituency.

Each chapter addresses one or more facet of the cultural work. Chapter 2 outlines the legitimizing work that Maroon cultural groups in Paramaribo are frequently charged with undertaking—negotiating categorical boundaries that situate them at regional, national, and cultural margins. Chapter 3 focuses on the work of galvanizing discrete communities that function in different ways within the same city. Chapter 4 delves into the creative and interactive work of performing awasa, the mainstay of all three groups' repertoires. Chapter 5 outlines the representational work of depicting the multiethnic nation and the sociopolitical structures that undergird it. In chapter 6 the work is not to disseminate multiethnic rhetoric, as it was in the previous chapter, but instead to cultivate collective sensibilities by signifying and theorizing one's place in the world amid multiple and competing social objectives. Chapter 7 concerns the creation of choreographic "works" that both satisfy consumer demands and problematize the premises on which they are founded. Finally, in chapter 8 I draw upon "work" as functionality and labor. I question the extent to which a common performative gesture is in fact "doing" the same thing as the contexts of performance change, while also considering what understandings and interrelationships between and among audiences and performers need to be upheld for this gesture to be socially affirming rather than ambivalent.

Together, these chapters constitute an interrogation of the ways that cultural performance mobilizes identities, both group and individual. Many of the book's main themes—ambivalence and ambiguity, strategic impositions on an archetypal image, and practices of cultural consumption—are based on individual and community reactions to discursive categories. They represent a concerted investigation of the ways in which Maroons' interpretive moves (Feld 1984, 7) can shift these categories and influence the ways that tradition is understood and perpetuated.

CHAPTER 2

Ambivalent Forms

African or African-American culture at any given moment was less an
achieved state, the end-result of a historical process, than an ongoing
argument about what elements of a shared past were relevant to a
current situation. And different African and African-American slaves
had differential degrees of access to shaping that argument as they
tried to incorporate the residuum of their past into the circumstances
of their present. The epochal transformation of African into African-
American culture was at the level of its everyday enactment cross-cut
by politics of gender, age, origin, etc., by a present struggle, that is, over
who had the power to define the relevant elements of a shared past.

—*Walter P. Johnson, On Agency*

This chapter introduces four ambivalent structures that shape the content
and meaning of Maroon cultural groups' performances, whether directly or
indirectly. First, ambivalence arises on the national level owing to Suriname's
conditional inclusion within both the South American and Caribbean geocultural regions. Second, as an ethnic group, Maroons have an ambivalent
relationship to the Surinamese nation-state, as the rights their ancestors
secured in eighteenth-century peace treaties with the Dutch are portrayed
as contradicting their status as national citizens. Third, Maroons living in
Paramaribo are caught in a structurally ambivalent position in that city life
is discursively juxtaposed with Maroon cultural identity. Fourth, I argue that
folkloric performance is an inherently ambivalent mode of presentation,

drawing together populations, aesthetics, and practices that are presumed to have diverging relationships to tradition, modernity, and political agency. Taken together, these ambivalent structures contextualize Maroon cultural groups socially and politically. In addition, the structures outline the stakes that inform contemporary arguments about, in Johnson's words, "what elements of a shared past [are] relevant to a current situation" and who is empowered to contribute to those arguments.

The Swiss psychologist Eugen Bleuler is credited with developing the term "ambivalence" in 1910—a word that literally translates as "strength on both sides" (from the Latin *ambi* [both, or on both sides) and *valentia* [strength]).[1] Bleuler theorized that there are three types of ambivalence: emotional or affective, in which the same object arouses both positive and negative feelings; voluntary or conative, in which conflicting wishes make it difficult or impossible to decide how to act; and intellectual or cognitive, in which a person holds contradictory ideas (Merton 1976, 3). To these classifications, Robert Merton proposed the addition of sociological ambivalence, which is concerned not with how ambivalence arises and ought to be addressed in a particular type or personality, but rather with how ambivalence comes to be "built into the structure of social statuses and roles" (ibid., 5). The four ambivalent conditions featured here each have a structural or situational component that reflects circumstances shared by a collective, rather than "the feeling-state of one or another type of personality" (ibid). The clearest example of Merton's sociological ambivalence is folkloric performance, in which both its adaptive and innovative components and its preservationist and authenticating roles are inherent in the work that cultural groups do. Other ambivalences (for instance, Suriname's geographic exceptionality or the social position of the urban Maroon) engage actively with issues of categorization, more closely approximating Zygmunt Bauman's characterization of ambivalence as an "acute discomfort," producing anxiety at the inadequacy of a categorical system "either [because] the situation belongs to none of the linguistically distinguished classes, or it falls into several classes at the same time" (1991, 2).

For those whose situation is not fully acknowledged or fully beneficial in any single established category (as with Suriname's situation within the geocultural region, Maroons' relationship to the Surinamese nation-state, and urban Maroons' relationship to prevailing discourses of Maroonness and urbanity), the ability to rearticulate those narratives and negotiate the terms of inclusion is both a functional necessity and an obligation. When granted, inclusion is often tempered by qualifications and caveats, or it demands reiteration for marginal actors to maintain a presence in discussions that would be "simpler" or more expeditious without their complicating the narrative. In such circumstances, repetition becomes a component of the representational labor of the marginal figure, employed either to reaffirm affiliations deemed tenuous, or to exercise a kind of vernacular cosmopolitanism (Bhabha 1996), carving out new identificatory space by articulating different truths or affiliations over successive iterations.

On multiple levels, then, and by virtue of their culture-representational character, Maroon cultural groups perform from a position of ambivalence. As they draw attention to themselves as marginal or otherwise "problematic" figures, they also expose the willing omissions and elisions that allow discursive categories to have the appearance of truth and self-evidence. While these categories may conjure up associations and classifications, in performance they have the capacity to remain dynamic, contestable, and open to negotiation. And as Bhabha has written, "The contribution of negotiation is to display the 'in-between' of this crucial argument; *it is not self-contradictory but significantly performs, in the process of its discussion, the problems of judgment and the identification that inform the political space of its enunciation.* . . . How does the language of the will accommodate the vicissitudes of its representation, its construction through a symbolic majority where the have-nots identify themselves from the position of the haves?" (Bhabha 1994, 24; my emphasis).

Music and dance prove to be ideal negotiating media, in that performers can demonstrate and embody the copresence of features that might otherwise be construed as opposites or even contradictions. As a case in point, through their performances the members of Maroon cultural groups in Paramaribo make it plain to their audiences that, contrary to prevailing discourse, urbanicity and Maroon cultural practices and identities are not at loggerheads. Beyond the "content" that they offer, cultural groups can assert a social presence through the frequency and predictability of their performances—for instance, on national holidays or at events promoting an entity to which Suriname Maroons are thought to belong. As cultural representatives, their visibility in a given context can impact the social subtext.

GEOGRAPHICAL AMBIVALENCE:
EXCEPTIONAL SURINAME

The first memory I have of Suriname coming up in discussion was as a graduate student in the musicologist Carol Hess's course on musics of the Americas. She had kicked off the semester by having us pool our collective geographic knowledge and fill out a map of the Americas. After several minutes we had correctly identified all of the South American countries, except for three unnamed territories above Brazil—the Guianas. She completed our map by providing the names, from east to west: Guyana, Suriname, French Guiana, former English and Dutch colonies and an overseas department under continued French jurisdiction.[2] Later that year, in anticipation of a trip to Peru, I picked up a travel guide to South America only to find the map on its opening pages mirroring the one my classmates and I had filled in months before: the South American continent was lit up with text, except for the Guianas, which were simply shaded in and not identified.[3]

Those three blank spaces and the representational predicament they posed stuck in my mind: to acknowledge the Guianas within South America meant resigning oneself to an untidy continental narrative riddled with exceptions, yet to omit them from discussion denies the fact of their geographic presence on the South American continent (see figure 2.1). The existence of the predicament

FIGURE 2.1 Suriname in geographical context.
Map created by the author via Google Maps.

Ambivalent Forms **41**

makes the subsequent choices politically performative—the acts of association and disavowal imply different priorities or beliefs.

G. A. de Bruijne describes the tenuous nature of Suriname's international identifications: "In South America, Suriname forms nearly an island, as it does not have a Latin American base. It only has a few economic and educational contacts with some Latin American countries. The only formal air connection is with Belém, Brazil. . . . If Suriname's ties to Latin America are rather weak, the same holds true for the Caribbean" (1979, 24). Although not an island and not located in the Caribbean Sea, Suriname has a demonstrated affiliation with the Caribbean both economically as a member of the Caribbean Community, or Caricom (an organization committed to economic integration within the Caribbean), and culturally via participation in Carifesta (the Caribbean Festival of Arts), Fiesta del Caribe, and other large-scale celebrations of Caribbean cultures and by virtue of its inclusion in various Caribbean-themed scholarly and literary anthologies.[4] Here, too, the country's belonging is exceptional, tempered by the very geographical features that would grant it a South American identity. (Maps of the Caribbean frequently indicate Trinidad and Tobago as its southernmost territories.) In either case, Suriname's alignment with these regional clusters is conditional, accompanied by the question of whether and why it "counts" and what is to be gained or lost based on the answer.

POLITICAL AMBIVALENCE:
MAROONS IN THE SURINAMESE NATION-STATE

> I see no contradiction between the State developing itself in one way or an-
> other for the benefit of its entire population, including indigenous and tribal
> peoples, and full respect for the rights of indigenous and tribal peoples. It
> sounds to me as if the State sees a contradiction here and I'd like to under-
> stand what it thinks that contradiction may be.
>
> Fergus MacKay, legal representative for the Saramaka Maroons,
> Transcript from the Inter-American Court of Human Rights,
> The Saramaka People v. Suriname (2007)

The second ambivalence concerns Maroons' relationship to the Surinamese nation-state—in particular, how they as a people can best defend their land and rights, as established by the treaties they signed with the Dutch in the eighteenth century and by the subsequent rulings of the Inter-American Court of Human Rights and the United Nations Committee on the Elimination of Racial Discrimination.[5] Maroons in the early twenty-first century can either work to expand representation of their concerns within the national government or present cases to international agencies and courts in opposition to the government, on the ground that it has denied their rights to land and systematically excluded them from decisions affecting their territories and ways of life. In practice, each position simultaneously requires and undermines the other: international court rulings, which supersede the national constitution, have affirmed Maroons' rights, but in practice little has changed, owing to the government's reluctance or refusal to meet the demands these external governing bodies imposed; and meanwhile, greater Maroon involvement in the apparatuses of the national government shows potential for effecting change, but with the possible side effect of weakening the case for maintaining a dual governance structure that recognizes Maroon sovereignty over Maroon lands. This is a prime example of what Merton referred to as sociological ambivalence: while the situation may lead one to develop mixed feelings on a personal or psychological level, the structural juxtaposition of factors at play make ambivalence inherent to the issue at hand.

As mentioned above, the treaties signed between the Dutch and the Ndyuka, Saamaka, and Matawai Maroons in the 1760s established the free status of each group, delimited their territories, and acknowledged their sovereignty over those designated lands. Over time, political circumstances changed—emancipation in 1863 rendered the Dutch-mandated return of newly escaped slaves a moot issue, and labor shortages in the nineteenth and twentieth centuries caused the colonial government to reverse its position on Maroon isolation and thereafter to attempt to absorb Maroons into the coastal economy as cheap labor, rather than restricting the frequency and volume of their travel to the coast.[6]

Throughout, Maroons have asserted their ownership of the land and operated within a dual authority structure, in which they recognize a relation and adherence to national laws and policies, while looking to Maroon traditional authorities in matters pertaining to their own communities and lands. Each of the six Maroon populations is led by a *gaanman* (a paramount chief) who appoints leaders (in decreasing order of rank, *ede kabiten*, *kabiten*, and *basiya*) who govern at the local level. These appointed leaders and advisors to the gaanman reside in areas outside of designated Maroon lands as well as within them, operating as community leaders from as far away as the Netherlands. While the gaanman and regional and local Maroon leaders oversee political matters, their roles cannot be glossed as equivalent to existing political positions within the Surinamese government; rather, their judicial and executive duties are integrated with spiritual and cultural components of society. As André Pakosie explains, "Maroon leaders are shown to occupy an intermediary position between the city-state and the people of the interior. Jointly they share responsibility for a good relationship between humans and the world of gods and spirits" (1996, 263). While Suriname's interior districts had no voting rights until 1963 (Cyriel Eersteling, pers. comm., 10 October 2009), present-day Maroons are registered citizens, are represented in voting districts, and are able to run for government office. In this sense their status is no different from citizens of other ethnicities. Maroons charge that their rights to the land their ancestors secured in the eighteenth-century peace treaties remains absolute, yet as the extraction of resources (primarily lumber, bauxite, and gold) becomes increasingly central to the national economy, these lands have become a source of ongoing debate and tension.

One of the most egregious disavowals of Maroons' rights to land occurred in the 1960s, when an estimated forty-three villages in central Suriname were flooded in the creation of the Afobaka Dam, a hydroelectric dam that services a nearby bauxite facility and powers much of Paramaribo. Plans for the dam were negotiated between the colonial government and a local subsidiary of the US-owned aluminum company Alcoa, without advance consultation or consent from the Maroon authorities who represented the affected areas. Richard Price estimates that approximately 6,000 village residents were forced to relocate as their houses and villages were destroyed, with their burial grounds, agricultural plots, hunting grounds, and historical sites submerged.[7] The government erected resettlement camps for the displaced Maroons, again without consulting the people for whom they were intended. As a result, these camps consist of a uniform grid of houses, demonstrating no regard for Saamaka social organization or their relationship with the environment. While the city benefited from inexpensive electricity and a localized boost in the economy, Price estimates that compensation for the Saamakas amounted to roughly $3 per displaced person (2011, 39). The Afobaka Dam and its subsequent fallout demonstrates on a large scale numerous characteristic problems between colonial (and later, national) parties that prioritize resource extraction and Maroon communities living in the land to be sourced: the former's efforts to reclaim territory that was never clearly or officially acknowledged to have changed sovereignty, the bestowal of contracts and concessions on foreign mining and logging companies without the consent or advice of Maroon leaders, the negligible compensation given to Maroon communities relative to the damage such projects inflict on their lands and livelihoods, the lack of avenues for legal recourse for affected communities within Surinamese law, and decision making that demonstrates an ignorance of or indifference to the distinctive features of Maroon societies' social organization and subsistence practices.

Since Suriname's independence in 1975, the national government's approach toward resource extraction on Maroon land has not diverged significantly from what came before. In 2006, Ellen-Rose Kambel submitted a report to the Inter-American Development Bank estimating that 60 percent of indigenous and Maroon communities are currently located within a logging concession, while another 40 percent are in or directly affected by mining concessions. Despite this, there are no established laws or procedures to ensure the participation of or consultation with the communities in the affected areas. Kambel notes, "In principle, the District Commissioner is responsible for consulting with the traditional authorities of affected communities as part of the concession granting procedure, but this often does not occur in practice and is not enforceable in law" (2006, 14). Extractive operations have had a dramatic impact on communities in the interior. Mercury, which is widely used in processing gold, has found its way into the rivers on which Maroon societies depend for their livelihoods. Still water left in mining pits creates a breeding ground for mosquitoes, leading to an increase in cases of malaria. Clear-cutting trees in the rain forest has dramatically affected hunting and agriculture.[8]

In addition to these ongoing issues related to control over the interior lands, conflicts between Maroon groups and the government are magnified by still-fresh memories of the trauma of Suriname's civil war (1986–92), fought largely between a national military government and Maroon insurgents. Anxieties persist not least because the leader of the military government during this dictatorial period, Desiré "Desi" Delano Bouterse, is at the time of writing serving his second term as the country's democratically elected president. Following a military coup in 1980, Bouterse and his administration demonstrated an increasingly dictatorial character.[9] In response, an opposition force called the Jungle Commando took shape under the leadership of Ronnie Brunswijk, a Ndyuka Maroon and formerly Bouterse's personal bodyguard. The civil war that ensued provided, in Richard Price's words, "a splendid opportunity [for city folks] to act on their long-standing prejudices against Maroons" (2011, 83). Fighting was waged largely in the interior, as Maroons selected primarily industrial targets to cripple the already floundering economy,[10] and the national military retaliated by attacking Maroon communities (including civilians) directly. Moiwana, Brunswijk's home village, was targeted in a 1986 attack that left 150 civilians dead. The following year on New Year's Eve, seven Maroon men were taken from Atjoni, a transportation hub along the Suriname River, transported to Moiwana, and murdered. The civil war and the damage it caused Maroon groups in the interior has been documented by Kenneth Bilby (1990 and 1997), H.U.E. Thoden van Velzen (1990), Edward Dew (1994), and Richard Price (1995 and 2011). It is of particular relevance to the issue at hand for two reasons: first, because rights to land and self-governance were deeply intertwined with reparations for human rights abuses during the civil war, and second, because wartime fighting in the interior caused the most recent mass migration of Maroons to the coast.

These are but some of the political events that have impacted Maroons' attitudes toward national governance. The anthropologist Saloman Emanuels—himself a Saamaka—has noted an ambivalence concerning Maroons' relationship to the nation-state: "Maroons don't deny the Suriname national identity, but they don't support it openly in a conscious way" (2011, 278). The strained relations between Maroon and national leaders no doubt contributes to this generally apathetic condition, which Emanuels suggests is manifested in attitudes toward national history and holidays that do not relate directly to Maroon narratives. The ambivalent position of the government is likewise perceptible in that the few Maroon leaders mentioned in national histories are often portrayed as criminals and outlaws (ibid., 289) and by the fact that 10 October, the anniversary of the first binding peace treaty with a Maroon group, was officially declared a national holiday only in 2011 and continues to be a source of significant animosity. Paramaribo residents' personal biases and frustration at yet another holiday interrupting the workweek combine with more targeted feelings of disapproval regarding the peace treaties themselves—a reminder of an earlier freedom that was established in part on the condition that newer runaways be returned to the colonial government.

Despite past and present antagonisms, some are optimistic that increased Maroon political representation in the national government is possible and can lead to better relations between the state and Maroon communities in the interior. The 2012 census saw a dramatic increase in the share of the national population who identify themselves as Maroon—from 14.7 percent in 2004 to 21.7 percent in 2012—thus making Maroons the second-largest ethnic group in the country.

As their numbers increase, they have the potential to effect significant political change, especially given the ethnic basis of Suriname's political parties (see chapter 5). Robert Connell terms this approach "state entryism" and suggests that it is primarily through the existing national governing bodies that the Ndyuka Maroons in particular have striven to protect their lands and social practices (2017, 138).[11] Yet while greater national participation can help Maroons safeguard their interests and livelihoods, it is accompanied by allegations that Maroons are in fact fully protected by and integrated into the national government, and therefore the government should not need to recognize the dual authority system that helps Maroon groups function as partially autonomous entities (R. Price 2011, 77). Not only does this argument propose a casual revision of the rights to which Maroons are entitled, but it also entails an oversimplification of the role and duties of the gaanman and his appointed advisors. Using government structures, then, can undermine Maroons' attempts to safeguard their sovereignty over their own territories, even as they may aim to protect those same rights and lands. Suspicion of and detachment from national politics deter a number of Maroons from voting, thereby decreasing their political influence on the national political stage.

However, Maroons have been effective in arguing for recognition of and compensation for damages done to their communities and lands by taking cases against the national government to international agencies and courts. The authority of these rulings supersedes Suriname's written national policy and constitution, but these international bodies have proven largely ineffective in implementing the changes they have mandated, owing to a lack of cooperation on the national level. For instance, Kambel observes that even after a 2005 decree by the Inter-American Court of Human Rights that ordered the government to "refrain from actions—either of State agents or third parties acting with State acquiescence or tolerance—that would affect the existence, value, use, or enjoyment of [Moiwana land, traditionally held by the Cottica Ndyuka]," new palm oil and bauxite mining concessions have been granted and their recipients have begun operations on this land (2006, 16). This is indicative of a larger trend in Surinamese politics to express a position while undermining it in practice (essentially saying one thing and doing another):

> Despite [making a written commitment to protecting the land tenure security of indigenous and Maroon communities and including these communities in consultations about extractive projects in and near their areas], the

government has suggested that it may be reluctant to take legislative and other measures to recognize and secure tenurial and other rights due to concerns about creating ethnic unrest. It is felt that the delicate balance between the different ethnic groups may be disturbed as other ethnic groups may feel discriminated against if indigenous peoples and Maroons receive—in their eyes—large tracts of land or are given any form of 'special treatment', such as recognizing collective lands that would apply only to indigenous and tribal peoples. (Kambel 2006, 18)

Rhetoric that celebrates the "delicate balance" among ethnic groups, championed as the key component in Suriname's distinctive national character, perpetuates the myth and misconception that all Surinamers receive equal treatment and rights, regardless of their ethnicity or location. It frames ethnopolitical relations as existing in an ideal state of equilibrium, even in the face of structural inequalities in, for instance, the provision of education and adequate health care.[12] It promotes the apocryphal idea that at present, discrimination may happen on an individual level, but it is not systemic in the laws and structures of government. The myth of equal treatment—a perpetual feature in nationalistic music and dance performances (see chapter 5 for abundant examples)—depicts those who are at a political disadvantage as being on equal footing with their colleagues of different ethnicities. The illusion of equality, perpetuated through both verbal rhetoric and performed nationalistic tropes, makes it possible for politically disadvantaged groups to then be charged with benefiting from various kinds of "favoritism."

URBAN MAROONS

In response to ongoing logging and mining activity on lands over which the Saamaka Maroons claim jurisdiction, Richard Price made this impassioned statement about the fundamental link between Saamakas' cultural practices and their ancestral land—a link characteristic of Suriname Maroon societies overall:[13]

> From the varied and complex ritual "guards" hung in fruit trees to prevent theft to the disposition of protective and curative plants around houses, from the snake gods and forest spirits who share garden spaces with Saramaka men and women to the river and sea gods who share their village landing-places (and who form an intimate part of their daily life), the relationship of people

and their territory is rich, ongoing, systematic, and ever-developing. For Sara-makas, their forest-and-riverine territory is their life—historically, spiritually, and materially. This [is] why they have reacted so strongly whenever their territory—from their perspective, guaranteed in the treaty of 1762—has been threatened by outsiders. (2011, 25)

To argue that "their forest-and-riverine territory is their life" raises the question, what of the lives of Maroons in the city? What kinds of cultural connections can they expect and experience? Living away from this land that has been and continues to be such a vital source of sustenance, knowledge, and spiritual connection, are their cultural practices and expressions of Maroon identity destined to be seen as deficient—appraised in terms of what they lack on account of their urban environment as much as what they keep vitally present?[14] Given claims that the rain forest interior is a culturally authenticating space—indeed, a homeland within the diaspora—Paramaribo in particular comes into focus as its discursive opposite. It is owing to the long-held and essential connection between Maroon societies and their lands in the interior that the urban Maroon is so often framed as a categorical incongruity, inherently out of place, despite the fact that over 83,000 Maroons live in Paramaribo and the surrounding area—thousands more than are now thought to reside in the interior.[15]

The extent to which Maroon collective identity is linked to both geographical and historical circumstances is made clear in the terms Maroons use to refer to themselves, including Maroon (or Marron in Dutch or French, meaning escaped slave), Businengee (Bush Negro), Busikondeesama (bushland person), loweman (runaway), and fiimanpikin (the child of free people), to list a few of the most common. Most of them are aligned with one of two primary themes: either the escape from slavery or the "bush," the rain forest interior. These themes might appear to present a choice between distinct parameters, either geography or a reaction against colonial power. However, the two are so historically intertwined that one essentially implies the other. Slavery was etched into the geography of the coast, and for nearly all of those who fled, escaping the conditions of slavery also meant escaping the coastal region for the interior. To identify oneself as a Businengee or Busikondeesama might not seem at first to have an explicit association with slavery, but consider that Businengee is used in contradistinction to Fotonengee (City Negro, another term for Suriname's Creole population), and in particular consider the origins of the word "foto." The historian and novelist Cynthia McLeod explains:

In the beginning [of the colonial] period Paramaribo consisted of [Fort Zeelandia], the governor's house, a few bars, some warehouses and a few houses. Social life took place some fifty kilometers further along the Suriname River, where the main square was located. . . . The fort was named in Nengre, the language of the slaves of that time, foto. Foto was notorious, because slaves could receive "light" punishments (up to a hundred lashes) on the plantation, but for more severe, read cruel, punishments they had to go to the fort. If the master or supervisor said, "Yu o go na foto" [You will go to the fort], then that amounted to nothing good. Foto, then, was first the name for the fort and the fort was in Paramaribo. So gradually it came to pass that the name for Paramaribo in Nengre became "foto." Paramaribo is still generally called "DE STAD" ["the city" in Dutch] and in the former Nengre and now in the language Sranan "foto" became the word for every city. (McLeod and Draaibar 2007, 30; my translation)[16]

Linguistically, the enduring use of "foto" among Suriname's African descendants points to an ongoing association between Paramaribo in particular (and cities in general) and colonial power. Maroons may have escaped from plantation areas outside the city limits, but Paramaribo was the place where they were sold and where they would be brought upon recapture, and it was there that slaves were subjected to the cruelest punishments. Paramaribo and the interior, then, are morally and ideologically weighted geographic areas.[17]

Maroons have never existed in complete isolation from the city, but their presence in Paramaribo has grown steadily over the years in response to a loosening of restrictions on their movements in the nineteenth century, increased opportunities for education and employment, and as they have been forced to move from their homes owing to war or dire economic or environmental circumstances. Theirs have been a combination of voluntary, coerced, and involuntary migrations (Shelemay 2011 and 2015, 163–200). Many have migrated in their own lifetimes, while an increasing number of Maroons are born and raised in the city. Some visit the interior often, whereas others have limited firsthand experience of Maroon ancestral lands or village life, or even none at all. Some can interact with elders and important people with a full command of Maroon languages and social codes; others (particularly those born and raised in the city) stop well short of fluency in these social and linguistic expectations. Maroons living in Paramaribo defy generalization as to their experiences, social and cultural fluencies, and relationships to Maroon communities within and beyond the city.

Regardless when or how they or their relatives came to Paramaribo, once there, most confront discrimination and prejudice on various levels. As Alex van Stipriaan asserts, "Maroons were mainly seen as 'dumb Djukas,'[18] who talked silly and who were easily fooled. Even now, that image persists among many, only now there is also the added stigma of criminal[ity]" (2009, 148). Poor-quality educational options in the interior (Kambel 2006) and the large-scale interruption of education altogether during the six years of civil war have done little to help dislodge these stereotypes. With fewer and on the whole less influential political representatives than their Hindustani and Creole counter-parts, Maroons have limited access to government jobs, which are among those with the most stability and the best pay in the country. Held at a political and educational disadvantage, a large proportion of Paramaribo's Maroon popula-tion gets by through *hosselen* ("hustling") or engaging in the informal economy (Jaffe and Sanderse 2009, 1574). Such activities might include selling produce or handicrafts and household items on the street, unofficial employment as a wage laborer or housekeeper, and (rarely) more illicit activities, such as prostitu-tion or drug dealing. Many neighborhoods in and around the city with a high proportion of Maroon residents (for instance Ramgoe, Abrabroki, and Sunny Point) suffer from substandard sanitary conditions and poor infrastructure. These factors combine with a general socioeconomic structure that pairs lighter complexions with privilege (Tjon Sie Fat 2009) to create a situation in which many Maroons experience hostility and ongoing discrimination, regardless of whether they are new arrivals to the city or lifelong residents. Even Maroons who have grown up in Paramaribo will often distinguish themselves from *fotosama* (city folk), indicating that though they live in the city, they are not 'of' it, nor do they identify with it.

Two accounts from my fieldwork, from 10 October (the anniversary of the first enduring treaty between Maroons and the Dutch, celebrated in Suriname as the Day of the Maroons) in 2011 and 2009, respectively, illustrate some of these social tensions concerning ethnicity:

10 OCTOBER 2011

Confrontational Space: A Small Window onto Ethnic Bias

Initially, I congratulated myself on my own good fortune to happen upon a room for rent in an apartment complex just a few blocks away from the Suriname Culture Center where Kifoko rehearsed twice weekly. Sure, the rehearsal areas for the cultural groups Saisa and Fiamba were nearly an hour away by public transportation, but this was a central location, in an area of the city that I knew fairly well, and the rooms were air-conditioned, equipped with internet, and moderately priced. Plus, I appreciated the fact that there was a security guard on duty most of the time. When I moved to the place, members of the Hindustani family that owned the property seemed welcoming and attentive. Things looked promising.

The first sign of a problem occurred when George Lazo, a Maroon and a policy advisor at the Ministry of Regional Development, agreed to stop by the apartment to greet me and answer a few questions. He called as he arrived, and I met him at the front gate, where he was talking with the security guard on duty. I did not hear their conversation, but by the time I reached them, Lazo was steaming mad. It had been a long time since someone had talked to him like that, he huffed. "Look at me," he said, indicating his neatly pressed slacks and oxford shirt. "I'm not a boy, I'm not *wisiwasi* [beggar]—I'm an important man!" Indeed, among his accomplishments, Lazo had founded a successful tour agency that was a major source of income for his home village, Santigron. He had used his considerable political network to advocate for a number of programs to benefit Maroons, and (of particular interest to me) he had been a crucial influence in the founding the cultural group Saisa. He stayed for only a few minutes, clearly bothered by what had transpired and eager to leave.

The situation escalated from there. As more of my Maroon friends came to visit, the owners of the property grew agitated, accusing one friend of stealing when a fellow guest reported something missing, and pointedly telling me that no drugs or solicitations were permitted on their premises, even though neither I nor any of my friends had done anything to give them cause for concern—mostly we talked on my balcony, plainly visible to other people. Then came 10 October, the first year that the Day of the Maroons was recognized as a national holiday. As I prepared to travel to Santigron (the hub of that year's Day of the Maroons festivities), I heard through my window the voice of a member of the construction crew that was laying the foundation for an additional building on the rental property. As the man worked, he declared loudly—seemingly to anybody and nobody in particular—"Waar zijn de Marrons, de weg-lopende besten [Where are the Maroons, the runaway beasts]?" He repeated this phrase incessantly, timing the words to his labor. On my way to the bus depot, I stopped at the nearest general store and picked up the classified ads. It was past time to relocate.

10 OCTOBER 2009

Unspoken Understandings

On 10 October 2009 (two years before the above incident took place), the drummers of the cultural group Fiamba were relaxing after finishing a midday performance in downtown Paramaribo. In a playful and celebratory mood after a job well done, Mano Deel, one of the drummers, decided to assume the role of a TV journalist and interview a number of his fellow drummers in turn. He called me over to videotape the proceedings, using one of the group's rattles as a microphone to comic effect. As he asked Errel van Dijk (one of Fiamba's newest drummers, to whom Deel had recently relinquished the role of *gaandoonman* (lead drummer), the tenor of the conversation changed from lighthearted to more somber, with van Dijk's telling allusions to the tensions he felt as a Maroon living in the city:

> Mano Deel: How do you feel to be an Okanisi, black child OK, a Maroon, even? How do you feel to say you're a Maroon, a free man's child, how do you feel?
>
> Errel van Dijk: Well the feeling . . . the feeling has to be in [yourself]. Because those . . . let's say . . . we don't say it to [make them] feel a [certain] way, but those . . . who live in the city here—
>
> *[Here, Deel departs from his initial lighthearted tone and assumes the role of a* pikiman *(a responder), and the two men fall into the rhythmic, responsorial speech patterns associated with serious talk]*
>
> MD: [Nodding] Yah yah yah.
>
> EvD: Then you know what I'm saying already.
>
> MD: Yah yah yah.
>
> EvD: Freedom's here.
>
> MD: Yah yah yah.
>
> EvD: We've come out of slavery, we're not in chains anymore.
>
> MD: OK! (pers. comm., 10 October 2009; my translation from Okanisi)

Van Dijk chose not to articulate what it was exactly about "those who live in the city here" that made it so important that one's pride in being a Maroon came from within, but the juxtaposition between city residents and this feeling of cultural pride was well established, and Deel seemed to recognize what he was saying and acted immediately. Reacting to the gravity of the sentiment, Deel underscored his message by responding as a pikiman, using a style of speech that amplified the mood of van Dijk's words and highlighted the shared cultural connection that was the topic of their conversation. Having moved to Paramaribo from Diitabiki (a village located deep in Ndyuka territory and the headquarters of the Ndyuka gaanman) only months before, it is perhaps not surprising that van Dijk chose to talk about the social strain of experiencing Maroon pride in the city, among city people.

As Maroons in Paramaribo endeavor to make space and time for traditional activities, they often invoke aspects of life and cultural practice in the interior. Above all in serious matters such as spiritual observances and funerary rites, how things are done in the interior serves as an ideal and a template that Maroons strive to emulate as best they can in urban contexts. But while the interior remains a perpetual reference point, it is worth recalling that many of the Maroons in the city grew up in these environments, and included among those who migrated are cultural practitioners with specialized knowledge and exceptional skill. (As a talented drummer, knowledgeable despite his young age, van Dijk is a great example.) Far too often people fail to differentiate issues of inadequate or less-than-ideal pragmatic constraints on cultural practice that are perpetual obstacles in an urban setting (such as time, venue, or noise control in a residential area) from issues of insufficient knowledge or expertise. This point was made abundantly clear during my fieldwork when, after telling me at length about the shallow cultural base of cultural groups in the city, a well-meaning contact suggested that I refer instead to the "more authentic" music on *I Greet the New Day*, a CD produced by the Maroon scholar André Pakosie (2002). Among the field recordings on the album was a song performed by Irma Dabenta, a long-standing member of the cultural group Kifoko. Though that song was not one that I recognized from Kifoko rehearsals or performances, formally and stylistically it aligned easily with the dozens of other songs I had heard Dabenta sing with the group. In this instance, the same performer was involved in performances at either end of my contact's spectrum of cultural integrity, and his judgment appeared to be based on assumptions about cultural groups and the authenticating aura of "the field" in Pakosie's recording.

Clearly, cultural change and fusion with foreign or cosmopolitan elements does not take place in the city alone. Among the people I met when I traveled inland were talented artists who would not perform outside a church context and others who belonged to formal groups that were much like Kifoko, Saisa, or Fiamba yet located in more remote areas, including Stoelman's Island and Maripasoula. Surely they, too, were engaged in adaptations that were comparable in character (or of a comparable degree) to those of their urban counterparts. A geographical mapping of cultural expertise and adaptive processes provides a convenient shorthand, but it depicts migration and cultural change in overly simplistic terms.

The cultural work Maroons do in the city spans a range as vast and varied as the experiences of those who live there. On the one hand, there are individuals with exceptional or specialized knowledge and training, and on the other hand, there are those who are not deeply enculturated at home or in their neighborhoods. The latter group is tasked in some ways with starting from scratch, learning through deliberate effort even those things that would seem basic or commonsensical had they grown up in the interior. Reaching the latter group, teaching them, and drawing them into cultural practice and community are tasks particular to the city and the broader Maroon diaspora, and they constitute an important component of the work that cultural groups do.

FOLKLORIC PERFORMANCE AS TRADITIONAL PRACTICE

Cultural groups' relation to traditional practice is the site of not one but several interconnecting sources of ambivalence, concerning the main themes of authority, authenticity, commodification, and consumption. The deepest anxieties and harshest criticisms emerge from the linked issues of their roles as cultural representatives and the extent of groups' knowledge of the genres they perform. For tourists and cultural outsiders, cultural groups function as an initial point of contact: they are often the first exposure these audiences have to Maroons and their performance traditions. Regardless of whatever claims a group does or does not make about its relationship to tradition, its performances can be instrumental in formulating impressions of and opinions about Maroons and their expressive culture. At the same time, cultural groups function as a resource for Maroons in Paramaribo who have not learned these genres at home or through their family and informal community networks. Instructing less experienced dancers and musicians involves formulating and articulating aesthetic norms and performance protocols, thereby establishing a genre's parameters. Both in terms of perpetuating these traditions and representing them to outsiders, cultural groups are therefore accountable to their broader community. Even if they may endeavor to pursue their own interests and creative directions, as cultural groups they are prefigured as occupying representative and authoritative roles.

In this sense, Maroon audiences are justified in appraising groups' activities in terms of adherence to tradition and in pointing out the potential ramifications of their use of creative license.

To perform genres that are essentially communal and participatory forms for a clearly designated (paying) audience (at times further delineated by their incapacity to interpret or respond according to social and aesthetic norms) is to reconfigure the use-value of performance, impacting its very character and content. Such performances initiate a transition from what Felix Hoerburger (1968) termed first-existence to second-existence folk dance, or from participatory to presentational performance, to use Thomas Turino's framework (2000 and 2008). Both authors have disavowed the notion that any one classification is inherently better than another, while using language that implies that the transition of a genre from the category of participatory or first existence to presentational or second existence constitutes a loss, if not a fall from grace.

Hoerburger defined folk dance in its first existence as "chiefly an integral part of the life of a community. It has an important function in the community. And to take it away from it is essentially to damage the life of the community" (1968, 31). In contrast, second-existence performance "is *no longer* an integral part of community life. It is not the property of the whole community *any more*, but only of a few interested people—as an occupation of their leisure time; as a hobby; as a sport; as a means of inter-human understanding; as a colourful performance or show; and so on" (ibid., my emphasis). Second existence, then, seeks to perpetuate dances that Hoerburger claimed were "rare to be seen" in their ("natural," socially "integral," and integrated) first-existence state (ibid.).

Turino's framework of participatory and presentational performance maintains this general categorical division, but he pays greater attention to the latter type of performance as directed toward an audience. His typology is broader in scope—he speaks about performance in general, rather than "folk" or traditional genres—and therefore a traditional practice's transition from a participatory to a presentational state is not addressed directly. Nonetheless, his opinions are easy to surmise amid what he is not claiming: "The truism that societies are always changing in creative ways does not imply that change is ethically neutral, nor that the power of nationalist states and transnational capital will not erode existing alternative indigenous ethics and aesthetics" (Turino 2000, 20). He goes so far as to propose an ethical disposition for these two categories that maintains the rarity and idealization of participatory music: "Participatory styles, practices, and values offer important alternative models for enriching life and community in places where presentational and recorded forms of music have become predominant, or at least most highly valued, modes—as in the modernist-capitalist formation. The lesson is not that we should replace these other modes of music making with participatory performance, thereby reducing music's potentials, but that we should learn to recognize, reinvigorate, and more highly value a type of music making and dance that, in many places, has proven key to social health" (ibid., 58).

Taking my lead from Stanley Fish's concept of interpretive communities (Fish 1980, chapter 3), if meaning resides not in the object itself but rather through its absorption and circulation within a network of interpreters, the existence of a stage (or a recording or other framework of mediation) tells an incomplete story of how a performance is to be consumed or, furthermore, what a particular practice of consumption will signify or how it will be used within a broader network of individuals.

When I consider Turino's s claim in relation to Maroons in Paramaribo, I am reminded of cultural groups' performances at funerary rites, with the intense community and solidarity that saturate these events and the relationships and interactions that enliven the perimeter of the performance space. I think back on definitively local and cosmopolitan backyard birthday parties. There, groups perform genres including awasa, songe, and bandámmba for partygoers who join in to a greater or lesser degree depending on the crowd. In particular, I think of the moments in rehearsal when the anticipation of a group's next gig dissolves, the pedagogical critique relaxes, and group members direct their full attention to performing in the moment—dancing and making music that is communal and participatory by its very nature, savoring an opportunity for playful interaction with one another and to show off their skills. All of these situations involved lively and familiar banter among performers (and often audience members, too) in situations that were intensely interpersonal and nurturing of community. Performances at funerary rites and birthday parties typically acted as a catalyst for community involvement rather than an alternative to it. These appear to be the very kinds of life- and community-enriching experiences that Turino advocates.

Yet cultural groups' performances are definitively presentational. They are painstakingly choreographed, and they are conceptualized as a show and fashioned as a commodity, with clearly designated performers who expect to be paid for their efforts. Maroon cultural groups can be shown in one light to function as community-sustaining collectives, doing the vital work of making space for Maroon social and creative expressions within the city, while at the same time they can be depicted as ushering in a shift in performance character toward commodification and passive enjoyment, forgoing the objective of creating the fullest expression of community in favor of making the most pleasing display. Turino indicated that his notion of participatory versus presentational performance is better figured as a process-product continuum than a binary model and that one kind of performance could have features of both types (2000, 47). Yet this conceptualization does not account for Maroon cultural groups, in that by changing the context or the aspect of one's perception (Wittgenstein 2009, 431), the same group (and even the same performance) can be shown to have contradictory functions or potentially to occupy different positions along a continuum, even simultaneously.

Crucially, the deepest ambivalences about authenticity are triggered not by the existence of an audience but by its composition. As I have established, cultural groups in Paramaribo performed for a wide range of audiences. Yet the dominant classifications used to categorize folkloric performance presuppose an "outsider" audience—typically of people with financial and political means but with limited knowledge, inclination, or capacity to take part. The interests that prompt outsider audiences to commission a "cultural show" tend toward cultural conservatism, entrenching a discursive juxtaposition between "authentic" Maroon cultural practice and urban populations and modernity. In turn, their expectations as consumers cause additional conditions of ambivalence. David Guss suggests that the label "folkloric" (and, I would add, "cultural") causes a double bind: "On the one hand, it stigmatizes whatever it is applied to, causing it to be viewed as marginal and backward. To be labeled 'folkloric' is to be premodern, preliterate, preindustrial. . . . Yet this second-class citizenship is maintained by the desire to 'preserve' the integrity and authenticity of these forms" (2000, 17). The assumptions of the folkloric designation align with preexisting characterizations of Maroons as possessing tremendous cultural richness while also being isolated from (and out of step with) contemporary trends and technologies. Both "ensnared and enabled" by cultural discourse (Sharp 2014, xviii), cultural groups face audience expectations that Michael Herzfeld likens to a pedestal and a tethering post (2004, 31), in which traditional practices are elevated and admired for their cultural and historical depth (the pedestal). However, with this admiration comes pressures to resist change, maintaining narrow interpretations and depictions of cultural practice (the tethering post). Running parallel to a desire to access the "real thing" are aesthetic interests in virtuosity and variety and a rather short degree of patience for performance events that unfold gradually over considerable time. The end result is that as consumers thirst for African cultural retentions (Herskovits 1941) and depictions of traditions forged in isolation, a great deal of cultural groups' ingenuity and compositional effort goes unacknowledged, accepted uncritically as the anonymous work product of the "folk."

Whereas little consideration is devoted to how foreign audiences require performers to adapt, there is a general awareness (or suspicion) that their presence as consumers diminishes the "authenticity" that they are so keen to experience. Given the role of isolation in Maroons' historical narrative, the most culturally authentic phenomena are thought to be those in which tourists and other non-Maroons have no part. This poses an ongoing dilemma in cultural consumption: the fact that cultural groups make traditional genres of music and dance available and (logistically and aesthetically) accessible to outside audiences is taken as proof of the performance's artifice. The notion of artifice takes further hold as it overlaps with suppositions that an urban lifestyle corrupts the authentic experience or expression of Maroon culture, making Maroon cultural groups doubly easy to discount. The "authentic experience" that so many tourists pursue is undercut by the fact that cultural groups' performances are intended for their consumption, compromised by, if nothing else, the glaring presence of their own cultural difference. Larry Shiner reports a similar paradox in the realm of visual art:

> What is conceptually interesting about this situation is that carvings *not intended* to be Art in our sense but made primarily as functional objects are considered "authentic" Primitive or Traditional Art, whereas carvings *intended* to be Art in our sense, i.e., made to be appreciated solely for their appearance, are called "fakes" and are reduced to the status of mere commercial craft. Thus, in the context of the Primitive Art market, the Art vs. craft distinction undergoes a paradoxical reversal. The utilitarian artifacts are elevated to the status of Art, and the non-utilitarian artifacts are relegated to the category of craft. (1994, 227)

As Sally Price and Richard Price have demonstrated (1999), aesthetic enjoyment and functionality find a ready coexistence in Maroon art forms, a point that I have no interest in contesting. Rather, I recall Shiner to draw attention to how categorizations—including those used by Hoerburger and Turino—describe nonstaged performance as being predominantly utilitarian (having an "important function in the community" and proving "key to social health"), with the unfortunate side effect of rendering its aesthetic attributes secondary by virtue of the classificatory schemas themselves. Cultural consumers are thereby able to enjoy music and dance from the first existence and participatory categories as a kind of "raw material" over which they can exercise their own aesthetic procilivities as interpreters, collectors, and samplers. When performers and/or cultural insiders attend to the aesthetic features of performance in a way that facilitates its wider circulation and consumption as a "product," too often their aesthetic efforts are dismissed out of hand as artifice or fakery, thereby denying performers the possibility of being considered "artists" on the same aesthetic plane and level as the consumers of their works. It is hard not to miss the romanticizing undertones of a touristic or scholarly quest (or conquest) here as well, in which functional or aesthetic adaptation and financial transaction and compensation are seen to diminish a thing's worth, as that which is not offered is preferred to that which is—perhaps because of its actual features, but also because it is withheld.[19] In particular, the issue of compensation for performance is reliably contentious. As Ruth Hellier-Tinoco points out, these ambivalences can be magnified when a tradition is absorbed into larger narratives of national culture: "Expectations that the musicians and dancers will perform for small amounts of money and for the honor of performing because their rituals and traditions are part of the patrimony prevail" (2011, 253).

In sum, consumer demand is seen as having a corrupting influence, while at the same time stigmatizing performers' compensation and disparaging their aesthetic contributions in their own processes of adaptation, personalization, and innovation. Within the discourse of commoditization, elements of composition, choreography, stagecraft, and showmanship that would serve as edifying dimensions in "classical" genres function instead as indications of fixity, dilution, and mass production—"tampering" with genres that might seem more "exotic" if consumed as though they were "raw materials."

In his canonic article "Aesthetics as Iconicity of Style," Steven Feld articulates what he saw as a troubling use by local evangelical missionary workers of culture-representational performance of the Kaluli of Papua New Guinea:

> Kaluli modes of expression are thus relegated to "custom", a term found both in Australian colonial usage (with the same condescending, romantic overtones as certain uses of "folklore") and in Papua New Guinea lingua franca, Tok Pisin as *kastom*. "Custom" is what Kaluli are requested, "allowed" (and occasionally paid) to perform, for instance, a half hour of ceremonial drumming

at the mission station airstrip on Papua New Guinea Independence Day. By the request for and tacit approval of this sanctioned version of expression, the mission people signal to visiting dignitaries (other mission officials, government agents, anthropologists) that the Kaluli (still) "have culture." But, more subtly, they communicate that *kastom* can be commodified. This is the process of hegemonic folkloricization: dominating outside parties legitimate condensed, simplified, or commodified displays; they invoke, promote, and cherish them as official and authentic custom, while at the same time misunderstanding, ignoring, or suppressing the real creative forces and expressive meanings that animate them in the community. (1988, 96)

Within Feld's description are many of the themes that have prompted anxiety and ambivalence in Maroon folkloric performance—commodification, simplification, the role of consumers with little cultural knowledge but significant financial and political power, the recurring issue of whether a people (still) "have culture," and what that implies politically. Feld argues persuasively that the strategic support or deployment of folkloric performance can be used as a mechanism for domination; it is an "allowance" that pays lip service to the continuation of cultural practice, while doing violence to those very practices by directing audiences' attention to "condensed, simplified, or commodified displays" rather than their "real creative forces and expressive meanings." His observations can function as a useful reminder that, whatever its contents, a "cultural show" can be solicited for strategic reasons and be taken to mean things beyond what the performers intend.

Along the way Feld makes a number of troubling but familiar assessments and assumptions. He demonstrates a clear disdain for folkloric presentations, based on the assumptions that their sole and unquestioned aim is to satisfy the expectations and desires of their elite audiences; that the performances categorically constitute shortcuts (not just shortened performance lengths, but ways of sidestepping the nuance, genuine character, and complexity of "authentic" practice that would give a performance "real creative force"); and that as cultural representatives, performers offer no commentary or social provocation, or any viable artistic expression. It is clear that he witnessed a folkloric presentation, but he gives no indication of what these performers actually did—he only invokes the absence of legitimacy. In fact, he portrays the performers as pitiable and totally disempowered, paid or not paid (as the case may be) to do the bidding of the missionaries, to whom Feld gives more credit (or blame) for the aesthetic and creative components of performance than he does the performers. Feld specifies that this is a symptom of "hegemonic folkloricization," leaving room for us to imagine other potential types of folkloric process and product, but he offers no alternative, nor does he direct the reader's eyes or ears to any specific aesthetic or interactive features by which this "type" of folklorization could be distinguished. Feld provides a clear case of what folkloric performance is being used (by missionaries and dignitaries) to do, but he omits entirely what the Kaluli performers are doing. I am suggesting that the critical vocabulary about the (foreign) consumption of folkloric performance has entrenched within it ambivalent structures and tendencies that discourage the practice of taking those performances seriously.

Feld's example underscores the benefit and importance of taking a broad-spectrum view of the cultural work of folkloric performance, not as a practice of "restoring" the agency to those thought to have none, but as a way of registering when, why, and how performers are directing their energies and to make sure these do not get left out of a conversation that is, after all, about them. Perhaps the best way to illustrate my point is by giving examples of performances from Maroon cultural groups that complicate the notion that folkloric performers are docile and unwitting. Not all performances have a subversive or provocative component to them, as do the three examples that follow. Yet each example I selected would be easy to overlook—especially since from other angles they could be described as being characteristic or representative of the awasa genre that forms their stylistic basis.

"Mi o trouw anga I yee," composed and performed by Fiamba
Kaba kelle kelle, kaba kelle kelle—the *gaan doon* (lead drum) finishes its opening phrases, calling the performers to attention. Faizel Pinas raises a song with an expansive, descending melody:

| *Mi anga I o trouw yee mama . . .* | Me and you will marry, mama . . . |
| *Mi anga I o meki wan baby . . .* | Me and you will make a baby . . . |

Two rows of dancers provide the chorus, stepping forward and back while swishing their hips, holding their arms as though they were cradling a baby:

In Holland.	In Holland.
In Ameeka.	In America.
In Faansi.	In France.

This song makes an overt reference to the ways in which romantic partnerships (marrying and producing offspring) can facilitate international mobility. Pinas's voice is warm and crooning, but his sweeping melody is answered by clipped responses that are spoken as much as sung, expressing a desire for travel in place of a desire for the individual who would facilitate it. The song is delivered in Okanisi, but with loan words—the Dutch word *trouw* for marriage, the English word "baby" instead of the Okanisi *pikin*—and an attentive outsider audience would likely recognize the names of the countries included in the chorus. Thus, the song speaks of how relationships and children intersect with mobility in a way that might be understood (wholly or in part) by an outsider audience. This does not mean, however, that the "you" to whom Faizel sings is imagined as a foreigner: the song could just as easily "speak to" a Maroon audience, with networks that often extend into diasporic communities in Holland and France.

Another song in Fiamba's repertoire was composed by Maranjaw, a young man loosely affiliated with the group who was from the neighborhood where they rehearsed. This aleke song, "A mi dugudugu," functioned as a way of airing a grievance against his employer, who he alleged had taken advantage of him, cheating him out of money he was owed. In the song, he appeals to the members of Fiamba for sympathy.

A mi dugudugu[20]

Lead: A mi dugudugu, a mi dugudugu	It's my dugudugu [nonlexical word]
Koor (chorus): Ayoo Fiamba	Ayoo Fiamba
L: Mi wroko gii en, a no wani pai mi	I work for him, he doesn't want to pay me
K: Ayoo Fiamba	Ayoo Fiamba
L: Saafu kaba, saafu de ete	Slavery ended, slavery still exists
K: Ayoo Fiamba	Ayoo Fiamba
L: Fiamba, Fiamba	Fiamba, Fiamba
K: Ayoo Fiamba	Ayoo Fiamba

The final example comes from the 2009 Awasa Festival in Saint-Laurent-du-Maroni, French Guiana, captured on video by Michel Ducoudray.[21] The cultural group Tangiba takes the stage to dance awasa—they are among the last groups to compete. Near the end of their set, Dyaga Plein, one of the group's two leaders, lies down in the center of the stage and stays still, as though he's unconscious. Other dancers mill about the dance stage, feigning their concern for him. One of the group's female dancers leans over him, inspecting him. She gestures an appeal to the audience—what should she do? Lightly, she touches the front of his *kamisa* breechcloth. (This is a rather shocking move, for while physical humor referring to sex is common enough among Maroons, for a woman to touch the private parts of a man of roughly the same age in public is nonetheless unexpected.) Dyaga springs up, revived by the touch, and dances energetically. Demonstrating his athleticism, he crouches low to the ground, balanced on the balls of his feet, his ankles remaining loose so he can shake his ankle rattles as he steps. He leaps down from the stage and approaches members of the audience, which is comprised almost entirely of Maroons from in or around Saint-Laurent-du-Maroni, where the contest is taking place. First, he walks up to a preteen girl in the front row, turns around and shakes his backside directly in front of her, pointing at it and telling her to touch it. She stiffens and does not budge from her chair, as the girl sitting next to her talks excitedly in her ear. He runs over to another woman. Standing over her, he isolates his hips, moving them forward and back. She leans far from him in her chair and looks away. Another male dancer from the group follows suit, instigating an array of playful but awkward encounters with women in the audience. Up until this point the audience had responded to performances with polite applause; now they cheer and roar with laughter.

From the moment of the female dancer's unexpected solution to Dyaga's "ailment," the routine continues to play with expectations, right up to its conclusion. Saisa's dancers are violating folkloric performance expectations by descending from the stage and soliciting reactions from audience members directly, encroaching on these women's space with their advances in such an overt and exaggerated way.[22] The uproarious response has less to do with their dancing skills (already demonstrated in previous numbers in their set) than with the physical comedy of the social encounters they have created, and the awkward and sometimes mortified reactions of the targeted women in the audience who become central to the performance. What this performance means socially is inextricable from its audience—the fact that Tangiba was performing for Maroons who were familiar with the various cosmopolitan and cultural codes the group transgressed led to the performance having a particular kind of resonance and satisfaction. To me, one of the most striking facets of this performance is the degree to which

Tangiba's dancers dominate the entire auditorium, taking command of the space and establishing their power to set their own agenda and relate to the audience on their own terms. I can't imagine a starker contrast to the image of (hegemonic) folkloric performance that Feld conjures.

Cultural groups are implicated in a series of power relationships: As hired entertainers, they perform in genres associated with Maroon traditions on command, and these performances are indeed used by people and organizations of means to make specific points about the place of culture. Cultural groups also create "culture shows" made of discrete works that can accommodate a short attention span, and they offer a sampler of genres in contrasting styles in quick succession. They make use of stages and streets as well as dance clearings, and they spend time creating a whole range of strategies that make consuming their performances as effortless as possible. Often audiences and critics assume the simplicity of folkloric performances, without ever pausing to consider that they could be otherwise. Yet as these examples illustrate, cultural or folkloric groups have at their disposal countless ways to meet the audience's or consumer's gaze head on—they can and do talk back to power.

In sum, there are a number of tensions that characterize culture-representational performance writ large: The label "cultural" or "folkloric" tends to both reify the historical grounding of a tradition while limiting the ways it can be interpreted and adapted. As cultural spokespersons, performers are accountable to the communities they represent, while at the same time they face scenarios and formats that are structurally or contextually incomparable with many tenets of traditional practice. (What would it take, for instance, to convey a sense of "authenticity" when performing in a casino or on a city street? What would critics expect or prefer during a three-minute performance segment within a larger work celebrating multicultural Suriname, or in the context of a parade?) Depending on the interpretive angle, cultural groups can be seen as sustaining community engagement and participation or hastening social and cultural dissolution in a modernist-capitalist structure. They contend with outsider audiences whose projections of authentic performance are undermined by their very existence and interaction. Demands for variety, innovation, and virtuosity clash with the task of presenting the generic and characteristic. By facilitating an outside audience's access to Maroon performance traditions, cultural groups produce performances that often fail to satisfy touristic desires for that which is not corrupted by (their own) outside influence. These features make folkloric and cultural groups the source of public anxiety and disdain while also making them very utilitarian: as cultural representatives who navigate an ambiguous and ambivalent social and political (and even geographic) terrain, they can be "taken to mean" many things.

In a Surinamese and Maroon context, cultural groups link and articulate various relationships between city and interior, and between Maroon nation and Surinamese nation. In nationalistic performance they can be used to promote a notion of multiethnic citizenship that obscures different ethnic groups' relationships to the power of the nation-state. Their rehearsals and performances in city contexts work against an assimilationist narrative, while giving group members opportunities to demonstrate that Maroon cultural practices do not present an inherent opposition to modernity. These groups and their performances claim or disavow affiliations as a matter of practice—not so much contradicting themselves as recognizing parts of a social situation that is complete and fluid but split by parameters that would locate power elsewhere. Groups may be for hire and mobilized by broader entities for their own purposes, but that does not prevent the groups from speaking their own truths and, to some degree, setting the representational agenda.

CHAPTER 3

Cultural Groups as
Interpretive Communities

As soon as Kifoko concluded its Thursday evening rehearsal, I would dash to the bus and across town to where Saisa's rehearsal was just beginning. I arrived at the second practice with sweat from the first still drying on my skin and clothes, but even so I had to reorient my mind and body to the task at hand, as though I had spent the previous hours doing something entirely different.

And in a way I had. Although I went from one Maroon cultural group's rehearsal to another, together they felt like a study in contrast. The venues, the air and light, the sounds from their respective neighborhoods, the conversations, and the ways that people interacted with one another were different. How we tied our *pangi* skirts and warmed up our bodies and the dialects and vocabularies group members used were likewise different. I was different in these spaces, too. My voice produced different sounds: I breathed deeper from my diaphragm in Kifoko rehearsals, taking to heart senior members' comments about posture and presence and savoring how our voices filled the resonant space of the rehearsal studio. With Saisa, I sang clustered together with other group members, taking pleasure in the way our voices created one powerful, piercing response to the lead singer's call. I sang with a brassier sound, from my throat, every so often breaking into harmony. Dancing with Kifoko, I corrected myself while watching my reflection in floor-length mirrors; in Saisa rehearsals I looked at the dancer opposite me, trying to match or complement his movements. Having first learned these dances under Kifoko's tutelage, I struggled at times to match the gait and the busier footwork that were characteristic of Saisa. I even listened differently.

In Kifoko rehearsals every drum stroke and footfall echoed off the cement walls of the dance studio. Saisa's open-air rehearsals gave the drums a clearer, drier sound, but I had to strain my ears to make out the calls from the low gaan doon amid a larger number of percussionists, performing in a faster tempo.

I began learning Maroon music and dance with Kifoko, and I can still remember emerging from my first Saisa rehearsal, astonished and bewildered that a dance I had spent months learning could seem so unfamiliar when practiced by a different cultural group. It has since occurred to me that members of these two groups might likewise be astonished at the dramatic changes in my actions and interactions during the course of a single evening, as I left one community of performers to join another. But then again, all three cultural groups with which I rehearsed regularly—Kifoko, Saisa, and Fiamba—were already well aware that, from certain angles, what they do is worlds apart.

At first glance it is similarity (not difference) that appears to characterize the relationships among these three cultural groups. All operated within a city of about a quarter-million people; the genres in their repertoires overlapped, with awasa dance serving as a mainstay of all three; and though in different proportions, the groups performed at the same kinds of events. These included funerary rites and birthday parties within Maroon communities; commissioned engagements for business openings or organizations' meetings; demonstrations for tourists; and performances for the general public coinciding with a holiday, festival, or competition. All told, as "culture shows," their performances were structured and could be consumed in a relatively uniform way.[1] From the stage, many of the distinguishing features of a group's practice are scarcely perceptible to a lay audience, registering only as a vague sense of stylistic variation.

The fact that these differences can at once have a profound effect and be barely discernible makes clear the importance of recognizing that cultural groups do so much more than put on the folkloric shows that are their most formal and public face. Not only do groups demonstrate communal performance styles, but they also constitute communities that are imbued with the full range of particularities borne of actual social relationships and experiences.[2] The groups attract members by appealing to diverse subsections of the Maroon population within Paramaribo, promoting disparate uses of cultural forms on both ideological and pragmatic levels. These forms, too, are not ready-made or self-evident but come into being amid innumerable social and situational idiosyncrasies. Seemingly small aspects of Kifoko's, Saisa's, and Fiamba's operations reverberate in their aesthetic choices, habits of relating to one another, and public presence to the point where, despite their abundant similarities, it becomes reasonable to ask whether they are in fact using cultural performance to "do" the same things—whether, in other words, they are mobilized to perform the same cultural work.

Here I illustrate how three such fundamental components of the groups' operations—designating a name, occupying a rehearsal space, and setting annual goals—become technologies of differentiation. They are all requisite for the normative function of a cultural group, and at the same time they generate durable particularities of practice and group identity. The very features and practices whereby they fulfill the generic expectations of a cultural group simultaneously establish each group as a unique node within the city's social and economic networks. They lead not only to specific modes of group identification but also to distinctive practices of interpreting and presenting tradition. In their weekly rehearsals, each group created performance practices that nurtured its individual character, while at the same time helping formulate ideas about common practice. By comparing the groups' approaches to these fundamental components of their operation, it becomes easier to see how traditional Maroon performance can be mobilized and applied to create various kinds of social meaning.

My ideas and choice in terminology are informed in part by Michel Foucault's *Technologies of the Self* (1988) and Ann Cooper Albright's discussion of "Techno Bodies" (2010). Albright reckons with the dancing body as simultaneously a sensory organism, a source of power, and an aesthetic object that is both the worker and the site of work but is fundamentally a tool and a vehicle of knowing and being known in the world. Foucault's technologies of the self "permit individuals to effect . . . a certain number of operations on their own bodies and souls, thoughts, conduct, and ways of being, so as to transform themselves in order to attain a certain state of happiness, purity, wisdom, perfection, immortality" (1988, 18). He discusses how seemingly small social gestures become "truth games" by which a person's self becomes known and cared for. Technologies of differentiation depart from Foucault's technologies of the self in that I focus on communal identities. Furthermore, the technologies of differentiation I discuss here have the additional structural feature of emerging from categorical parameters, establishing a seemingly paradoxical relationship in which satisfying the requisites for belonging entails engaging with the particulars that will set one group apart from others.

Also central to my analysis is the literary critic Stanley Fish's concept of interpretive communities (1976 and 1980). Fish argues that meaning does not reside in a text alone. Rather, it emerges experientially, in dialogue with the interpretive faculties of an individual, which are inherently shaped through a person's socialization in a particular community. His approach is phenomenological in nature, prioritizing emerging, experiential meaning over and above any notion of the intrinsic meaning of a static text. Taking into account the role of the interpreter as well as the work to be interpreted, Fish concerns himself with issues of impact and function—he returns perpetually to the question, what does the text *do*?[3]

Fish's examples come almost exclusively from literature, yet the same principles can be applied constructively to other expressive works and their interpretation. He acknowledges that performance is ideally suited to such a phenomenological approach, claiming that "the great merit in kinetic art is that it forces you to be aware of 'it' as a changing object—and therefore no 'object' at all—and also to be aware of yourself as correspondingly changing" (Fish 1980, 43). In the present case, I suggest that Paramaribo's cultural groups each constitute a discrete interpretive community with its own practices of creating and making sense of Maroon music and dance. The relevance, satisfaction, and utility of performing these Maroon genres are all constructed and envisioned collectively through the particularized aspects of each group's operation. The "works" in which these groups involve themselves might be considered their public performances or the genres that make up their repertoires, but in either case, Fish's analytical lens encourages consideration of what happens as those works are experienced by an interpretive community, above and beyond their intrinsic properties. In other words, we are invited to forgo the notion of a self-contained meaning of a work and instead investigate the ways in which it is made meaningful.

What I call technologies of differentiation—the particular practices that arise as a means of fulfilling generic expectations—help create interpretive communities. It is through them that a group becomes recognizable as a cultural group, while also having self-contained and internally consistent logics of operation and objectives. Ultimately, as Max Weber points out, "ideal types" (such as the category "cultural group") cannot exist independently of the particularities that make their exceptions.[4] The very mechanisms by which Kifoko, Fiamba, and Saisa become fully recognizable as cultural groups are the same ones that make one group distinct from another. Technologies of differentiation might have in common that they help build interpretive communities, but they, too, have distinctive functional tendencies that shape a collective in specific ways. A group's name states its intention and ideology, its rehearsal location dictates elements of the group's public interface, the venue influences pedagogy and choreography and shapes a rehearsal's social interactions, and a group's goals inform ideas about the relevance and ideal application of Maroon performance in relation to society at large. The net result of their differences are collectives that on one level may appear similar to the point of being interchangeable but nonetheless have a character and communal feeling that distinguishes one from the next. Through the specific practices of interpretive communities, the artistic work of performance and the social work of community building are rooted in unique sensory experience and are made to make sense.

Recognizing the different social motivations and expressive aims that propel individuals toward one cultural group as opposed to another makes it clear that Maroons living in Paramaribo are hardly a monolithic population. Likewise, it discredits the idea that cultural groups exist solely to provide one kind of performance product—a cultural show—that is likely to exhibit a limited range of variation that may be difficult for the untrained eye to discern. The work with which a group concerns itself can have any of a number of relationships to the works that its members present for their various audiences. This distinction becomes increasingly evident through focusing on rehearsals not as a means to one particular end, but as the creation of social and ideological space for self-expression in a cultural idiom.

NAMES

Devising a name is one of the preliminary and fundamental steps in founding a cultural group. Though it is obligatory, and most groups draw from cultural-symbolic vocabularies in predictable ways, it is also a process that involves great care and intention and has the potential to set an ideological trajectory for the group to follow. As a distillation of a group's character, the group's name articulates features, priorities, and ideals that its members, and its leaders in particular, find meaningful. Collectively, Kifoko, Fiamba, and Saisa provide a clear example of how a name functions as a technology of differentiation, making aspects of their character and social or creative vision immediately evident. A comparison of the meanings of their names illustrates fundamental distinctions between each group's approach to cultural practice and performance.

Kifoko

The visual artist and cultural group founder André Mosis first used the name Kifoko to refer to his workspace, which he occupied from 1981 to 1990. Over time, the name was used to refer to various groups and projects that emerged from this space, such as the Kifoko House Band, which specialized in aleke music; and Kifoko Productions, which made Maroon culture–themed items for retail. The cultural group Kifoko is the last remaining venture from this place and time associated with Mosis and his Kifoko workshop.

In Mosis's native Okanisi language, "kifoko" is the name of a designated corner of a house where broken or unused things are put to be later repaired or shared with neighbors.[5] Eddy Lante interprets this to mean that people should hold on to their culture—they should not discard their heritage or forsake it in favor of other flashy or novel forms. Yet a closer consideration of the term reveals telling aspects of the group's approach to cultural practice. All culture-referential and tradition-based performances use a retrospective lens to some extent, but the term "kifoko" invokes the past explicitly, while implying a certain degree of cultural estrangement on the part of the current generation.

Items placed in the kifoko have undergone some variety of damage, suffered imperfections, or fallen into disuse. Typically, they need care and attention to be restored to working order. Using the term as an analogy places group members in a stewardship role, working to safeguard and maintain practices that are either underused or have sustained some kind of damage and must be rehabilitated in order to once again be found useful and valuable. As Jeff Todd Titon notes, central to stewardship is "the idea that humans are caretakers, not owners, of resources" (2009, 121). The moniker "kifoko" emphasizes collective use over individual ownership and frames cultural practice as something external rather than embodied. As with the items in the kifoko, performance practices can be taken up and modified, used, or shared, but the practices and practitioners never fully merge.

The analogy prefigures unrealized potential, but it also implies a sense of deficit or immediate inutility, whether because the item in a kifoko has fallen into disrepair or there is no person present who would appreciate and have a use for it. The name's rehabilitative framework provides a ready link to folkloric performance strategies that emphasize nostalgia and cultural preservation efforts. It also aligns with African Diasporic experiences of separation from an African homeland and the social fracture and loss of cultural continuity that resulted from the traumatic and restrictive processes of slavery. The institution of slavery instilled a sense of an irreparable longing and loss that resonates with the notion that a kifoko would never be empty, and the contents extracted therefrom could always be made more complete, more whole.[6]

At the same time, as established in chapter 2, urban Maroons are susceptible to allegations that their cultural resources are lacking relative to Maroons in towns or villages further inland. City residents are presumed to have comparatively limited skill in or knowledge of traditional music and dance and fewer opportunities or inclinations to congregate as a community and engage in their own cultural practices. In this light, the restorative implications of the term "kifoko" can function as a response to the challenges an urban lifestyle and location are presumed to pose, while also speaking to a larger and more general diasporic process of cultural reclamation.

As individuals, Kifoko members practice cultural stewardship by learning and striving for accuracy and excellence in the group's featured genres. Collectively, research and educational projects have played a large role in the group's self-image. Beginning in the mid-1980s, Mosis and several other Kifoko members conducted independent research, recording oral histories and documenting information about the dances in their repertoire.[7] Their prior research informs many aspects of the group's practice and presentation, from the ordering of their performances and rehearsals (following the same order as the gaansamapee, the sequence of genres traditionally performed on special occasions) to the communication between drummers and dancers and the manner in which they wear their clothes and style their hair. Most of the group's large-scale research projects took place in the first decade of Kifoko's existence. However, these early projects continue to serve as one of the group's signature features, distinguishing them from the other groups active in Paramaribo.

Fiamba

"Gaansama de vanouwdu, ma . . . ifu I wani do nyun sani, da I á man do en nanga gaansama. Da I abi fu wroko nanga yonku sama [(The performance traditions of one's) elders are important but . . . if you want to do new things, you can't do it with older people. Then, you have to work with young people]."

—Erwin Alexander Tolin (pers. comm., 3 December 2009)

Fiamba song "U n'á gaanwan," composed and sung by Jemi Sikanar

Lead:
O ye yee, u naa gaanwan, fa u fika ja u n'a gaanwan [O ye yee, we don't have elders, how we're left here, we don't have elders].

Chorus:

Ooo yee, u n'a gaanwan, fa u wanwan fika ja u n'a gaanwan [Ooo yee, we don't have elders, how we're left alone here, we don't have elders].

Lead:

O ye yee u naa gaanwan, Fiamba uman fika ja u de sondee gannwan [O ye yee, we don't have elders, Fiamba women are left here, we're without elders].

Chorus:

Ooo yee, u n'a gaanwan, fa u wanwan fika ja u n'a gaanwan [Ooo yee, we don't have elders, how we're left alone here, we don't have elders].

Whereas the name Kifoko emphasizes heritage and stewardship, Fiamba places the focus on youth and creative potential. Fiamba is the Okanisi name of an ovenbird common in Suriname's rain forest interior.[8] Despite the fiamba's small size, it is known for making large and elaborate nests. Louise Wondel, the group's founder, explained the meaning of the name this way: "Mi sikin nyoni ma mi sa du bigi [I may be small but I can do big things]." In a line from her poem "Sabi," Wondel gives a further insight: "Fiamba taki, Nyoni fu sikin, a ná nyoni fu neesi. Sabi de a gaandi, ma a de a pikin wan tu [(The bird) Fiamba says, smallness in size does not mean a small nest. Knowledge is with the elders, but it's with the young ones too]" (1998). Whereas "nyoni" (smallness) has multiple possible applications, Wondel's explication of the meaning in her poem makes a clear link to youth, and this meaning carries over to the name of the cultural group Fiamba. In 2009, Clifton Asongo, the group's leader and Wondel's nephew, noted that Fiamba's demographics had always been young—a feature of its membership that had only become more pronounced over time.

This youth affiliation was not only evident in the group's roster, it was also reflected in various ways through Fiamba's presentational strategies and activities. Women's performance outfits were typically styled to indicate a younger population, with shorter pangi skirts and tops that exposed the dancers' midriffs. Fiamba's repertoire featured the popular genres aleke and loketo, thereby presenting a more contemporary and youth-oriented take on traditional performance.[9] Some of the songs the group regularly performed referred to youth and young people's concerns. The most explicit of these songs was Jemi Sikanar's "U n'á gaanwan," cited above. In some of Fiamba's performances, members also made their youthful identity explicit—most notably at the World Kinderfestival, which they attended in Antwerp, Belgium, in 2001 and a subsequent CD recording with fellow participants, the Ghana Junior All-Stars (Ghana Junior All-Stars and Pikin fu Fiamba 2001)). In this recording, Fiamba was billed as Pikin fu Fiamba (children of fiamba) instead of its regular name, further emphasizing the group's identification with youth. The group's performance calendar showed the extent to which young people's activities were influenced by the academic calendar, with breaks coinciding with school vacations. Asongo saw this youth affiliation as beneficial: "I find that it's a good thing to really work with the young ones. You see? Because you're helping them form themselves, to take a good path in society" (pers. comm., 17 September 2009; my translation from Okanisi). In turn, he noted that working with young people gave the group a special kind of energy and enthusiasm—what he deemed an "apart sfeer" (distinctive ambiance).

The name Fiamba speaks of potential and ambition. The "big things" that group members can do could be interpreted as their capacity to impress audiences as dancers and musicians within the group. Sheryl Tesa, a singer and dancer in Fiamba, embodied this attitude in conveying her family's reaction to her participation in the group: "Up to now they tell me—maybe I'm singing awasa or something—they tell me, 'look now, you can't sing those kinds of songs there, you don't know how to sing them' . . . then you don't respond. They'll see, when you go sing. Really" (pers. comm., July 2009; my translation from Okanisi). Tesa framed her participation in Fiamba as a way to realize her potential and show what she is capable of achieving, despite her family members' skepticism.

Taken another way, Fiamba helps equip members with the tools that will allow them to do big things later in life. As Erwin Alexander Tolin, a founding member who is no longer with the group, remarked, with the youth identity of the group came an expectation that members would leave once they reached a certain age (flying out of the nest, to extend the analogy). Several former Fiamba members have gone on to become recognized public figures and cultural advocates in various ways. Tolin has received international recognition as a playwright. He has coordinated a number of large-scale performance events in dialogue with the Ministry of Culture, while also directing programs for youth outreach and empowerment through theater. Norma Sante has become one of the best-known faces and voices in the national entertainment industry as a lead singer in the popular kaskawi band, Naks Kaseko Loco. Kaskawi has multiple cultural influences, but by singing nearly exclusively in Okanisi, Sante has given this particular group a distinctly Maroon voice and character. Sante was "discovered" by Naks Kaseko Loco through her performances with Fiamba in 2007. And Wondel became widely known as a performer, poet, and scholar and was deemed a rising star in Maroon cultural performance and advocacy from the mid-1990s through the mid-2000s. Within the group, then, a number of individuals have made impressive achievements, arising in part from the cultural foundations that Fiamba instills.[10]

The names Kifoko and Fiamba set no clear musical or choreographic parameters. Instead, they chart particular social trajectories and organizing principles. Beyond the groups' daily practices and aesthetic codes (which may well share a number of characteristics), these names give a sense of vision and purpose that structure those actions toward different ends. Both names mobilize ideas of social productivity. Kifoko frames group participation as a way of sustaining valued aspects of Maroon culture—preserving, safeguarding, and disseminating music and dance for the good of the community. Fiamba introduces the cultural group as a kind of proving ground for young people, at once demonstrating "big things" they can do and giving them performance skills and experience that they can use as a basis for realizing future ambitions.

Saisa

Instead of articulating a stance or vision, like the names Kifoko and Fiamba, the name Saisa refers explicitly to performance content and a community affiliation. Saisa is an acronym for "Songe and Awasa in Santrigron" (pronounced "Santi-goon" in the Saamaccan language).[11] Songe and awasa are two well-known dance genres of the Ndyuka Maroons, and Santigron is a village roughly an hour's drive from Paramaribo. Nearly every member of the group had some affiliation with Santigron, either living or having lived there themselves or having immediate family members there.

Whereas village connections, however distant, tend to serve as cultural authenticators for urban Maroons, the ambiguous status of Santigron as a village with a more heterogeneous and "suburban" character prompted some people to question Saisa's grasp of traditional performance practices. Having a sense of Santigron's particular history and character helps clarify the particularities of Saisa's image and social function. An introductory description of the village is therefore warranted.[12]

After Suriname abolished slavery in 1863, greater numbers of Maroons came to the urban coast in search of work. Maroon laborers' knowledge of the rain forest and Suriname's rivers made them desirable to lumber contractors and other employers interested in harvesting Suriname's natural resources. In response to these new demands, a Saamaka man named Tangiba Kwao founded the village of Santigron around the beginning of the twentieth century.[13] This new village attracted Maroons whose work drew them to the coast and the outlying plantations, but who wanted to maintain a village lifestyle.

As the product of postabolition conditions, Santigron's founding narrative is profoundly different from what might be expected of an older village. Santigron was created by Maroons moving toward the city, rather than by newly escaped slaves moving away from it. Whereas the inaccessibility of earlier Maroon establishments was a strategic advantage, Santigron's proximity and easy access to Paramaribo, outlying plantations, and lumber areas was an intentional and desirable feature. The population of this new village drew together Maroons from various groups and lineages, all of which were well established by this point. While the village had a Saamaka majority and fell under Saamaka political jurisdiction, the Matawai and Ndyuka populations in particular were also well represented.

Despite these anomalies, Santigron retained a number of social and structural characteristics representative of Maroon cultural practice in general. Although its residents recognized colonial rule, Santigron founded and maintained traditional Maroon authority structures. Local conflicts continued to be addressed through conferences (*kuutus*) with the village kabiteni and basiya (assistants to the kabiteni), appointed by the Saamaka gaanman. In the center of the village is a *faaka tiki*, a place where offerings are made to ancestral spirits. Kenneth Bilby (1990, 153) noted that every Maroon village has a faaka tiki, and this is an easy way to distinguish a village from a *kampu*, a Maroon community that may not be officially recognized as autonomous by Maroon leaders and is generally smaller in size than a village. Santigron also has a *faagi*, a menstrual hut where some women still seclude themselves while menstruating, in accordance with traditional practice.

In the 2000s and 2010s, the interplay of traditional practices and urban influences was readily apparent. The village's dirt roads and pathways wound around an architectural patchwork of houses, from cement constructions with several rooms and running water to traditional one-room houses with slanting roofs, low doorways, and few or no amenities. Many residents had cars, and a public bus ran regularly between Santigron and Lelydorp—the capital of Wanica, a district on the outskirts of the greater Paramaribo area. The village's bars and general stores were well stocked, and in the evenings several houses enjoyed central electricity. The continuous low groan of power generators that was part of more distant villages' evening soundscapes was noticeably absent. Santigron's close proximity to the city provided residents with easy access to goods, materials, and amenities that were more expensive and difficult to obtain further inland.

In many ways, Santigron is ideally situated to take advantage of Suriname's growing tourist economy. It is one of the few Maroon villages that make a convenient day trip for tourists, and multiple tour operators have erected lodges nearby for those who wish to stay overnight. Santigron is particularly appealing to visitors who are curious about Maroon culture or about the rain forest interior, but who could do without the added time, discomfort, and expense of a journey further inland. One of the highlights of day and overnight tour packages is a performance of traditional song, drumming, and dance by Santigron residents. Arinze Tours, one of the largest and most prominent agencies working in Santigron, enlisted the help of local children in such performances, and many of the younger members of Saisa started performing for formal audiences through this organization. Not coincidentally, it was George Lazo, founder of Arinze Tours, who advocated most strongly for Saisa's founding.

At the same time, Santigron is not a cultural attraction just for tourists. City-based Maroons also travel there to learn about Maroon culture. In fact, Kifoko members conducted research here in the 1980s under Mosis's direction. More recently, the contestants of the SaDumma (can-do woman) Talent Contest went there as part of their educational training in Maroon culture. Through initiatives such as these, Santigron provides Maroons whose travels within Suriname are limited with valuable exposure to Maroon customs as practiced in a village setting. Before the 1980s, the practice of indigenous religions (and Afro-Surinamese religions in particular) was subject to censure in Paramaribo, a result of colonial hegemony and independence-era ethnopolitical power disputes.[14] Both Creole and Maroon religious pracitioners would travel to Santigron to conduct their rituals and ceremonies, located outside of the city's immediate jurisdiction yet accessible to city residents. Although practitioners of Afro-Surinamese religions are no longer subjected to the same kind or degree of censure for their beliefs, Santigron continues to be a popular site to hold religious functions, including *wenti pees*, Maroon spiritual rites involving possession.[15] Of the three groups profiled here, Saisa was the only one to include music associated with kumanti (war spirits) in its regular repertoire. This gave their performances for Maroon audiences an air of unpredictability, as it was fairly common for a person to be overtaken by a spirit in the course of performance.

In sum, there are abundant examples of Santigron's dual nature, with several features characteristic of Maroon villages on the one hand and numerous particularities owing to its proximity to Paramaribo on the other hand. One might notice the faaka tiki and faagi, the multiple kabiteni and basiya representing local jurisdiction, and the abundance of Maroon visual or performance art and be struck by these markers of residents' active engagement in Maroon traditions. However, by focusing on the fact that the village was established relatively recently (after abolition) and has a particularly heterogeneous population, an unusual degree of infrastructure, a number of commuter residents who divide their time between Santigron and Paramaribo, and the ways in which the arts are linked to the tourist economy, it becomes easy to see why some allege that the village and the cultural practices of its residents are not representative of traditional Maroon practices and lifestyles.

Whereas Maroons and non-Maroons alike at times dismiss city dwellers categorically as "not really" being practitioners of Maroon culture due to their existence outside a village setting (and therefore at a remove from the traditional practices and modes of interaction that a village environment facilitates), the residents of Santigron risk being discredited not because they are alienated from village life, but because their village appears untraditional in so many respects: it was founded too recently, its population is too heterogeneous, and its location is not quite remote enough to "count" as authentic.

Though Saisa rehearsed in Paramaribo, its members' affiliation with Santigron reverberated in their rehearsal and performance practices. Songe and awasa, the two most prominent of the dance genres that the group performed, are both associated with the Ndyuka Maroons of Eastern Suriname rather than the Saamaka Maroons, under whose political jurisdiction Santigron falls. Such cultural intermixture is commonplace in Santigron, whose founding residents were from various Maroon groups. Saisa rehearsals were conducted in the Saramaccan language, yet song texts for their two marquee genres were in Okanisi, the language of the Ndyuka. Saisa members spent a substantial amount of time debating the correct pronunciation of song lyrics and various performance conventions, demonstrating awareness that their most immediate cultural and linguistic references were anomalous in the degree of their heterogeneity. The inclusion in their repertoire of music and dance associated with spiritual practice resonates with Santigron's history as a place where religious ceremonies such as wenti pees could take place without fear of censure.

By virtue of their proximity to Santigron, Saisa members participated in village social life in a way that distinguished them from other cultural groups. Whether in Santigron or in the city, Saisa performances for Santigron residents had a kind of intimacy to them, owing to the fact that the performers and audience members tended to know each other so well. When Cheke Pinas, a crowd favorite, would begin to perform a solo, he was greeted with the cheers of an audience already familiar with his extraordinarily high jumps and his explosive energy. Flirtatious scenarios acted out between group members who were family members resulted in laughter based in part on the dissonance between the relationships of the individuals in daily life and those in the scenes they depicted. Songs that alluded to local politics sparked commentary that lingered after a performance had finished.

Having a name is a compulsory element of being recognized as a cultural group in Paramaribo. An audience need not grasp the full meaning or significance of a group's name for it to function, yet as with the iconography on flags or currency, a group's name often narrates key priorities, allegiances, and ideals that serve to consolidate identity within the group. Far from being arbitrary, the names Kifoko, Fiamba, and Saisa are important orienting agents that affect the groups' repertoire, the kinds of public engagement they pursue, and their approaches to performance practice. These names activate enduring principles and concepts that can stay constant as groups expand, change leadership, and reckon with the logistical matters that affect their day-to-day operation.

SPACE

Space and performance practice are perpetually shaping and shaped by one another. In the physical space of rehearsal, aesthetic and pragmatic issues ground a group's more abstract, ideological aims. A venue's specific dimensions and features impact learning processes, informing choreographic decisions and structuring social interactions. A rehearsal's location can enhance a cultural group's ability to attract both members and supporters. Likewise, if their presence is deemed a disturbance, the location can aggravate social tensions with other individuals and institutions in the area. Cultural groups occupy closed or intimate rehearsal spaces while simultaneously appealing to broader social networks for performance opportunities or to recruit new members. They are collectives that are in some ways self-contained while also striving for accessibility. Their rehearsals are audible beyond the physical boundaries of the rehearsal space, reaching into the private, daily routines of people who frequent the surrounding streets and buildings. In these and other ways, cultural groups garner a sense of public intimacy, often blurring distinctions between public and private and between individual and collective ownership in the process.

On a fundamental level, rehearsals constitute a primary site for "bodily ways of gathering information," joining together processes of sensing and reasoning—processes in which physical surroundings play a crucial role (Geurts 2002, 3). Through rehearsing, group members make sense of traditional performance practice in a literal way, using their sensory experiences to inform broad notions of common or correct practice. As repeated, spatially grounded phenomena, rehearsals cultivate a group-specific understanding of the expectations and satisfactions embedded within performance practice. Likewise, the formal and informal ways of occupying a rehearsal space provide valuable indications of a member's social standing or level of ability relative to the group as a whole.

In Paramaribo in the 2000s, the Creoles had the NAKS Cultural Center, the Javanese had the Sana Budaya Cultural Center, and the Indian and Chinese embassies sponsored cultural events and programming, but the people of Suriname's interior—the Maroons and Amerindians—had no comparable public place that was explicitly recognized as a social and cultural headquarters. In absence of such a center, Maroon cultural groups have done their best to organize independently. At some point this process posed challenges for all three of the groups I studied, but it also allowed them to claim or reclaim urban space in ways that contributed to each group's distinctive image and social impact. As groups form, they alter the ways in which Maroons circulate within this urban environment, demonstrating their adeptness at organizing and congregating despite conditions that might seem inhospitable to these activities.

For a space to be a suitable location for rehearsals, it must satisfy a few basic logistical requirements. The area must be large enough to accommodate all the group members, with enough space to set up the drums and for the dancers to move freely. Dancing requires a smooth surface suitable for bare feet. Whether indoors or in the open air, the sound of a rehearsal extends beyond the immediate space, calling for tolerance on the part of local residents. Weekday rehearsals necessarily take place in the evening hours, so as not to conflict with most members' school or work schedules. Though these requirements may seem modest, Kifoko, Saisa, and Fiamba have all struggled at some point to find a reliable space, and each group had moved at least once by 2007. During 2008–9, Kifoko was located in the historic section of downtown Paramaribo, whereas Saisa and Fiamba rehearsed in two distinct neighborhoods in the Wanica district—Ramgoe and Hanna's Lust, respectively.

Saisa and Fiamba both started off rehearsing in public venues before relocating to the private residences of their leaders. Initially Fiamba held rehearsals in a soccer field at a local secondary school in Hanna's Lust, before being asked to relocate. Wondel interpreted the group's eviction as an act of discrimination against Maroons: "We left the school and practiced at the [school-owned] soccer field, but then [the management] told us 'This is not a Djuka place' . . . so we came to this Djuka place here [gestures to her front yard]!" (pers. comm., 30 August 2009). As she recounted these events, "Djuka" is clearly meant as an insult, following the term's established usage among coastal Surinamers as an expression of contempt (S. Price 1993, xxix—xxxi). Given that these cultural groups focus explicitly on Maroon culture, and also given the degree to which Surinamese society operates along lines of ethnic affiliation, opposition to groups' rehearsing can easily be interpreted as emanating from some degree of bias or hostility toward Maroons in general—an effort to restrict their organizing efforts and minimize their public presence—whether or not these were in fact contributing factors.

Saisa, too, was asked to relocate. After it was founded in 1991, the group rehearsed at a public school in the Wanica district. The group was able to use this space thanks in part to the facilitation of Ronald Venetiaan, then minister of education and human resources and subsequently president of Suriname.[16] Three years later they were asked to leave by the police chief at a nearby station. According to Eduard Fonkel, co-leader of Saisa and a policeman, the reason given was that when the group rehearsed, it created enough of a disturbance that thieves and other criminals could misbehave without police officers knowing they were doing so. After that point, the group rehearsed a few blocks away, at the house of Dansi Waterberg, its director. For both Saisa and Fiamba, permission to practice in public venues was rescinded as the groups were judged to be undesirable and/or disruptive. Regardless of whether their eviction was the result of bias, as was Wondel's impression, or of logistical challenges, as Fonkel argued, both cases reveal the tenuous and conditional nature of groups' arrangements with outside organizations as they sought a suitable place to gather and rehearse.

Transitioning to private residences afforded these groups greater control over rehearsal space—Wondel's front yard and the clearing in back of Waterberg's house were both adapted to fit each group's particular needs. At her home in Hanna's Lust, Wondel poured concrete over one area so it could serve as a rehearsal stage for dancers. Halfway down the long driveway to the house, between the rehearsal area and the road, was an inlet with a few benches where friends of group members could socialize among themselves during rehearsal. At the mouth of the driveway were signs advertising a number of staple foods, including cassava and *podosiri* (a thick liquid made of açai berries) that Wondel's mother and sister had for sale. The addition of the group's rehearsal space further enforced the house's function as a hub for cultural products and practices. After Asongo took over leadership of the group in 2006, Fiamba's presence became even more visible. He created a second rehearsal area closer to the road and installed a banner with the group's name near the mouth of the driveway. The net result of these alterations was that although the house was technically a private residence, it had a semiprivate character, with a heavier than average amount of foot traffic. Frequently people who were not members of the Wondel-Asongo family (above all, area youngsters) used the space as a meeting point and place to socialize. Asongo had worked his way up in Fiamba over the years, moving from playing the shakers to performing increasingly difficult drum parts, and he was particularly sympathetic to the boys and young men searching for opportunities to practice the various drum parts in Fiamba's repertoire. Aspiring drummers were free to practice in the rehearsal space with the group drums on their own time, often without direct supervision. Asongo's only stipulation was that, since he and the members of his family were devout Christians, music associated with Maroon spirits and spiritual practice was not allowed.[17] Even when the group was not actively rehearsing, then, Wondel and Asongo's home had a clear and consistent identity as the group's headquarters. It merged private and public uses of space, accommodating Fiamba members' creative expression and musical exploration within parameters that were set by the family.

In comparison to Fiamba's rehearsal space, Saisa's retained a more private character. It was located at the end of a dead-end street, whereas Wondel and Asongo's home sat at a moderately busy neighborhood intersection. Waterberg posted no sign claiming affiliation with the group, and members of the group and spectators had to enter the gate and walk behind Waterberg's house to access the rehearsal area. Although the group did not actively advertise its location as Fiamba did, it still had a significant presence in the neighborhood. Group members' friends and relatives would venture into Waterberg's backyard to watch the rehearsals, as would a number of neighborhood kids—some already dressed in their pajamas. Some rehearsals drew as many as a dozen spectators and others only a few, yet the presence of onlookers at rehearsals was a regular occurrence despite the group's inconspicuous and private location.

Waterberg did alter his living space to suit the needs of the group, but in a more subdued fashion than the signs and the brightly painted additions in Asongo and Wondel's yard. Near the entrance of Saisa's rehearsal area was a blackboard that listed upcoming gigs and relevant information and was also used on occasion in creating and teaching new choreography. Women used a shed separated from the main house as a changing room. Drums were set up at the far end of the space, and Adirondack-style wooden chairs lined one side of the perimeter. A corrugated metal partition provided a small alley in back of the drummers where men would duck out to smoke or answer a phone call. In rehearsal, the male members who performed in rehearsal congregated near the drums. Those who weren't playing instruments would sing the chorus (koor), and dancers would stand nearby when they weren't rehearsing. The women occupied the chairs, with those who had no place to sit standing or perching on the chair arms. The two group leaders (Fonkel and Waterberg) and senior members who participated less often sat on tables opposite the drummers and often mingled with friends and relatives who dropped in to watch.

The clearing for dancers was small, and Saisa's choreography reflected this. Only rarely would a routine feature more than six dancers at a time. The group's signature shifting geometrical patterns could be rehearsed far more easily in this space than could the longer horizontal lines of dancers featured in Kifoko's and Fiamba's routines. Saisa's relatively cramped, roughly circular rehearsal space translated well to performances in a clearing rather than a stage, where bystanders pressed up against each other and the performers, straining to get a good view of the action.

Saisa and Fiamba arose from the creative visions of their founders, subsequently gaining members and finding a space. However, with Kifoko it was the availability of a space where people could gather that gradually led to the group's founding. This group emerged as a formalization of activities that arose more or less organically in Mosis's studio, which had become a meeting place for individuals—young men in particular—interested in cultural uplift and affirmation. Mosis named his studio Kifoko and worked there in the period 1981–90. Beyond its function as his own workspace, the Kifoko studio gave rise to both formal and informal activities. Mosis describes the overall atmosphere and expansion of the cultural projects that transpired there:

> The cassette recorder in the workshop was in constant use, playing Afro-Surinamese music, reggae, soul, and folk tales. There were traditional percussion instruments there [in the studio] as well, for example apinti drums. On June 3, 1983, a new development began, involving a number of young musicians from

the aleke band Clemencia, which had not been active for roughly two years. This visit led to the further involvement of singers Abele Albert Malon, aka Bote, Rudolph Anaje, and percussionist Atiye Balimoi. Thereafter, there were regular "jam sessions," which then became the "Kifoko House Band." On an irregular basis, the group would convene on Sundays to rehearse aleke music. [Through these rehearsals t]he Kifoko House Band further solidified. Young Maroon musicians, singers, and dancers became registered members.

In early August, 1983, my wife Laetitia Tojo and I, along with our five children, moved to Christoffel Kerstenstraat, number 26—thus, next to the workshop. In the yard there were a number of empty and dilapidated homes. [My colleagues] Cognac, Tjonfoli, and I converted this area into a space for various activities. . . . This space was named "Kifoko Garden" shortly thereafter. The music rehearsals and discussions that [formerly] took place in the workshop were now held in Kifoko Garden. (Mosis 2012; my translation)[18]

The cultural group Kifoko emerged after Mosis created Kifoko Garden. The group was founded as a continuation of a successful workshop given by the respected performers Da Tipa Tojo and Baa Nalibi Abani. Mosis's description of the workshop makes clear once again his concern with presenting an authoritative version, his efforts to formalize activities that were initially informal, and his commitment to community outreach:

I knew my father-in-law, Da Tipa Tojo, to be a known apintiman and respected master drummer within the Paramakan community. I asked him to instruct young musicians in awasa and songe music. On August 25, 1983, I invited him to oversee a rehearsal. We invited all of the previously registered young singers, musicians, and dancers [to take part]. In turn, Da Tipa brought with him to the rehearsal another percussionist, Baa Nalibi Abani. My request to Da Tipa was to give a workshop for these young musicians, allowing them to learn the steps and music of awasa and songe correctly.

Taken together, Mosis's recollections illustrate the importance of having a physical space where Maroons could gather and socialize. With the availability of space came opportunities for creative expression, first undertaken on a temporary or impromptu basis and later formalized, with registered members and regular meetings. Though Mosis was the sole owner of the property, his workshop changed character and was physically transformed as a result of the people who frequented it.

Whereas Saisa and Fiamba transitioned over time from rehearsing in public to doing so in private space, Kifoko eventually left Mosis's property, reestablishing itself in rented public spaces. First the group rented a rehearsal room at the Wie na Wie Community Center. Later it rented space at the NAKS Cultural Center and then at the Thalia Theater, before occupying the rehearsal space where I met its members in 2006—a dance studio in the back of the Suriname Culture Center (CCS). All of these moves have put Kifoko in dialogue with other cultural institutions and organizations in Paramaribo, some with Afro-Surinamese affiliations and others without. Mosis indicates how the group benefited from resources and training opportunities available through the NAKS organization and the Thalia Theater. Training did not just broaden the group's skill set; it also helped members establish viable working relationships with other organizations and a common aesthetic vocabulary that facilitated future partnerships and collaborations. These long-standing relationships, built up over the group's thirty-year existence, helped make Kifoko the go-to group for numerous high-profile performance engagements in the 2000s through the mid-2010s, including international engagements like the Caribbean Festival of Arts (Carifesta) and Fiesta del Caribe in 2013.[19]

Kifoko's rented rehearsal space contributed importantly in distinguishing it from the other cultural groups that were active during the 2000s. The fact that Kifoko could afford to rent a dance studio for its twice-weekly rehearsals was a sign of prestige, as well as an indication that the group remained strong and active even decades after its founding. The rehearsal studio that Kifoko used was a bare room with wooden floorboards. Benches lined one wall and full-length mirrors another, and ballet barres were bolted into the two remaining walls. Kifoko shared this space with hip-hop, ballet, and theater groups, and this placed the group in an atmosphere where training, conditioning, and the idea of the professional performer were familiar concepts, evident in the layout of the space itself. Clearly, the studio was set up to facilitate transitions from rehearsal to performance on a proscenium stage. While in some ways the room was definitively designed for certain habits of use and presentation, the space bore no enduring mark as a meeting location for Kifoko specifically—all groups' equipment and personal effects were stored off the premises, leaving no indication of their use of the space outside of their rehearsal time.

Kifoko was the only group that rehearsed in front of mirrors—a feature that had a significant pedagogical impact.[20] Dancers arranged themselves in staggered rows and were encouraged to use the mirrors to correct aspects of their own alignment or their position in relationship to other performers. The mirrors provided direct, useful feedback, but in some ways they took attention away from different interactive cues, such as developing an attunement with other performers in the space or listening to kawai ankle rattles as opposed to looking to determine whether people were out of sync.

Kifoko provides a particularly clear demonstration of how securing a rehearsal location and venue (requisites for any functional cultural group) become key technologies of differentiation, exerting influence over the structures of logic that buffer an interpretive community. Both of Kifoko's leaders and several other key members of the group lived in Sunny Point, one of the city's outermost suburbs. Holding rehearsals in the center of Paramaribo was undoubtedly an inconvenience for them, but it did allow them to capitalize on their extensive network and attract publicity and new recruits with relative ease. The CCS, the group's longtime residence, was located on Anton Dragtenweg in Paramaribo's historic district, within walking distance of several important organizations concerned with the arts including the Thalia Theater, the Ministry of Culture, and the Department of Culture Studies. People affiliated with these groups would often drop by rehearsals to observe or discuss arrangements for future performances with Lante and Dewinie, the group's leaders. For reporters, tourists, and others who did not have an immediate connection with any of the existing cultural groups, Kifoko's public location and extensive network made it the easiest group to contact and locate.

The same held true for new recruits, of which Kifoko had a steady stream. The majority of them were children and teens who would come for a few rehearsals and then stop, although others stuck with it on a sporadic or short-term basis. Girls and women who demonstrated particular skill or showed dedication to the group by their regular attendance over months and years were gradually absorbed into the group's core membership.[21] The group had far fewer male members, and new male members were often invited to perform as percussionists or dancers after less time. The number of individuals who participated in Kifoko rehearsals but never or seldom performed with the group makes it clear that performance cannot be assumed to be the sole or most important objective for taking part in a group. Having a large and fluctuating membership with the regular presence of new members and inexperienced dancers affected logistical and pedagogical components of rehearsal. A woman dancer could discern her status in the group relative to other members based on where she was physically placed in relation to others and what tasks she was assigned—a full rehearsal would feature one line of novice dancers and another one of more skilled dancers. Those who followed instructions well would be put on the ends of each line, and senior dancers typically arranged newer or less skilled dancers so people of comparable skill would dance opposite each other. Aspects of one's status, then, could be discerned through how one occupied rehearsal space.

Given that this group was in some ways the most available to newcomers, it might not come as a surprise that Kifoko was the most protective of specialized knowledge. Finer points of, for instance, the drum phrases to which a seasoned dancer might respond were shared only among long-standing members of the group. Trust had to be earned. Senior members could find a ready cultural justification for their guarded approach, as secrecy and suspicion helped the early generations of Maroons protect themselves against spies and intruders as they sought to establish their own societies in the interior reaches of the country. Never sharing all of what you know continues to be a guiding principle for many Maroons. For most of Kifoko's public performances, only the most experienced and talented dancers were selected to take part. Whereas Fiamba and Saisa spent the lion's share of their rehearsal time preparing material for upcoming gigs, Kifoko devoted more attention to pedagogy and general training, thereby enforcing its members' conviction that, as Graciella Dewinie put it in chapter 1, "Kifoko na wan sikoo [Kifoko is a school]." While there was some overlap between the songs and dances worked on in rehearsal and those performed publicly, a number of the routines that were regularly featured in Kifoko's performances were never practiced in rehearsals. When a group member was invited to participate on a regular basis, these choreographies were learned informally.

It's easy to see how elements of the group's practice have a direct relationship to both the location and the venue of rehearsal. The central location garnered more students and proved more accessible to foreigners and institutions. With a steady stream of interested but inexperienced dancers, many of whom did not remain in the group for long, rehearsal roles tended to be divided more noticeably between long-standing and incoming members. The most coveted performance opportunities, involving travel or an increased media presence, often provided sufficient funds for only a dozen or so members. This further enforced a divide between traveling members and those who attended rehearsals but performed with the group seldom if at all. The ways in which the group controlled certain kinds of knowledge was in part a by-product of having a significant number of participants who had no immediate connection to the core group members—a feature that was once again enforced by Kifoko's greater visibility on account of the group's institutional connections. It would be too simplistic to say that the group's location and venue were responsible for the characteristics and features of its operation that I've outlined here. Nonetheless, it is clear how the spatial components of the group's rehearsal became absorbed into the internal logic of Kifoko as an interpretive community.

GOALS

Rehearsal routines were perpetually affected by important upcoming performances and projects. These focused a group's attention on a common and specific task, shaping the contents of its repertoire in the process. It is telling, therefore, that the events that members designated as the highlights of 2008–9 differed in character so dramatically from one group to the next. These differences affirm each group's established priorities and illustrate the variety of uses to which cultural performance can be put. Kifoko's high points involved participation in international cultural celebrations in Guyana and French Guiana, as well as efforts to showcase the Eastern Maroon storytelling genre mato. Fiamba's yearly activities culminated in the Avondvierdaagse (AVD), a four-day, citywide parade through the streets of Paramaribo. And Saisa recorded its fourth album.

During its 2008–9 season, Kifoko participated in two international events aimed at highlighting the cultural diversity of the Caribbean. In August 2008 group members traveled to Guyana to participate in Carifesta, and in February 2009 they traveled east to Kourou to participate in the Parade du Littoral, the largest carnival-themed event in French Guiana. In the former, a select group of Kifoko members performed as part of the larger nationalistic music and theater project Alakondre Dron, while in the latter Kifoko performed as an independent entity, both marching in the parade and then giving a staged performance in the evening under the group's name. Both events placed Kifoko in an ambassadorial role, representing Suriname and the Suriname Maroons in particular amid other international performers and in international settings. Traveling to neighboring countries allowed Kifoko's members to interact with new audiences, both with and without ties to Maroon culture. In Kourou, the group took particular pleasure in connecting with Maroons living there, many of whom had migrated to this coastal town in search of employment at the Centre Spatiale Guyanais (Guiana Space Center). After their performances, many residents approached group members to connect through mutual acquaintances and share their observations and experiences concerning Maroon music and dance.

International performance opportunities were inherently selective and competitive, both among cultural groups and within Kifoko. The significant expenses these performances required (including for performers' travel, food, and lodging) often meant that only select group members were able to attend. Such high-profile engagements helped secure a group's status as a semiprofessional as opposed to amateur organization (Turino 2000, 52). Perhaps it is not coincidental that Kifoko, whose members traveled internationally with greater frequency than did those of Saisa or Fiamba, spoke often of professionalism, whereas this was not a dominant discourse in either of the other groups. Ideas of professionalism were applied in relation to the group's training and skill set, its members' general level of accountability and responsibility, and their performance fees. Senior members often talked about the importance of staying still on stage when not actively performing so as not to distract an audience, demonstrating spatial precision through straight lines in evenly spaced rows, and in general maintaining discipline onstage and off. The training they had received in collaboration with other groups, the importance of warming up, and the research they had conducted in the group's early years were all used as evidence of their professionalism, entitling them to certain standards of payment and respectful treatment by the individuals or organizations that hired the group. As professionals, Kifoko members prided themselves on their capacity to be flexible—to put on a good show regardless what challenges they encountered—but that flexibility in performance was also used to substantiate taking a hard line regarding payment and accommodations. The group's need to advocate for fair treatment for its members speaks to real and well-founded suspicions that sponsoring organizations would not adequately care for or compensate performers, or that their compensation would be less than that of other, non-Maroon cultural groups for comparable work.

Kikofo's second major undertaking in 2008–9 was a *mato neti*, an extended session of storytelling, featuring intermittent music and dance as well as spoken narrative. Typically, these events are highly interactive, involving multiple storytellers inserting their own story fragments—what Sally Price and Richard Price call "tale-nuggets" (1999, 271)—into a grand narrative. Lante, who was the driving force behind putting Kifoko's mato events together, saw them as an opportunity to showcase one of the lesser-known Maroon performance genres, while with luck allowing the group and the community at large to learn from each other. Although Kifoko's members had not managed in recent years to conduct fieldwork on the scale that they had in the 1990s, events like mato netis made it possible for them to continue to learn from elders and knowledgeable Maroons in their midst and to create a public forum from which they and members of the community alike could benefit.

The deeply interactive nature of mato presented its own challenges, however. By calling for greater audience participation in a highly improvisatory form, the group lost the ability to predict or control the outcome. As Kifoko's members discussed their impressions after their first mato neti attempt in October 2009, they expressed both positive feelings about the event and also frustrations at not being able to control the contributions of audience members that were either dull, poorly timed, or deemed in poor taste. Ultimately, though this was (and was intended to be) a community event, Kifoko bore some degree of responsibility for the outcome of the performance, including the contributions of group members and nonmembers alike. Thus, these performances involved a greater degree of risk than did other performances in which the group maintained creative control throughout. Segments performed and rehearsed by the group as a whole were used to structure the event and function as transitions, implying order that facilitated the genre's insertion into public events and spaces. Both Kifoko's international performances and mato netis presented opportunities for community engagement, with the potential to forge connections with new audiences, while also connecting with Maroon communities on a broad level.

For Fiamba, the AVD parade has become a long-standing high point in its performance calendar. Discussed at length in chapter 5, the AVD is a four-day event with the goals of promoting health and wellness, marketing local businesses and industries, and showcasing various social and cultural groups active in the city. Despite ongoing attempts to attract the attention of tourists and foreign businesses and organizations, the event remains intensely local in character. Each day of the parade carves a different path through the various regions of the city. A large turnout and extensive coverage by the local media enabled Fiamba to extend its audience beyond established networks of relatives, friends, and classmates to a wider swath of the city's population. The event functioned as a way of recruiting new members, both from young people who were eager to participate in the AVD in some capacity and by attracting potential recruits during the event. This aspect of the event was particularly appealing in 2009, a year in which the group's dancers were relatively few and inexperienced. Along with new members, a few former members returned to the fold, affirming an enduring connection to the group.

Fiamba has participated in every AVD from 2008 to 2019. On account of the considerable logistical coordination and endurance the AVD demands, preparations begin months in advance. Members devote time to recruiting and registering new members and planning the banners, props, and matching outfits—ideally multiple sets to provide some visual variety over the span of the four days. As the event approaches, increasing amounts of rehearsal time are devoted to tailoring the group's repertoire to fit the parade's structure. Specifically, this involves practicing marching in formation, preparing material for short performances when the group is stopped along the parade route, and planning how best to showcase the group during its few minutes of hypervisibility at designated media hot spots.

Fiamba's focus on the AVD not only informed its choices in developing new repertoire (songs and routines that could be adjusted for the parade format), but it also impacted the flow of new members to the group, with Fiamba's numbers often doubling as parade time came closer. As the AVD is an annual event, the group's preparatory activities have become part of the annual rhythms of its operation, as have school vacation periods and exam schedules. Such events impact these young performers to a greater degree than other groups, in which a broader spectrum of ages is represented. In fact, the physical challenges of not only walking but dancing over these long distances were more appealing and more easily met by Fiamba owing to the group's young demographic.

For Saisa, the creation of new recordings was a perennial activity. Their four audio recordings and one DVD were of some interest to tourists and international music and culture enthusiasts, but for the most part their market consisted of Maroons. Their recordings were most readily found in bootleg music stores and stands aimed at a neighborhood audience. Occasionally, tracks from their CDs would be aired on Radio Koyeba, the only radio station in Paramaribo explicitly targeting a Maroon listenership. Aspiring dancers often used these recordings as they attempted to learn or practice at home. Several of the dancers in Saisa recalled practicing with recordings at home before approaching Saisa leaders about joining the group. The utilitarian aspect of their recordings was not lost on the group. During the recording process for their fourth CD, members continually "tried out" the tracks by dancing to them in the studio to verify that they established an appropriate tempo and that a dancer would have enough time to listen and respond to the various cues and rhythms offered by the lead drummer.

Each CD brought into circulation a new set of songs, most of which were original compositions sung by the composer. An emphasis on recording projects reflected and perpetuated the group's drive to create new material. The addition of songs to its repertoire in turn drove Saisa to come up with complementary choreography that fit the particularities of the melody or the song's subject matter. As with the new songs, many of the new choreographies were associated with specific individuals within the group—either the choreographers or the particular dancers who most often performed the pieces at gigs. The group's 2009 CD release was especially important to members because it was a way of distinguishing themselves from Tangiba, a "rival" group that had been founded by two former Saisa members. The CD made it clear that Saisa continued to be active, while also staking a claim on lyrics and musical settings that group members believed were distinctive and did not want to be credited to Tangiba, which had a similar aesthetic. The opening tracks of the CD went a step further, making oblique mention of their grievances against Tangiba. The first song states, "It's a lie they're telling, we haven't broken up. We're playing right now—come see for yourself (A lei de lei, u á booko. A now we pee ete, da u kon luku yee)." Another track alleges that Tangiba garnered success by pretending to be Saisa, using the lyrics, "[You can] eat but don't eat with our name, [you can] dance but don't dance with our name (Nyan nyan oo ma á nyan anga wi nen, dansi dansi oo ma á dansi anga wi nen" (Saisa 2009). Tangiba, in turn, developed a song challenging Saisa to deny the group's strength and talent: "If we're not dancing well, say so." (Delia Waterberg, pers. comm., 21 October 2009). In this way, producing recordings focused Saisa's energies on creating original, personalized compositions and trademark dances. Through them the group was able to reach out to potential patrons, budding dancers wishing to practice at home, and their social networks in Paramaribo and Santigron.

CONCLUSION

To a large degree, my research on Maroon cultural groups has been propelled by the simple but profound experience of going to rehearsals and being struck by the degree to which the groups felt completely different from one another. Undoubtedly, part of this difference had to do with the influential personalities and gifted performers who have shaped each group over the years, but it remains worth asking about the relationship between the character of the doing that happens in rehearsal and what is done. Are these groups in fact forming the same types of communities? Despite engaging in what might seem like the same activities, how might groups' rehearsals and performances be generating different social and cultural content or using performance to achieve different objectives? At what point and through what means do stylistic distinctions enter the realm of form and function?

Fish's interpretive communities offer a useful approach to these questions, in particular through his insistence that meaning and sense are made through the inherently dynamic convergences of texts (or what might more constructively be considered "works" in the performing arts), contexts, and interpreters. I suggest that technologies of differentiation—in this case, choosing a group name, securing a regular rehearsal venue, and readying performances and recordings for public consumption—are key processes through which interpretive communities come into being and are maintained. They consist of actions that are simultaneously expected or requisite components of a group's function and the sites in which the particularity of practice is fully manifested. In a single gesture, then, technologies of differentiation construct and deconstruct ideas about common practice at different social levels. As they accumulate, they establish a group's distinctive character, but insofar as groups and their expressive output continue to exhibit large-scale resemblances, their differences are often easier to feel than to articulate.

Beyond helping explain how interpretive communities come into being, each of the technologies of differentiation I've outlined here sheds light on a separate aspect of Maroon identity politics within Paramaribo. Group names, for instance, all uncover different ambivalences to which cultural performance can help respond or counteract. The name Kifoko speaks to two different perceptions of lack—a general feeling of cultural loss that is part of the legacy of the slave trade and challenges concerning deficiency in cultural knowledge that are leveled with some regularity against Maroons who live and work in a major urban center. Fiamba asserts the capacity of young people to achieve impressive feats despite their age and relative lack of experience, and Saisa calls direct attention to a village that demonstrates the contradictions in local discourse concerning cultural authenticity. Even as each group remains open in their membership and inclusive of multiple Maroon groups in their repertoires, their names respond to particular pressures that are likely to affect different subsections of the Maroon population to varying degrees.

Groups' struggles to secure a rehearsal venue reveal challenges to cultural expression that are still very much at work in Paramaribo. Without a cultural center or other sanctioned gathering place, groups' efforts to form a community and practice traditional performance genres remain contingent upon the cooperation of a wider range of communities and institutions. Cultural groups are centering activities, drawing Maroons together through their shared interests, but they are also decentralized—groups are scattered throughout the city and remain independent, small-scale ventures. This keeps them localized, tied to neighborhood and social networks in ways that can be intimate and affirming but that also limit their reach and visibility.[22] Reliance on group leaders' privately owned spaces might allow for greater control of a space, but it also keeps the group's stability dependent on that member's cooperation and involvement, as well as the stability of their home situation.

Groups' goals serve as focal points, building upon more general interests and ideals in concrete ways and over extended periods of time. Cultural groups adapt and develop within the various genres in their repertoires not only in relation to abstract aesthetic notions of cosmopolitianism, professionalization, or modernization, but also in relation to the more immediate tasks of situating performance in the existing structures and networks that comprise the city's entertainment industry. Just as groups strive to best occupy the available spaces in their physical surroundings, so too must they formulate their activities in relation to existing modes of encounter with existing audiences.

POSTLUDE: CHANGING TIMES

A lot changed between the eighteen months of my primary fieldwork and the writing of this book. Saisa disbanded in 2011. Its breakup coincided with another crop of performers leaving Saisa in favor of a newly formed group, Oséle. Like Tangiba, Oséle had in its membership a number of former Saisa members and new recruits, while retaining a strong affiliation with the village of Santigron. In hindsight, many Saisa members seemed to anticipate the group's dissolution in 2008, and the difficulties Tangiba and Oséle caused in maintaining performance commissions and retaining members ended up being too much to overcome. While Saisa may have disbanded, Santigron continues to foster a vibrant community of performers that remains influential in Paramaribo. In contrast to Kifoko and Fiamba, these Santigron-affiliated groups make clear that multiple cultural groups can function as similar (or joined) interpretive communities. Their broad similarities in terms of aesthetics, goals, affiliations, and target audiences have placed these groups in a more intense kind of dialogue and competition.

In 2008–9, Fiamba had hit what Asongo described as a low point. As was the case with Saisa, a number of Fiamba's members had recently left to found a new group (Wenoeza). While Fiamba's percussion section maintained its vitality, owing largely to the recent addition of a few talented and enthusiastic new recruits, most of the group's strongest dancers had left to join Wenoeza. In 2008, shortly after Wenoeza's founding, Fiamba's dancers had been few and of inconsistent ability. Ten years later, many of the percussionists who had joined in the mid-2000s remained active members in the group. Now in their late twenties and even early thirties, these men were beginning to test the prediction that Tolin had made about the group several years before—that given Fiamba's reputation as a group for young people, members would eventually "age out" and leave. Fiamba's age range has continued to skew narrower and significantly younger than that in most of the other cultural groups in Paramaribo, but as group members stay for longer durations, the Fiamba's youth group identity begins to seem more malleable.[23] Thanks to the AVD and their independent recruitment efforts, by 2017 Fiamba had established a strong roster of both male and female dancers. In the 2016 AVD, their ranks swelled to over a hundred participants, including past and present members and temporary participants with the ability and inclination to join in.

Whereas Asongo had maintained a stable presence in the group and took the lead on logistical matters, he claimed no particular expertise in the music and dance genres in the group's repertoire or desire to act as the guiding force behind its artistic vision. His relatively less authoritative approach allowed group members to take the initiative and exercise significant influence on the group and its creative direction. By 2017, his open approach to leadership appeared to be facilitating positive change. A group of five members emerged as leaders, taking on responsibilities that included running rehearsals, communicating with members in anticipation of performances, recruiting new members, and overseeing new rehearsal practices and new content in the group's repertoire. As a result of this group's collective efforts, Fiamba's regular repertoire had expanded to include the genres mato and songe, its membership had increased, and members exhibited a greater degree of technical proficiency and grounding in traditional practice.[24]

Just as Suriname was hit with massive inflation in 2017 (Alleyne et al. 2018), Kifoko's longtime rehearsal venue, the CCS, raised its fee for renting studio space, thereby forcing the group to find an alternative arrangement. As of October of that year, the group had relocated to Sunny Point, a neighborhood on the outskirts of the Paramaribo metropolitan area, where members rehearsed in Lante's driveway. This new rehearsal space was small and could not accommodate the choreographies or rehearsal practices the group had established in the CCS. Dancers and drummers squeezed their rehearsals into an area scarcely larger than two parking spaces. As one of the dancers, Graciella Dewinie, put it, "To rehearse here—it drops the quality. Because you can't do what you want. . . . The actual thing that you want to do—that you want to work on—on rehearsal day you won't get it" (pers. comm., 12 October 2017). The group's longtime members had sufficient experience rehearsing and performing in large spaces to anticipate the adjustments that they would need to make come performance day, but there was no way of simulating those experiences or marking them out in space at the rehearsal location.

Kifoko's new location also prompted dramatic changes in membership. Up to this point, Kifoko had differentiated itself from groups that had a neighborhood, family, or regional focus, claiming that it was open and accessible to all. As the group moved away from its studio space in the city center to a residential area on the outskirts of the city, the number of participants without ties to the area or to long-standing members of the group dwindled, while new recruits were local to Sunny Point. As of that October, the number of dancers had shrunk to seven or eight of Kifoko's longtime members. With the move, the group had lost the suburban and middle-class young women and girls with a casual interest in Maroon dance forms but no preexisting personal connection to a cultural group. Kifoko did have more success in recruiting young men and boys as drummers. Recruiting male members had been a longtime objective for the group, but of late it had become a necessity owing to the recent departure of two of the group's strongest male performers: The brothers Minio and Herman Tojo had left Kifoko in favor of the newly founded Gadoe Talentie, a group that infused traditional Maroon music and dance styles with Christian thematic content.[25] Whereas dancers closer to the city center were unlikely to make the trek out to Sunny Point, the new recruits from the neighborhood were just as unlikely to go to rehearsals in the city center but were happy to participate as rehearsals moved closer to their homes. Finally, as a result of moving away from the city center, Kifoko members reported having to work harder to secure coveted gigs or catch the attention of tourists and organizations. Beyond the logistical benefits of the central location of the rehearsal and the larger studio space, Lante regretted losing the psychological benefits of rehearsing in a space designed specifically for rehearsal, with features including a wall of mirrors and a smooth wooden floor: "You take a different kind of energy when you rehearse at a place like CCS; it doesn't feel like you're just rehearsing at home" (pers. comm., 12 October 2017).

These changes serve as a reminder that cultural groups exist in a constant state of flux. No technology of differentiation acts as a clear and stable determinant of a group's operation or creative direction, but as groups change over time, their past and present routines and founding narratives continue to exercise influence and inform their character. Kifoko, Saisa, and Fiamba had clearly differentiated social and creative priorities. They all created cultural shows that resembled one another in numerous ways, but group members and their local networks recognized that they were serving different communities and serving them differently.

CHAPTER 4

Awasa

An Integrated Analysis

Even without any prior introduction to awasa or any understanding of the Okanisi language or the genre's salient features, it is easy to become captivated by its performance. Drums maintain a flurry of sound in kaleidoscopically changing patterns, and a lead singer and chorus cut through the dense percussive texture. The air buzzes with anticipation as each new dancer emerges from the perimeter, infusing the dance's bent and angular positions with their own character and stylistic touches, and every step adds the sound of ankle rattles to the musical mix. Yet whether or not a person understands the communicative work that undergirds the performance, collaboration is the prerequisite for all other aspects: it lays the groundwork for each expressive utterance, showcasing and amplifying performers' talent.

The analysis presented in this chapter is my attempt to introduce the structural and interactive scaffolding that orders the more immediately accessible sounds and movements of awasa performance.[1] Through analysis, I aim to give a sense of the character and complexity of the genre, shedding light on the kinds of social and musical awareness, performance skills, and creative license associated with each performer's role. A structural analysis makes clear how the connections and conversations between performers shift constantly throughout the duration of each piece. In an effort to maintain the liveness and improvisatory quality characteristic of awasa, here I highlight the aesthetic logic that governs decision making: I focus on elements of "common practice," whereas elsewhere in the book I describe particular choreographed "works" in groups' repertoires and chronicle what transpires during specific performances. These three factors—the interactive scaffolding of a given genre, a group's particular compositions, and the specific circumstances of a performance—combine to make each performance by a cultural group familiar and predictable in many ways, while also offering something perpetually new, brimming with social and expressive possibility.

This chapter delves equally into musical and choreographic detail. The fact that music and dance are often inextricable components of a performance event is by now a relatively well-rehearsed assertion, particularly in relation to many performance traditions in Africa and the African Diaspora. Yet despite the widespread acceptance of this general claim, the character of interactions between dancers and musicians and a technical understanding of the nature of their relationship are topics that continue to receive only the broadest treatment.[2] While ethnomusicologists, dance scholars, and anthropologists frequently make explicit their focused interest in the sonic, choreographic, or textual dimensions of performance, I maintain that this kind of selectivity risks bypassing crucial logical, logistical, and creative facets that not only enhance but help constitute their chosen points of focus.

The tendency to separate aural and kinesthetic realms of performance risks distorting the communicative play that ultimately renders a performance effective or satisfying. What is more, this selective erasure is often gendered, particularly in musical analysis. As the ethnomusicologist Kyra Gaunt notes, "Musical analysis tends to be about sound, texture, and a composer's or a performer's intention. But, by doing this, male (and many female) scholars have been 'invisibilifying' (Lott 2000, 75) girls and women in histories of African American musical practice and discourse" (2006, 11). Paying attention to the improvising body, supporting as well as soloistic roles within the ensemble, the gendering of sounds and movement in Maroon performance discourse, and the ways in which these structures can be (and often are) transgressed in performance all contribute to a more gender-balanced analysis.

In awasa, the instrumentalists, singers, and dancers are deeply interdependent: a conversation initiated through sound is often continued through dance, and vice versa. Given the musicians' intense physicality and the dancers' audibility through their kawai ankle rattles, awasa is an ideal genre through which to explore the possibilities of integrated analysis. To that end, while I divide this chapter into discrete sections based on the various roles a performer can assume (drumming, singing, and dancing), each section reaches beyond these divisions to address the ways in which the players occupying these roles interrelate.

Awasa is the most ubiquitous dance style of the Ndyuka Maroons and is widely performed by all the Eastern Maroon groups. It is characterized by its fast pace, clearly defined pulse, and strenuous dancing style, performed by dancers wearing kawai ankle rattles made from seed shells.[3] The dance can be performed on occasions with or without any religious or spiritual subtext: it is equally suitable for birthday parties or casual entertainment and for spirit possessions and Sunday church services. In the gaansamapee—the progression of dance genres performed at funerary rites and other major social gatherings—awasa is the last dance performed, often marking a culmination of the event's energy and excitement. The genre highlights gendered ideals, with women exhibiting their grace and suppleness and men demonstrating their strength and agility.

My analysis of awasa is based primarily on practice and observation, as well as interviews with leading members of cultural groups and other Maroon practitioners and cultural advocates within and beyond Paramaribo. I focus on attributes and communicative structures that were consistently evident in performance, regardless of who was performing and in what context. It is worth noting, however, that there were evident differences in how each cultural group rendered awasa—for instance, in their instrumentation, the cues the lead drummer used to signal the dancers, and nuances in dancing technique. I indicate instances of diverging interpretation throughout. Performers frequently commented that, more than the other dances in their repertoires, awasa is able to accommodate a tremendous amount of stylistic and expressive flexibility: Sections of the dance can take more or less time, movement and playing qualities can be finessed in nearly infinite ways, and the genre readily absorbs theatrical allusions and other stylistic references (see chapter 7). No doubt these are features of the genre that contributed to its centrality in the repertoires of all the Maroon cultural groups in Paramaribo during the late 2000s. Above all else, it was the communicative aspect of each part in relation to the whole that people looked to as the authentic and characteristic basis of the genre, allowing it to remain recognizable and accessible to Maroon audiences despite particularities of its rendering and the demands of a given performance context.

My efforts to characterize a genre for those not already familiar with it require that I engage with a politics of representation that relates directly to issues of folkloric and ethnographic ambivalence that I laid out in the opening chapters of this book. Specifically, generic representation assumes a definitive, authoritative voice as a matter of course, while the task of describing or representing a tradition in its wholeness and multiplicity inevitably falls short of the mark.[4] In light of this, the present chapter is best seen as a point of departure for getting to know a genre that has proven to be exceptionally malleable, both in its performance contexts and its content.

AWASA DRUMMING

The core of the percussion section in an awasa ensemble consists of three drums—*tun, pikin doon*, and gaan doon.[5] To this core ensemble can be added a rattle (called a *saka* or *sek'seki*). Saisa, Tangiba, Osélé, and occasionally Fiamba also included a wooden bench (*kwakwa* or *kwakwabangi*) that is played with two sticks, but this is not widely considered standard instrumentation.[6] Each of the three drums is similar in construction and appearance and is made from a single log, typically standing approximately two feet tall. The drum cavity ranges from a cylindrical to a conical shape. The drum's head, most commonly made of deer or goat hide, is fastened to the drum shell with wooden pegs, while the other end cinches at the bottom to a small opening. The gaan doon and pikin doon are generally played at an angle, while the tun is played either at an angle or upright, with the resonating hole at its base completely blocked. The sides of a drum are adorned with *tembe*—carved or painted geometric patterns. Many established performance groups include the group's name or other words or phrases alongside these patterns (figure 4.1).[7]

FIGURE 4.1 Tangiba performs in the village of Santigron in October 2011. At the far right are the saka and the kwakwabangi.
Photo by the author.

Drums of this construction are known popularly as *apinti doon*, but apinti refers more precisely to the language that can be conveyed through the instrument. Technically, only instruments specially designated for that purpose can be classified correctly as apinti doon.[8] Just as, in popular usage, the word "apinti" can refer to a drum or the language communicated through the drum, a terminological overlap occurs when discussing the tun, pikin doon, and gaan doon. Each of these terms can be used in reference to the name of a drum, its musical function, and its characteristic rhythmic pattern. For instance, a person can play (the musical pattern) tun on the tun (drum), thus performing the tun (timekeeping role) for the ensemble.[9]

Drumming is designated as a male activity, and a drummer is referred to as a *doonman*, or the man of a specific drum in the ensemble—for instance, *tunman* or *pikindoonman*.[10] Opinions vary as to what level of involvement with drums and drumming is acceptable for women. In all of the three groups with which I worked, women were free to touch the group's drums, and on occasion they would practice simple patterns. Yet at no point during my fieldwork did I witness a woman performing publicly as a member of a Maroon drumming ensemble.[11]

THE DRUMS AND THEIR ROLES

Tun

The name "tun" (pronounced "toon") is onomatopoetic, emulating the sound of the low, steady beat this drum provides. In other Maroon genres—for instance, songe—the tun repeats a short rhythmic pattern, much as the *gankogui* does in an Ewe drumming ensemble or the *clave* does in salsa and various other types of Latin American popular music. In awasa, however, the tun drummer provides a constant, uniform pulse. Singers, drummers, and dancers all orient themselves to this regular beat, which should be played at a loud volume and at a tempo that accommodates the dancers. (It should be fast enough to provide an exciting performance and to not wear the dancers out unduly, yet not so fast that the grace and nuance of the movements are compromised in an effort to keep up. Tempos usually range from 130 to 155 beats per minute.) Whereas the gaan doon player often dictates the pulse at the outset of a song, moving on to other styles of playing as soon as he is sure that the tempo has been communicated, it is the tunman's primary responsibility to maintain the established tempo for the duration of the piece (see figures 4.2 and 4.3).

FIGURE 4.2 and 4.3 Kifoko drummers (left to right: Henny Tojo, pikindoonman; Fabian Asidjan, tunman; and Herman Tojo, gaandoonman) demonstrate drumming postures on 14 October 2009. Each performer's physical stance and the direction of his attention makes clear which part he is playing. On the left, the pikindoonman's fingers are loose and slightly curved, and his attention is directed toward the gaandoonman and Lucia Pinas, the lead singer for this event (the woman at the far left). The tunman performs with a characteristically solid, grounded stance and downward gaze. On the right, the gaandoonman's gaze is directed outward. He follows the actions of the dancers as they perform in front to him, ready to guide them or enter into dialogue with them as the situation demands. Kifoko's use of drum stands is anomalous: typically, drums are played by seated musicians. Photos by the author.

The tun is generally higher in pitch than the gaan doon and lower than the pikin doon, but more important than the pitch that the drum produces is the quality of its sound. Most ensembles cultivate a tun sound that is timbrally distinct from the other two drums. Sometimes the tun is designated as such by virtue of its being the least resonant of the three. Further differentiations in the sound are achieved through the previously mentioned practice of playing the drum upright instead of angled away from the drummer, so that it further loses some of its resonance, or by playing the tun with a stick instead of the more common practice of striking the drum with a player's hand.[12]

Pikin Doon

Although not always noticeably smaller than the other drums, the pikin doon (literally, "small drum") is the highest pitched of the three drums in an awasa ensemble. Like the tun, the pikin doon provides a continuous musical texture for the duration of each song. In many ways, this highly syncopated supporting role is the most rhythmically challenging of the three drum parts. In between the strong beats of the tun, the pikin doon plays one of two core rhythms (example 4.1).

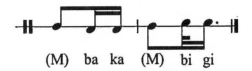

(M) ba ka (M) bi gi

Basic pikin doon pattern. The text in
the example is explained below.

These two rhythmic ideas are closely related—the difference between them a mere thirty-second note, going by at a fast pace—yet a competent pikin doon player must differentiate clearly between them. Both rhythms are played using open tones, placed either in the center of the drum or at its rim—which produce a lower or higher tone, respectively.[13] The drummer Georgio Mosis explained that these rhythmic and tonal ideas can be articulated verbally using the syllables "mbaka, mbigi." Here the "m" sound indicates the low, dry downbeat provided by the tun (thus, for the pikindoonman, a felt but unsounded rest on the downbeat), while the vowels in "baka" and "bigi" retain both the subtle pitch differentiations between the rim and center of the drum and the slight variation of the rhythmic values in the two cells.

When they begin learning the pikin doon, players tend to alternate regularly between the rhythmic cells and pitch centers in the example above. As they become more advanced, their combinations of rhythms and tones become more irregular, allowing for the creation and development of longer, more complex musical ideas. Within this narrow range of musical material—two pitch centers and two rhythms—drummers are able to create a subtle yet important layer of dynamism and phrasing in the musical texture. In moments when the gaan doon is absent from the musical texture, the pikin doon helps sustain the listener's interest.[14]

Example 4.2 is a transcription of a pikin doon demonstration played by José Tojo, a former Kifoko member. I include his demonstration in its entirety to better illustrate how, just after he establishes a tonal or rhythmical pattern, he modifies its content, keeping the ordering of these cells unpredictable. In this case, he does repeat the material of the opening pattern (the first nine beats) verbatim, starting on the second beat of measure 6. Specific combinations of cells that they find most comfortable to play or most aesthetically pleasing recur throughout the playing of many pikin doon players.[15]

Pikin doon demonstration performed
by José Tojo (transcription of audio track 1).

In the basic *boli wataa* dance step discussed later in this chapter, dancers step left, together, right, and together again to the steady beat of the tun, thus reinforcing a four-beat cycle over a supporting structure that would otherwise seem unmetered. (This is reinforced aurally through the kawai ankle rattles—the sound of stepping left or right being slightly stronger than that of the together steps—and visually, with the full-body swaying of the dancers emphasizing beats 1 and 3.) While the basic pikin doon part (see example 4.3) emphasizes this sense of meter, more complicated, irregular combinations of the rhythmic and tonal units can offset this sense of metrical regularity, at times stressing "weak" beats or even reorganizing the common pulse of the music into groups of three, rather than the duple organization implied by the dancers' boli wataa.[16]

Through his perpetual response to the ongoing pulse of the tun, the pikin-doonman provides a supporting role in establishing "The Time."[17] Meanwhile, through the strategic combination and variation of the two rhythmic ideas and the two pitch centers, an accomplished pikindoonman can respond to the gaan doon through musical phrasing over several successive beats. In this way, the pikin doon player maintains two distinct yet related and complementary musical conversations simultaneously.

An example in which the tonal contours of the gaan
doon part are echoed in the pikin doon part.

Gaan Doon

More than any other player in the ensemble, the gaandoonman structures and
narrates the events of a performance as they unfold. As the leader of the percussion section, he engages in dialogue with fellow instrumentalists, singers, dancers,
and even onlookers throughout the course of a performance. His multiple roles
include structuring the events of a performance, supporting the vocalists and
dancers by providing complementary rhythmic motives, suggesting rhythmic
frameworks that a dancer might choose to incorporate into her solo dancing
and punctuating the overall musical texture with short, virtuosic solos. In what
follows, I narrate the changes in the content and function of the gaan doon part
over the duration of a single song.[18] With the exception of the lead singer's opening solo, the gaan doon is an active part of the musical texture for the entirety of a
piece, its changing roles narrating the changes in the dance event as they unfold.[19]

The gaandoonman opens a performance with an introductory sequence in
apinti. He begins by honoring the drum, naming its various components, and
thereby honoring the natural and spiritual elements that make performance possible. After delivering this initial message, a skilled apintiman will acknowledge
individuals in attendance or craft a message that pertains to the performance
occasion. Proverbs can be used to refer to these events or give more generalized
commentary.

Such introductions are not exclusive to social dances but rather are common in
a variety of contexts. Table 4.1 compares two apinti transcriptions to illustrate how,
despite the different circumstances of performance and the many individuals whose

composite interpretations are rendered here, these introductory segments convey similarities both in content and structure. Table 4.2 shows text common to both transcriptions. In an awasa performance, the gaandoonman typically concludes his introduction with the phrase "kaba kelle kelle,"[20] indicating to those present that he is finished and the lead singer can proceed with her unaccompanied solo.

TABLE 4.1. Comparison of apinti translations

Performance A		Performance B	
Transcription	**Translation**	**Transcription**	**Translation**
Odyan Koobuwa be si ankama	**Odyan Koobuwa**	Ting: tjekele gín din gín din . . . gilíng	"Listen"; opening call.
Mi **Odyan Koobuwa** be si ankama Fu **osiosi wataa dyande** Domba	I, **Odyan Koobuwa** **Of the river** Player of the consecrated drum,	**Asantí kotoko bu a dú okáng, kobuá, o sá si watera dján de**, djantanási, dum de dum; **kediamá kédiampon** ódu a sási ódu a keémponu sasi nana betie	**Recital of the drum's "praise name," including words for its parts** (wooden body, pegs, ties, head); **call to supreme god** and the earth
Asanti Kotoko boadu Asanti Kotoko tintin Asanti Kotoko man ntenbuwa Falamanpopo Kwansa	**The unity drum of the Ashanti** Which consists of drum wood, The drum skin, The cord and The drum pin Made of cedar wood	Opete nyán opete; sembe sindo gede gede gede, sembe sindó gede hía. Gídi gídi kúndu bi a kúndu; opete nyán opete; **kokóti bái batí.**	Call to junior assistant headmen; remark that "many people have sat down." Call to senior assistant headmen; call to junior assistant headmen; **call to headmen**
Afiamantanta Akan Gbolokoso gbologbolo Msi agama gbologbolo	The spokesman of the Akan Venerable ancestors The consecrated drum asks permission	Kásikási têgètêgèdé. Keí keí dí día, kêtekí dí día, kilinkilíng, kiding tjêkele ding,	Call to senior women. Good morning; **call to the paramount chief;** proverb("However great the problem,

Performance A		Performance B	
Transcription	Translation	Transcription	Translation
Futi-uti fili fili fili fili	To speak	tjêkeleding,	the paramount
	He has been away,	ding din . . . ;	chief can take care
Futi-uti bilimba	But now he is back	**kilíbe tente, odú**	of it"); prayer.
Uyumuna keeku,	A new day has	**akásambile** fu wán	
keeku uyummuna	broken	pandási; sekúinya	
Ketekei keenki,	He greets you	kata kái na tí	
ketekei keenki		sekúinya; [begi].	
ampo			
Keedyamaa			
Keedyampon			
Odamankama			
nanti,			
Odamankama			
bala,			
Odamankama			
betele			
Odyuwa Bunsu			
Bunsu Bunsu obala			
Mi Odyan			
Koobuwa be si			
ankama			
Fu osiosi wataa			
dyande			
Kelebe ten ten			
ten ten Odun			
Akansangele			
Kelebe ten ten ten			
Odun Akansanbili			
Kokotibaibati,			
kokotibaibati fu			
Asanti ako			
Uyemuna			
keeku, keeku			
uyemuna			
Ketekei keenki			
ketekei keenki			
ampon			

Performance A		Performance B	
Transcription	Translation	Transcription	Translation
Keedyamaa Keedyampon Odamankama nanti, Odamankama bala, Odamankama betele Odyuwa Bunsu Bunsu Bunsu obala **Mi Odyan Koobuwa be si ankama Fu osiosi wataa dyande Kelebe ten ten ten ten** Odun Akansangele **Kelebe ten ten ten Odun Akansanbili Kokotibaibati, kokotibaibati** fu Asanti ako Uyemuna keeku, keeku uyemuna Ketekei keenki ketekei keenki ampon	**God of the universe,** The gods, The dead nd the living, He greets you mother Odyuwa Bunsu **Strong Odun tree on which everything leans** Bearer of the staff of honour of the Ashanti **I, Odyan Koobuwa, greet you with all respect.**	Kediamá kédiampon ódu a sási ódu a kêèmponu sasi naná bêtiè. **Kilíbe tente, odú akásambile** fu wán pandási; alíbête benté, bébetiêbenté a falí; otíbilíbití tja ko bêèdjô; killíng king diá keng dia kéng eti; kásikási têgètêgèdé; fébe tutú máfiakata bánta nási betê; [piimísi]; atupeteezú atuá petee zú ahuun wásikan djáni bobo; [piimisi] **Kokóti bai batí;** asákpa a pênde, makáiya pênde; gídi gídi bú a fô. Ahála ba tatá gánda volabutan; Dabikúku misí améusu; [begi]; [piimísi]; **kokóti bai batí; kilíbe tente, odú akásambile** fu wán pandási; ma in tene, ma in tênè búa.	Call to the paramount chief; proverb ("The water hyacinth floats down- stream with the ebb tide, but the tide will bring it back up as well"); call for liquor; apologies to the elders; call to senior women; proverb ("When the mouth starts moving, hunger is afraid"); apologies (for anything bad that might have inadvertently been drummed); call to "headmen of the river" (gods); apologies. **Call to headmen;** call (by name) to two important ancestors. Call to city officials; proverb ("Smoke has no feet, but it makes its way to heaven"); prayer; apologies; **call o headmen; call to the paramount chief;**

Performance A		Performance B	
Transcription	Translation	Transcription	Translation
			proverb ("When a leaf falls in the water, it's not the same day that it starts to rot").

Notes: The translation of performance A is from Pakosie (2002, 129). This article highlights the cultural connections between the Akan groups of Ghana and Suriname's Maroon populations. Pakosie recorded both drummers in the 1990s. Performance B comes from apintiman Peléki, recorded at a Saamaka tribal meeting in 1968. Translated by S. Price and R. Price (1999, 258–59). An audio recording of this performance is available on R. Price and S. Price (1977). One additional stanza from their transcription is excluded here for concision. The spelling and wording in both examples is as it appears in the publications cited. Bolding indicates shared words. The comparable sequence of events is easily discernible in the English translations.

TABLE 4.2. Words or phrases in both apinti transcriptions (Table 4.1)

Transcription A	Transcription B	Translation
Asanti Kotoko boadu Odyan Koobuwa Fu osiosi wataa dyande	Asantí kotoko bu a dú okáng, kobuá, O sá si watera djɑ́n de	Both Pakosie and S. Price and R. Price identify these phrases as components of the drum's praise names, though the order in which they are performed and their translations differ slightly.
Kokotibaibati	Kokóti bai batí	Call to headmen
Kelebe ten ten ten Odun Akansanbili	Kilíbe tente, odú akásambile	Call to the paramount chief
Keedyamaa Keedyampon	Kediamá kédiampon	The supreme god or god of the universe

Note: To date, the most extensive listing of Maroon esoteric language, as well as apinti language, is an appendix in R. Price (2008, 309–89). As Price notes, this is only the "tip of the iceberg."

Following the lead singer's solo, the gaandoonman reenters with the supporting drummers. Should the tempo be unsteady, he will reinforce the tun, either by mirroring this part or by drumming simple rhythms that emphasize the pulse. Once the ensemble has settled into a stable musical texture, the gaandoonman is then free to be more adventurous in his improvisations. Whereas the pikin doon and tun provide a nearly continuous texture, the gaan doon player can destabilize and offset the musical texture at will. In these moments of free improvisation, drummers convey a great deal of their performance style and musical strengths, which may include their physical strength and stamina; their ability to create an exciting musical buildup; or the speed, complexity, and precision of their rhythmic patterns.

After the drummers and singers have established their musical roles and performed their initial improvisations (see figure 4.9), the dancers become the focal point of the performance. It is the gaandoonman's responsibility to cue the various phases of the dance, including when dancers should advance into the performance space or move back into the crowd, and at what points to transition between the "resting" boli wataa dance move and more vigorous dancing, described as *paata*. He does this and conveys additional information or commentary through drumming phrases in *kumanti'pinti*, a subcategory of the apinti language that is less formal and less nuanced than its counterpart, *anwanwi*, but well suited for providing dancers with basic information during the course of their performance.

Once a dancer has entered the performance space and has begun to paata—to "get down" and dance energetically[21]—a particularly dynamic opportunity arises for communication between the dancer or dancers and the gaandoonman. Any of these performers can suggest patterns to be seized upon and interpreted by the other performers. To suggest a pattern is to *gii futu* (literally, to "give foot"). A dancer does this by incorporating a rhythmic pattern into his or her dancing, and the gaandoonman does this by repeating short rhythmic phrases that lend themselves to dance. The performers are under no obligation to seize upon any single rhythmic or kinesthetic pattern—any specific *futu* that they are given—but they are expected to stay attuned to each other for the duration of a solo passage. Due to awasa's physically strenuous dancing positions, solos tend to be brief, with the longer ones lasting only a few minutes. Even within this short timeframe, a solo does not stay fixed in the same sounds and motions for long before a new variation or futu is introduced.

The gaandoonman concludes the soloistic portion of the dance by instructing the dancers to *waka gwe* ("walk go away"), or return to the edge of the performance space. When he wishes the performance to conclude, or for there to be a pause between segments of dancing, he signals the performers to stop with a few high-pitched slap strokes on the drum's rim. The brief pause between pieces is filled with cheers, exclamations, and congratulatory hugs from fellow performers and audience members. Performers mop the sweat from their bodies with towels and handkerchiefs, take a quick drink,[22] and reposition themselves in preparation for the next piece.

Throughout a performance, the three drums in an awasa ensemble combine to provide a dense and continuous musical texture in which the main pulse, though at times syncopated by the gaan doon and counterbalanced by the rhythmically complex pikin doon, is clearly articulated. When the shakers or kwakwabangi are included in the ensemble, they further accentuate the pulse by doubling the tun or offering simple rhythms that land heavily on the beat.

SONG

Awasa songs are delivered in a call-and-response format between a solo lead vocalist and supporting vocalists, which the Paramaribo-based cultural groups referred to as the koor. The response phrases (*piki*, in the Okanisi language) are predominantly heterophonic, intermittently breaking off into separate harmonized melodic lines. The ending note of each phrase is habitually elongated, overlapping with the following phrase so as to create a continuous vocal presence even while the lead vocalist and koor alternate.[23]

These songs span a wide range of subject matter, drawing from proverbs; everyday activities and scenarios; and social relationships between friends, relatives, neighbors, employers, and lovers. The texts provide an emotional frame that, directly or indirectly, contextualizes the creative efforts of all the performers, infusing each piece with its own character. Individuals and small groups of dancers may develop certain movements that borrow subject matter from the song text, either rehearsing such moves before the moment of performance or developing thematic material on the spot. Many formal awasa groups build upon this practice, incorporating sung themes into choreographed routines (see figure 4.4 and example 4.4).

(wave)

FIGURE 4.4 and example 4.4 A Fiamba dancer illustrates a choreographed move.
The lead sings, "Fa u kon ja [How did we come here]?" and "Fa u kon ja tide [How did
we come here today]?," to which the koor responds, "U á kon suku toobi [We didn't come
looking for trouble]." Here, the collective of dancers enact their message—they did not
come looking for trouble—both by singing the koor and giving a wave that indicates
refusal. They retain this wave in their dancing for the duration of the song, even as they
lower themselves into the more strenuous paata dancing position, as shown here.
Photo by the author.

Beyond literal interpretations of the text, a song can influence the creative
output of dancers and drummers in more subtle ways. Various songs make possible different rhythmic groupings and, as a result, have an influence on the
variations both drummers and dancers employ. In the above example, the song

establishes two phrases of triple groupings (a full call and response cycle lasting twelve pulses, divided into two groups of six each). Guided by the melodic structure, dancers further emphasize these metrical implications by waving every six pulses.[24] Whereas solo dancers, the pikindoonman, and the gaandoonman are able to change between affirming and destabilizing these metrical implications, the call-response format between the lead singer and koor offers more structural stability, providing a consistent framework for the duration of a song. Drummers and dancers can orient their actions to the song's call-and-response framework as well, for instance by generating their own response to the lead singer's call (see example 4.5).

A gaan doon part that is based on the rhythm of the sung material.

Singers can be male or female. Dancers and (less often) percussionists in Kifoko, Fiamba, and Siasa doubled as koor singers, though this can be considered a diversion from awasa's practice in a village setting, in which people typically do not sing the response phrases while dancing (André Pakosie, pers. comm., 2008). In Kifoko and Saisa, a few singers would stand close to the lead singer and lead the koor, thereby designating singing as their primary mode of engagement, but other performers were nonetheless free—if not expected—to join in the singing.[25] Among Fiamba's members, the female dancers were often criticized for not singing loudly enough as they danced, to the point where—for audiences that were not likely to understand the Okanisi language—sometimes the (male) lead singer would even use the word "koor" in his calls, giving dancers a particularly pointed reminder that they were expected to perform this role while they were dancing.[26]

To be heard over the dense, continuous rhythmic texture of the drums and the overall hubbub of the crowd requires a powerful voice, one capable of producing a volume and timbre that can cut through the sound environment of a performance. No matter how strong a lead singer's voice is, during the height of performance it becomes difficult to make out their words. For many of the larger performance events—both those featuring awasa groups and those performed by a community at large—a microphone is made available for the lead singer, with an additional microphone for one or a few other performers to provide the koor.[27] Even so, having a strong and distinctive sound that can be projected over the many competing sounds of an awasa performance remains a valued characteristic of a singer.

SONG STRUCTURE

During the lead singer's opening solo, which directly follows the gaandoonman's opening message in apinti, the audience can contemplate the message on which all the performers will "play" as the piece gets going. This is the only point at which the lead singer is unfettered by the insistent pulse of the tun and the measured call-and-response interchange that is introduced once the koor begins singing. Here, the lead singer gets their best opportunity to explore the text and melody of the song, using pauses and elongated syllables, vocal ornamentation, variations in volume, and vocal timbre to dramatic affect.

A common practice for cultural groups is for the songs to mark episodes in an overall performance, with a short break between each song during which performers can change places or prepare for a new choreographed idea. Multiple songs can be performed without a break in between them as well, the drummers sustaining the musical texture while the lead singer transitions from one song to the next. In the latter case, the lead singer should take care not to switch between songs while a dancer is in the middle of a solo. Such a move registers as rude, communicating indifference to the dancer's efforts. The two songs discussed below illustrate common formal features that exist between call and response.

"Jang joe njang" ("Eat Your Food")

This contemporary song, composed by the members of Saisa, emerged in response to tensions they experienced in relation to a rival group (as discussed in chapter 3). The lyrics ("[You can] eat but don't eat with our name; [you can] dance but don't dance with our name; when we find food we show off)" (Saisa 2009) insinuate that this new group, of which several former Saisa members were part, was "eating" with Saisa's name—using Saisa's connections to achieve their own success. The transcriptions in examples 4.6–4.8 show, respectively, the complete statement of the song, presented in the lead singer's solo at the outset of a performance; the basic koor response; and an abridged call-and-response pattern used intermittently once the performance is well under way, to intensify the overall mood and create variety. Among the features of this song that are characteristic of awasa singing more generally are:

- A limited tonal range.
- Phrases that can be sung comfortably in a single breath, starting out with a high pitch and gradually descending.
- A koor response with the same general melodic contour as in the opening call.

The same melodic contour is reworked in subtle ways as the song progresses from the opening solo to the call and response and, as the more strenuous dancing gets under way, in the abridged call-and-response phrases. Notice that the combined call and response take half as long as one statement of the initial koor phrase, making it easy to switch between the two without disrupting the overall time feel of the performance. The lead singer signals this switch with the second note of their call—repeating the initial note indicates the long version, while descending three semitones marks the transition to the abridged call and response. This transcription and all subsequent song transcriptions should be seen as a melodic and textual outline of the song, subject to embellishment and improvisation during the course of performance.

Lead Singer

Nyan nyan oo ma a nyan an ga mi neng   Dan-si dan-si oo.— ma a dans' an-ga mi neng, ta-ki

Di u fen-de nyan, da w'e poo-lo,   Di u fen-de nyan ee da w'e poo-lo.

Koor

Nyan nyan oo ma a nyan an-ga wi neng,   Nyan nyan oo ma a nyan an-ga wi neng.

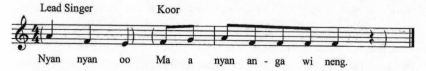

Nyan   nyan   oo   Ma   a   nyan   an - ga   wi   neng.

Lead, koor, and abridged call-and-response parts for Saisa's composition "Jang joe nyan."

"Sa Asenowe"

"Sa Asenowe," one of the best-known traditional awasa songs, narrates the physical beauty and dancing prowess of a woman by that name. This song maintains the musical features listed for the previous song, yet here the lead and the koor are exchanging sung phrases in quick succession from the outset. To create variety, then, the lead singer can opt to return to the beginning tonal area in subsequent choruses or to repeat the last two tonal areas, ascending to the highest pitches only occasionally (see example 4.9).

Lead

Oo   yee   oo   yee yee   yee yee yee   oo   yee yee

Koor

Sa A 'senowe   Sa A   'senowe   Sa A   'senowe   Sa A   'senowe

"Sa Asenowe" basic melody.

VARIATIONS: TEXT AND MELODY

The quick alternation between the lead singer's call and the koor's response for the duration of a song results in a highly repetitive framework. A talented singer can prevent this repetition from becoming overly monotonous by modifying the words and the melodic and rhythmic content of her calls. Through these variations, the singer becomes an important source of musical variety, often shaping the social and dramatic trajectory of a piece in the process.[28] This feature of (sometimes slight) variation sustained over many repetitions fits well with the particularly keen appreciation for word play for which the Maroons are known. As Sally Price and Richard Price observe, "Playfulness, creativity, and improvisation permeate conversation, and spontaneously invented elliptical phrases frequently substitute for standard words" (1999, 238). The call-and-response format gives a lead singer an excellent opportunity to play with word substitution and such elliptical phrases: "Bai wan keti fu mi, mi á poi bai en! Bai wan keti fu mi, mi á poi bai en! I sa akisi mi baa fu mi bai en gi yu, ma I á mu tek' a tori ya fu feelanti anga mi yee [Buy a necklace for me, I can't buy it! Buy a necklace for me, I can't buy it. You can ask me to buy it for you, but you mustn't take this story here to quarrel with me]."

Henny Tojo would lead this song occasionally during Kifoko rehearsals in which time was devoted exclusively to singing. Though I never heard the group perform this song publicly, I include it here because it provides a good example of the lead singer's capacity to change a person's understanding of a song as he goes on to vary its text. As Tojo leads the song, he keeps its overall melodic structure relatively constant, while substituting different articles that this other person (presumably a lover) is asking him to purchase in place of the necklace. By listing more expensive items (such as a house or a washing machine) or inexpensive items that could reasonably be expected to be within a person's budget and social obligations (staple foods, for instance), the singer allows the listeners to develop an evolving understanding of the initial request for a necklace, which is repeated by the koor between each call. Larger items might suggest that the demands are unreasonable and inform people's imagination of who is making the request, while smaller items could lead to an interpretation that the man is either stingy or quite poor. I find that the persistent asking and refusal built into this song give it a poignant quality, coinciding as they do with the ever-present struggle to make ends meet that is so familiar to many Maroons and, indeed, Surinamers of other backgrounds.[29] The song also alludes to gender tensions and expectations in that it highlights the practice of gift exchange between romantic partners, which is an important custom that is broadly observed among Maroons (see S. Price 1993).

Another way in which singers create variety and interest is by making specific reference to individuals in attendance—either fellow performers or onlookers— or by referring to the performance occasion at hand. The ability to improvise these calls involves making timely observations about the individuals present and the circumstances of the performance, all while adapting their message to the timing and melodic structures inherent to the song. The ability to negotiate these various considerations in the moment of performance, whether drawing from the subject matter of the song (as demonstrated by Tojo's song) or from the circumstances of a given performance (as do the singers in the following examples) is one hallmark of a great singer.

"Kon go diingi labaa" (Audio Tracks 2 and 3)

This song tells the story of a person of modest means who offers a guest *labaa*, a kind of homemade bitters, for lack of more elaborate food or drink. (The song's title means "Come [let's] go drink labaa"). The humble but gracious tone of this traditional song, combined with its simple, spacious melody that sits comfortably in the middle of most singers' range, accounts for its enduring popularity. Singers can add their own stylistic touches to a standard piece. Through participants' musical (and social) sensitivity, even a well-known text and melody like this one can be a source of interest and excitement, rooted in the moment of performance.

Several abovementioned structural characteristics and methods of variation are present in recorded versions of this song. Lead singers make ample use of a distinctive style of vibrato or trill (termed *loli*) specific to the Eastern Maroon groups at the ends of their phrases.[30] Like both "Jang joe njang" and "Sa Asenowe," this song has a shorter variation to which the singers switch after several repetitions of the initial call and response. But unlike the previous examples, the abridged section of "Kon go diingi labaa" differs significantly from the opening material in terms of text; melody; and the metrical implications of its call-and-response structure, which changes from a duple to a triple feel.

Irma Dabenta Performing Informally in a Hotel Room in Georgetown, Guyana (Audio Track 2)

Kifoko members Irma Dabenta, Maria Dewinie, Lucia Alankoi, and I were relaxing in a hotel room between performances at the tenth iteration of Carifesta, the Caribbean Festival of Arts, which took place in Georgetown, Guyana in August 2008. Irma, one of two Kifoko's lead singers, had agreed some days before to help me learn some of the songs in the group's repertoire. With the heat of the day waning and the evening's activities concluded, an appropriate time was finally at hand. While we perched on the hotel beds, Dabenta sang several songs for me to record, pausing in between to offer a few words of explanation. Dewinie added her own voice to my tentative koor, while Alankoi talked quietly on her cell phone in the background, offering instructions to a friend on how to add minutes on her phone from Guyana.

Carla Pinas and Losen Abente, Recorded by André Pakosie
(Audio Track 2)

I chose to use this example, recorded by André Pakosie in 2002,[31] because it illustrates just how interactive and personalized participants' vocal contributions can be. We hear some characteristic interjections as the recording progresses—after the initial response phrase, several individuals offer exclamations of praise and satisfaction at Carla Pinas's sensitive interpretation of the text. At 0:25, Pinas calls out to Losen Abente, the man who takes over the role of lead singer in the second half of the recording. Abente responds, "Ayoo, ay baa uman," in acknowledgement of her "shout-out" to him. Roughly ten seconds later, a woman exclaims, "Ay! Baaya ee!" (a standard congratulatory expression indicating a job well done). In live performances *baaya ee* is often accompanied by a friendly embrace or waving one's hands overhead. Participants' impromptou phrases and exclamations have an improvisatory character to them, but nearly all of them are timed to occur as the "call" phrase ends and its "response" begins. Thus, in between the established antiphonal structure of the song as a whole, a singer and her audience can initiate other, personalized dialogues.

Another notable feature of this second recording is the textual, tonal, and rhythmic variety in the response phrases.[32] In particular in the slow, introductory part of the song, the supporting singers split off to harmonize with one another. Once the song transitions to the faster section, the loudest and largest response is the phrase "labaa mofu ee labaa [labaa, a little labaa]." Yet other people can be heard singing "labaa labaa labaa," another common response to the same song. Yet another variation is audible, in which a few singers respond instead, "labaa mofu ee labaa yee." Adding the syllable "yee" to the phrases grants further affirmative stress to the message, while also changing the vocalized patterns of emphasis in the response phrase. "Kon go Diingi Labaa" is a very well-known piece, and these different approaches to the koor or piki are likely the result of both creative decisions favoring a heterophonic musical texture and differing understandings of what the "standard" response pattern is. Thus, this recording serves as a useful reminder that beyond its general thematic content and tonal contours, a song may exist in many variations as opposed to a singular, authoritative version.

DANCE

In transitioning from the resting boli wataa step to the paata, the vigorous dancing that characterizes awasa, the energy and excitement of a performance surge. The uniformity of the resting step dissolves into captivating demonstrations of character and skill. One dancer rolls his shoulders and wrists smoothly, the fluidity of these upper body movements counterbalancing the constant activity of his feet and ankles. His face shows no indication of the strain caused by dancing in a deep knee bend while balancing on the balls of his feet. Another dancer demonstrates his athleticism by leaping up into the air and then appearing to fall recklessly to the ground in a move that could have come just as easily from a b-boy dancing on a New York City street corner.[33] A woman dances as though moving against a current, the slow, supple flow of her hands, shoulders, and back seeming to work against some invisible form of resistance. Her hips sway languidly as she steps in place, maintaining the deep squatting position for which awasa is known. A man and woman approach each other flirtatiously, the man making stylized advances and dancing energetically as though trying to catch his partner's attention. The woman smiles while keeping an indirect gaze, her whole foot stamping the ground powerfully with each step as she seems to create her own sphere of energy that these flirtatious advances cannot penetrate.

The core of awasa dancing can be located in a single posture, its fundamental step—sideways left, together, right, and together again—is simple enough for even a beginning dancer to grasp.[34] Whether in spite or because of this core simplicity, awasa dancing accommodates a seemingly limitless spectrum of technical and expressive virtuosity, which ranges in scale from subtle nuances to gymnastic feats and moments of audacious theatricality.

Despite the diverse array of movements employed in awasa and the variety of ways that performers use a dance space, there are several dimensions of the dance that are well suited to analysis. These include the structure of the dance, the dramatic arc of events, the characteristics of the general steps and their function in performance, and the interaction between drummers and singers. Through studying these components, it becomes easier to recognize when and how dancers are engaged in manipulating form and content in constructing their own distinctive performances.

The simplicity of the basic footwork is counteracted by an overall posture that is extremely challenging to sustain for a long time and to mobilize throughout a performance space. Onlookers' satisfaction in watching a dancer navigate space or perform a challenging move is intensified by the performer's ability to make the inherently taxing, initially awkward positions and steps appear comfortable, even graceful—a site of play rather than of struggle.[35] To gain this kind of physical fluency, beginning dancers spend most of their time practicing the squatting posture for which awasa is known, trying to appropriate its characteristic angles and quality of movement into their own physical frames and kinesthetic vocabularies. This command over a challenging posture (won over time) lays the foundation for the movements described in the exercise below.

Exercise: Experiencing Awasa's Basic Posture

I developed this exercise as a pedagogical tool in the United States, finding that through this sequence of movements, newcomers to the dance were able to assume the angles and alignment characteristic of awasa posture.[36] I recommend that readers try the exercise themselves, as physically experiencing the posture fosters a greater understanding and appreciation of the challenges dancers face and the strength, flexibility, and agility the dance demands.

1. Stand with your feet your hips' width apart, toes facing forward.
2. Reach upward, keeping the back straight and lengthening the spine, then slowly bend forward at the hips until your torso is parallel to the floor.
3. Maintaining a straight back and long spine, bend your knees, coming into a deep squat.
4. From this position, raise your rib cage and upper torso so they are facing forward (as opposed to facing the ground). This should create a deep curve in the lower back. Bend your arms at the elbows, keeping them loose and close to the body.

Upon arriving at step 4, you will experience what many consider the cornerstones of awasa dancing posture—a deep knee bend and grounded stance, with the characteristic curve in the lower back. Take a moment to notice what muscle groups are strained and what other parts of the body maintain a relatively wide range of motion. Experiment with bending your knees more or less—how does this change your experience of the posture? Try taking steps forward and to either side, noticing how changes in foot placement and weight distribution can produce dramatic changes in the positions of the legs—in particular, the angles of the knees.

AWASA IN MOTION: BASIC MOVEMENT
VOCABULARY AND STRUCTURE

While awasa dancing accommodates a diversity of moves and choreographies, nearly all performances have the same core sequence of events. Interspersed with the boli wataa resting dance step, dancers approach the main dancing space (shuffling forward with the step *waka kon*), engage in several successive spurts of virtuosic dancing (paata), and return once more to the outskirts of the performance space (waka gwe). They do this individually, in pairs, or as a small group.

Once they have arrived in the center of the dance space, dancers can orient themselves in a number of ways in relation to the drummers, onlookers, and one another. Traditionally, onlookers surround the performance space, so a dancer can expect to be observed from all sides as she performs. Isolations of the hips and lower back (in addition to the face and front of the body) are points of interest for audience members, mitigating any need for solo dancers to keep a frontal orientation to onlookers and ensuring that there is no one ideal vantage point from which to view a performance. When dancers face away, onlookers have a moment to admire the finery of the dancers' clothing, which often boasts ornate cross-stitching, appliqué work, or decorative crocheted borders. Often, dancers face the gaandoonman when communicating directly with him, whether that communication is through instructions delivered in *kumanti'pinti* or through the mutual play of the gii futu exchange (discussed below). When the dance space is shared between multiple performers, however, dancers most frequently directed their attention toward one another.

Boli Wataa

Boli wataa can be translated as "boil [or cook] water." As both a kind of movement and an action, it refers to an upright side-to-side step, which creates a gentle swaying motion in the body. As she sways, the dancer bends her arms and circulates her hands close to her body in front of her, keeping her wrists relaxed and fluid in their movements. (This motion reminds me of the alternating circular movements of turning the ropes in a game of Double Dutch, but at a more relaxed tempo.) The boli wataa step is the first movement a dancer performs and the step to which she returns after each bout of strenuous dancing. I call this a resting step because it counterbalances the taxing knee bend required for the waka kon, waka gwe, and paata. Upon hearing the name, I associated the rolling, circular movements of a dancer's hands and wrists with the way boiling water circulates in a pot, yet none of the people I interviewed interpreted the boli wataa movement as directly correlated to the domestic action of the same name.

Although this step gives dancers a chance to rest, it also affords them opportunities to demonstrate their grace and musicality, particularly in the subtle bouncing of the knees and the practiced nonchalance with which they circulate their hands. The attention paid to such details is evident in the differentiations made between the boli wataa step as performed for songe and that performed for awasa, which differ slightly but explicitly in foot and arm positioning and cadence.

Dancers are seldom the only individuals to boli wataa during an event: singers and onlookers often adopt the step as well, or an understated version of it. Many people find it easier to sing in time when performing this step, which causes a performer to move sympathetically with the basic pulse as provided by the tun.[37] The communal movement of the dancers and singers can be contagious—in some of my video footage from fieldwork, it is clear that the person operating the camera (sometimes me, sometimes a friend or generous acquaintance) adopted the swaying motion of the boli wataa step while filming.

When performing in groups, particularly in cultural groups like those I studied in Paramaribo, dancers often aim to synchronize their swaying with those next to and across from them, thereby creating a visual show of unity. In the rehearsals I attended, dancers who stepped left when the next person stepped right, or vice versa, would be informed that they were "boxing"—bumping into their neighbors because they were out of sync with the group. Concern with this phenomenon seems to be a larger issue in formalized group performances than in performances involving the community at large.

Waka Kon, Waka Gwe

Waka kon and waka gwe are moves of locomotion, carrying the dancer toward or away from the dance space, respectively. Groups and individuals perform this move in a variety of ways. Kifoko and Fiamba dancers used flat-footed steps as they navigated through space, stepping with each beat of the tun. Saisa dancers, in contrast, knocked their heels against the ground between each step, subdividing the main pulse into two.[38] When transitioning from boli wataa to mannengeefutu—the male soloistic style—a dancer performs a variation of waka kon by lifting the heel of whichever foot did not receive the weight of a step, angling the heel and ankle away from the body (see figure 4.5). In so doing, he shifts his weight forward in anticipation of the dancing that is yet to come, in which he is precariously balanced on the balls of his feet.

FIGURE 4.5 Waka kon or waka
gwe in mannengeefutu style.
Drawing by the author.

PAATA: UMANPIKINFUTU, MANNENGEEFUTU

The dance section of this chapter opened with a description of some of the ways in which dancers add character to their performance as they paata—"get down" and dance soloistically. This virtuosic dancing is divisible into two gendered styles, umanpikinfutu ("woman child foot"; see figure 4.6)[39] and mannengeefutu ("man foot"; see figure 4.7).

In comparing the two foot positions, the greater range of motion possible in mannengeefutu is immediately apparent. The comparatively small range of

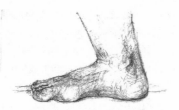

FIGURE 4.6 Umanpikinfutu.
Drawing by the author.

FIGURE 4.7 Mannengeefutu.
Drawing by the author.

flexion in umanpikinfutu results in a body posture that remains fairly constant throughout a performance—though it, too, is subject to perpetual nuance and inflection. Mannengeefutu, in contrast, allows dancers to crouch close to the ground or stand nearly upright, and to turn or travel through space in a short amount of time. While some dancers maintain the characteristic awasa posture throughout their solos in mannengeefutu style, many other dancers transition constantly between this posture and a variety of other positions, taking advantage of their larger range of movement.

With the addition of the kawai ankle rattles (see figure 4.8), this difference in kinesthetic range registers aurally as well as visually. Mannegeefutu allows the ankle to move horizontally and vertically while the ball of the foot maintains contact with the ground. As most awasa dancing involves stepping in time with the beat of the tun, the added ankle flexibility of mannengeefutu allows the dancer to articulate subdivisions of this pulse as he changes the position of his ankles. Dancing umanpikinfutu, the sound of the kawai varies depending on the force with which the foot hits the ground (in fact, the dynamic range of the kawai is greater in umanpikinfutu than in mannengeefutu), yet articulating metrical subdivisions between steps is not possible while the heel maintains contact with the ground.

The change in movement style as dancers transition from the preparatory boli wataa and traveling steps to the virtuosic umanpikinfutu and mannengeefutu is coupled with a changing relationship between these dancers and the gaandoonman. Whereas up to this point the dancers had listened to the gaandoonman for directional cues (we might even think of this as the dancers' response to the gaandoonman's call), the paata and gii futu performance practices signal a transition to a much more fluid, free-form dialogue, in which the gaandoonman and the solo dancer(s) offer each other rhythmic or choreographic patterns on which to play.

FIGURE 4.8 Kawai ankle rattle.
Photo by the author.

GII FUTU

The term gii futu was introduced above in this chapter in relation to the gaandoonman. Gii futu is an exchange between dancers and the gaandoonman in which rhythms conveyed by one performer are incorporated into the performance of the others. A rhythm given by the drummer might be answered in a way that registers both visually and aurally.

In thinking about the social and structural functions of gii futu, I find it instructive to think about other things that are "given" in Okanisi language constructions. Two of the most common examples include thanks (*da*) and greeting (*odi*).[40] To give thanks or greeting is a voluntary act, though it is often required in order to fulfill social expectations. It is thus a contribution to an important social and/or creative structure. Yet for these social gestures to be successful, they have to be acknowledged by the audience to whom they are directed. In traditional Maroon social practice, giving thanks or giving a greeting involves entering into a complex and structured interchange between the initiator and the recipient: the gesture's social efficacy requires the participation of both members.[41]

Likewise, gii futu acquires its meaning and function as the kinesthetic or rhythmic pattern one performer suggests is taken up and interpreted by others. As with giving thanks or greeting, each futu a performer suggests is both voluntary (in terms of content and timing) and required (in terms of fulfilling the social and aesthetic expectations of the dance form). If neither drummer nor dancers varied their performance during a solo, with the expectation that this variation would in turn change others' performances, the result would be a decidedly flat and uninteresting performance. While the act of suggesting creates variety and interest, other performers' responses to these suggestions heightens the overall effect, while also attesting to the skill and experience level of the performers or the ensemble as a whole.

Given the amount of attention placed on the feet, it is worth noting that the dancing surface can have a dramatic effect on a performance. Consider how one might dance differently on sand versus wood or on smooth cement versus asphalt, and how these surfaces would be more or less accommodating indoors or outdoors, after a heavy rain or while baking in the midday sun. Another consideration that has a major impact on a dancer's alignment is the distribution of weight, either over the dancer's whole foot or on the ball of his foot. Not only do seemingly subtle adjustments resonate across a dancer's entire frame, but they are also often magnified, creating widely differing shapes—particularly in the position of a dancer's knees.

Although a dancer's feet are clearly a point of focus, especially in terms of the rhythmic dialogue of gii futu, the unsounded manipulations of a dancer's body are likewise involved in establishing or playing with a rhythmic idea. To communicate effectively with a dancer, the gaandoonman has to watch the dancer's movements as keenly as he listens to the rhythms they produce, a fact to which the intense outward gaze of the gaandoonman in figure 4.2 attests.

GENDERED MOVEMENT

As mentioned above, awasa is a dance that showcases gendered ideals—Maroons within and outside of cultural groups were consistent in noting that the dance highlights a woman's grace and sinuous movement ("fa a mooi [how she is beautiful]") or a man's strength, endurance, and improvisatory gifts ("fa a flexi, fa a dansi taanga [how he's adaptable, how strongly he dances]"). Umanpikinfutu and mannengeefutu steps are both explicitly gendered, and these foot positions reverberate throughout a person's body as she or he dances, impacting a person's range of movement and contributing to whole-body differences between the two styles. In addition to these, there is a series of stylistic nuances (movements of the hands and torso, positioning of the head, aspects of the timing of the dance—see table 4.3) that are not a direct result of the feet but nonetheless tend to affirm the overarching gendered ideals awasa conveys—grace and suppleness for women, strength and agility for men.[42]

TABLE 4.3. Gendered movements in awasa

Female gendered movement	Male gendered movement
Pronounced curve in the back	Straight or upright torso
Indirect gaze	Quick rotations of the wrist (a flicking or switching motion)
Emphasis on fluid movements and rounded shapes	Arms move farther from the body, often extended in front of the dancer and angled slightly toward the ground
Hip movements include a side-to-side "swishing" motion	Vertical levels range from upright to crouching
	Fingers held together or in fists
	Inserting dramatic pauses, acrobatic stunts, or theatrical gestures in the middle of a solo

As they paata, dancers often exhibit a great deal of gendered movement, yet the boundary between masculine and feminine often constitutes a site of play and experimentation rather than one of strict enforcement. Few if any attributes of either the male or female style are explicitly off limits to the opposite sex. It is particularly common for women to transition from umanpikinfutu to mannengeefutu over successive spurts of dancing. Even when a dancer performs a step that is aligned with the opposite gender, many of the nuances of the style—including the positioning of the hands or the angle of the head—can inflect the perceived femininity or masculinity of the dancer's performance style or rendering.

SYNTHESIS

Figure 4.9 is my attempt to create a framework through which different pieces of a performance can be contextualized and compared, without overdetermining the content—which can vary dramatically from one event to the next. Up to this point in the chapter, my description and organization of awasa drumming, singing, and dancing corresponds with a horizontal reading of figure 4.9. The graphic rendering makes it easier to trace the weave of connective threads of performance, both in terms of the progression of events for each part (the horizontal plane), as well as the co-occurrence and interactions between performance roles (the vertical plane). An understanding of the structural and interactive features of awasa requires an appreciation of the dynamic interplay between the warp and the weft.

Reading the Graph

If one segment of this structure is to characterize awasa, it is section C, in which all performers are fully engaged and the amount of interactivity between parts is at its peak. Although the durations of all of these sections are highly flexible, the paata is consistently the longest, often lasting longer than the other segments combined. In some performances, especially when a community collectively mounts a performance, rather than commissioning a formally designated dance group, sections B and D can be very short, with abridged communications between solo dancer(s) and the gaandoonman.

Though it is easy to interpret the gaandoonman as dictating the activities of a dancer (or, at least, a dancer who is attentive to his directions), the character

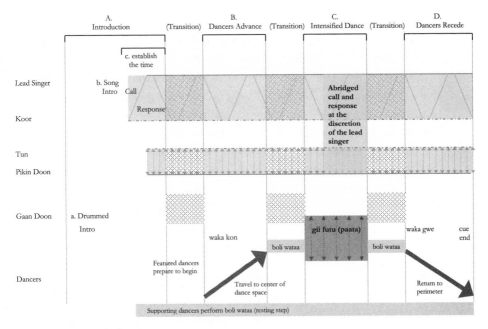

Key to Figure 4.9 (above)

A dancer's movement through a performance space (upward indicates movement from perimeter to the center of the space; downward a return to the perimeter).

A call and response framework in which the end of the caller's phrase typically overlaps with the beginning of the response and vice-versa.

Indicates heightened attention and communication between two musical roles.

A supporting role with limited opportunity for variation and a primary objective of maintaining a constant musical texture.

A role that features ongoing interaction and potential for dialogue with multiple other roles within the ensemble.

A role that helps to establish the metrical structure and time feel.

A field of heightened interactive and/or improvisatory potential as a result of a thinner sonic texture.

A field of intensified interactivity and improvisatory potential, heightening the excitement of a performance.

of their interaction is not a unidirectional flow of information from drummer to dancer; the gaandoonman also responds to the dancers' actions. Dancers are more likely to dictate the timing and duration of each section and a given piece. A dancer who tires easily will prompt a drummer to make the paata section shorter, while a dancer who clearly wishes to continue dancing will do so of her own accord. Likewise, the duration of sections B and D are dependent on the amount of time dancers take to reach the center or periphery of the dance space. The directional arrows on the graph indicate these two parts' dialogic function.

This interactive feature is related to a broader point about the variety and character of interactional forms that can be described as call and response. Although call-and-response forms have in common some degree of dialogue between two parties, there are a number of ways of calling and responding within a performance context that are differently structured and can enact various social and musical roles. Some indication of the range of functions of call-and-response forms is evident within awasa. Consider, for instance, the differences between the call-and-response interaction between the gaandoonman and dancers and that between the lead singer and koor, or between tun and pikin doon. In the latter examples, the two parts "lock into" one another, creating a dense and interactive sonic texture, yet should one performer or performance role not enter at the expected time, its complementary part is to keep on without any drastic alteration in timing. Different rules of engagement are exercised between the gaandoonman and the dancers, in which the roles of caller and respondent can change within the course of a piece. While it is most common for the gaandoonman to cue a solo dancer, it is by no means rare for the dancer to initiate a new rhythmic or choreographic pattern, or futu, for the drummer to follow. Furthermore, when a lead singer calls attention to another individual or group in her song and that individual, in turn, acknowledges the singer (as with Carla Pinas and Losen Abente in "Kon go Diingi Labaa"), they are taking part in a variety of call and response whose function is nearly opposite to that of the steady exchanges between the lead and koor or the tun and pikin doon. While the latter establishes an ongoing musical texture, the former punctuates it.

Interrelations

On a broad structural level, the various roles that performers can assume in awasa are timekeeping, providing a constant pattern with limited variation, and performing patterns with a great deal of improvisatory freedom and minimal timekeeping responsibilities. Broken down in this way, we can see that all three roles are performed by each section of the ensemble.[43] Table 4.4 organizes performance parts in terms of their functional affinities, but there are ways in which the function and communicative profile of each performance role is distinctive.

TABLE 4.4. Functional affinities between percussion, song, and dance

	Percussion	Song	Dance
Timekeeping (maintaining the *tactus*, or pulse)	Tun and pikin doon (also kwakwa and saka)	Lead and koor	Boli wataa
Constant pattern with limited variation	Pikin doon	Koor	Umanpikinfutu
Improvisatory	Gaan doon	Lead singer	Mannengeefutu

Although I did not hear performers talk about the group in terms of these strata, some clue of the perceived interrelation of musical, choreographic, or affective functions between singers, percussionists, and dancers is evident in the verbs used to describe the "doing" of various performance roles. In addition to the commonly used verbs—*naki* (hit), *singi* (sing), *dansi* (dance), and pee (play)—other words describe more specifically the interactive or structural characteristics of a given part. Many such words are ascribed to performers in multiple sections of the ensemble. For instance, *koti* (cut) is a verb that can be linked to dance moves involving quick, assertive, and abrupt articulations, usually of the hips or midsection.[44] It can also be said that a lead drummer will koti gaan doon, exercising a level of virtuosity and a crispness of articulation that is similar to its danced counterpart. Likewise, waka (walk) is implicit in the dance moves waka kon and waka gwe, yet a pikin doon player can also be said to "waka" pikin doon. All these actions have continuous motion as a common feature. To give a third example, the response to a call is termed "piki" in Okanisi. In awasa performance, this term applies both to singers in performing the koor and to the pikindoonman as his part responds to the incessant beats of the tun and potentially to the larger phrasal units of the gaandoonman.

Considering these structural continuities between discrete sections of an ensemble draws our attention to likenesses between various performers and performed material. It may help us recognize states of awareness and potential sites for dialogue common to performers with a shared performance function, or in experiencing awasa, these different strata might help an onlooker process what is happening in a performance.

Yet at the same time, alongside these similarities are several important differences. A dancer, for instance, is in the unique position of inhabiting two or three of these different performance functions within a given piece. Furthermore, a dancer performing umanpikinfutu does not necessarily accompany or occupy a role that is subordinate to a dancer performing mannengeefutu, and she can be engaged in dialogue with the gaan doon in much the same way as a dancer performing in the mannengeefutu style.

To cite another example, singers and supporting drummers have a structural or functional likeness (indicated by the striped fields on the graph), yet the pairs differ in terms of their communicative and improvisatory capacities. Both the singers and the drummers maintain the time in two parts, in which one member of each pair (the lead singer and the pikindoonman) has the potential to communicate across sections, while the other (either the koor or the tunman) stays comparatively stable. The difference arises in light of the latter group. In some instances, as in audio track 3, koor singers are able to implement some subtle variation in pitch, rhythmic contour, or even text while collectively maintaining a response to the lead singer's call with relatively constant rhythmic and tonal character. By contrast, the tun remains unchanging throughout the piece. Although the lead singer shares with the gaandoonman and a dancer performing mannengeefutu a great deal of improvisatory freedom, she is beholden to the metrical structure of the piece being performed. Improvisations must fit into a regular, finite number of beats or the balance of the call-and-response exchange with the koor will be disturbed.

In his important and controversial work, *Representing African Music*, Kofi Agawu states emphatically the close relation between rhythmic timelines and dance: "No one hears a *topos* without also hearing—in actuality or imaginatively—the movement of feet. And the movement of feet in turn registers directly or indirectly the metrical structure of the dance. Conceptually, then, the music and dance of a given *topos* exist at the same level; the music is not prior to the dance, nor is the dance prior to the music" (2003, 73).[45] Agawu's statement that a *topos*, or timeline, is equally dependent on music and dance is an idea that I think warrants continued attention and could bring about far-reaching changes in the analysis and dissemination of African and African Diasporic music and dance genres. While the structural or functional properties of the tun in awasa lie somewhere between *tactus* and *topos* (or engages properties of both simultaneously), Agawu's observations here speak to the central importance of the kinesthetic ordering of sound in creating a sense of "The Time," which David Locke describes as "[the parts that] articulate and embellish the key musical phrase which 'sculpts' time into a distinct 'shape,' thereby implicitly establishing the music's meter" (1998, 11).

Even so, often it is insufficient to mention dancers in a general sense. To give an example, although it is in conversation with the music's steady pulse, the often erratic dancing of the mannengeefutu style would not necessarily lead one to a more grounded experience of the tun. Here again it becomes important to consider different structural and communicative functions within and between sections of an ensemble. Likewise, Locke's conception of "The Time" can be implemented effectively in an analysis of awasa only if performers other than percussionists are considered. The ordering of the pulse into a larger shape is the role of the supporting dancers (through their kawai and swaying bodies) and through the alternating call-and-response phrases of the singers—not the drummers. The structure I have illustrated in figure 4.9 is intended to help organize the sounds and movements of performance, but I wish to emphasize that each part is distinctive. With the organizational schema I introduced above, my intention is to produce a framework through which both commonalities and differences will be easier to identify.

Given the uniqueness of each part, it might be reasonable to conclude that an awasa performance could not seem complete without the participation of all sections of an ensemble. "Completeness" is a subjective matter, yet I want to point out that dancers, singers, and drummers can and do practice and perform awasa with one or even two sections of the ensemble absent. I consider this a testament both to performers' awareness of and their complicity in the other realms of performance.[46] Lyrical, rhythmical, and choreographic sensibilities are drawn upon by every section of the ensemble, as are structural, soloistic or improvisatory, and supporting performance roles.

What is the purpose of analysis and transcription, particularly in an era when audio and video texts can travel with increasing ease alongside written accounts? Throughout this chapter I have illustrated, graphed, and analyzed various technical and communicative features of performance with the goal of helping readers gain focus on specific phenomena. Performers operate with attention paid to prescribed moves and postures, but the lines between prescribed and improvised, or between conformity to distinct ideals and the expectation of stylization, are especially hazy. As I witnessed and performed this dance genre, I came to understand the pleasure and excitement of performance as existing not in the technical prowess of the performer alone, but also in how, through those technical skills, a dancer could demonstrate awareness of and participation in the event as a whole. Talent was most satisfying as a social and poetic technology, rather than as an end in itself.

With this in mind, I consider analysis's greatest service to the genre to be introducing the technical and interactive structures that order the more immediately accessible sounds and movements of awasa performance. Through taking a performance or performance practice out of "real time" and examining its composite parts and its creative, communicative, and historical links, we get a glimpse of the satisfaction afforded connoisseurs of the genre. We also get a sense for the complex mixture of timing, musicality, improvisation, rhythmic sensibility, and physical discipline that talented performers wield. These are impressive when outlined in a detailed fashion, but they also bears testament to the phenomenon of bodily knowing, for the often complicated visual and sonic responses that are produced in the moment of performance owe a great deal to the cultural-performative conditioning that is physically acquired and deployed as a result of long-term practice and exposure.

CHAPTER 5

Alakondre Dron

Embodying Multiethnic Discourse

Did you notice that I immediately started to talk about my ethnicity
when I spoke about identity? That is so deep in our Surinamese
genes. In a country that so beats its breast as a multiethnic paradise,
we are very busy with those compartments. And we think that
ethnicity is the most important characteristic for a person.

—*Sharda Ganga, "Identiteit? Bij Kid Dynamite" (my translation)*

You can't just be concepts. Like you can't suddenly call us a rainbow
nation and then, we must be a rainbow. We [South Africans] have to break
down these concepts *as* this rainbow nation. Otherwise, it means nothing
to us, you know? We have to know, what does this rainbow mean?

—*Thandiswa Maswai, Late Night with Kgomotso Matsunyane*

In an effort to explain the ways that ethnicity is mobilized in Suriname, the
journalist and playwright Sharda Ganga recounted to me an experience she had
in 2000 while attending Carifesta (the Caribbean Festival of Arts). Upon their
arrival in Saint Kitts (the host country for that year's celebration), the members
of the Surinamese delegation—including politicians, visual and performing artists, poets, and playwrights—were instructed to come to the evening's ceremony
in traditional dress. Ganga recalled how, evidently, everyone else had known to

squirrel away in their luggage an outfit that signaled their respective ethnicities. She had some ambivalence about broadcasting her ethnic heritage in such a manner and had packed no such outfit. Realizing that to ignore the instructions would not go over well, she asked a friend of hers—an Amerindian woman—if she could borrow something to wear. At the opening ceremonies, several members of the Surinamese delegation came up to her, confused and distressed as to why she, a Hindustani, would be dressed in the traditional apparel of another ethnic group. She recalled how one of her Hindustani colleagues was particularly upset, chastising Ganga and saying that she would have "wrapped her up" like a proper Hindustani woman had she known about the wardrobe problem. "That's how it is here," Sharda concluded (pers. comm., 10 June 2014).

In this case, "how it is here" has less to do with the spoken rhetoric of multiethnic nationalism than with its enactment. The theme of "unity in diversity," common throughout the Caribbean and beyond,[1] becomes particular to Suriname as it is embodied and set into motion by the country's citizenry. As Ganga's anecdote makes clear, the norms and expectations that guide performances of nationalism are firmly established and actively regulated, even if they are seldom articulated. In this case, each member of the Surinamese delegation was expected to embody as fully as possible a singular cultural "ingredient" in the multiethnic national mixture—one that resonated with his or her phenotypic features, thereby enhancing ethnic legibility. The particular multiplicity in this multicultural vision resulted from creating a collective of individuals representing singular ethnic units, rather than an intermixture of influences synthesized in individuals' identificatory practices—for instance, in their comportment and self-styling. Ganga's challenge to this expectation and the distress it caused further demonstrate the point: despite abundant cross-cultural dialogue and ethnic intermixture among the population at large, practices of cultural representation in Suriname have remained staunchly oriented toward ethnic compartmentalization.

Understanding why ethnic performativity is such a preoccupation, and why ethnocultural identifications seem to warrant such intense regulation, requires some knowledge of the country's political structure. The historian Edward Dew dates the division of political parties along explicitly ethnic lines to 1948, when Suriname was parsed into voting districts that reflected the geographical distribution of the country's major ethnic groups.[2] This ethnopolitical framework merged with a Dutch consociational model of governance in which a number of parties, none of which has a decisive majority, form temporary or nonbinding alliances to promote or temper legislation in accordance with party interests.[3] Given both the diversity of Suriname's population and the fact that no ethnic group has managed to secure a clear majority, ethnic partisanship maps rather easily onto a consociational framework, resulting in what Dew has termed *apanjaht* consociationalism—"apanjaht" meaning "one's own ethnic group" in Sarnámi, a dialect of Caribbean Hindustani.[4] Dew posits that although a number of additional factors prevent voters' decision making from being wholly predictable, ethnicity has remained their dominant mode of political party identification into the twenty-first century.[5] Rosemarijn Hoefte observes that as parties with no explicit ethnic affiliation become more common, the ethnic partisanship that until now has dominated the political scene may be waning. Yet she notes, "Even [President Desi] Bouterse's acclaimed panethnic NDP [Nationale Democratische Partij (National Democratic Party)] is a careful mixture of different ethnic backgrounds, thus enabling voters to choose a candidate on the basis of ethnic preference" (2014a, 139).

As Paul B. Tjon Sie Fat reminds us, apanjaht consociationalism is not entirely descriptive, but prescriptive as well: "[It] is not just the result of ethnic pluralism but also the generator of ethnic identity; in other words in order to participate, one cannot but be ethnic" (2009, 22). Tjon Sie Fat argues that as both a cause and a symptom of the given political structure, ethnic performing is a requisite and inevitable part of political participation in a national sphere. He takes care to clarify that the kinds of performance demanded of Surinamers has to do with sociopolitical legibility, rather than necessarily reflecting an individual's experiences, cultural practices, or chosen modes of identification. Tjon Sie Fat illustrates his point using his own experiences: "Born in Suriname of part-Chinese descent, with a Sino-Surinamese surname, I share the experience of inescapable 'Chineseness' with many Surinamese, of being placed in a universal, ubiquitous, self-evident Chinese category, without actually being an insider to the 'Chinese community' in any way" (ibid.). Ganga, too, conveys a sense of the inescapability of ethnic identity, claiming, "I have resisted the straitjacket of being a Hindustani for a long time" (2014). As someone who participates in a broad range of cultural activities in Suriname beyond Hindustani practices, she describes herself as aligning intentionally with a Hindustani identity only at certain moments. (She used as an example her desire to specify her relationship to her newborn nephew not just as an aunt, but as a *phoewa* in the Hindustani tradition: "the woman who will be allowed to sit in the front row at every memorable life event" [ibid.].) Despite her own inclinations, as a Surinamer her ethnic legibility is often treated as a matter of some social importance, a point made abundantly clear by her experience at Carifesta.

Ethnic identification for political ends has remained one of precious few ways of gaining access to resources (including various licenses and permits, housing, jobs, and educational opportunities) in a country where the formal infrastructure is weak. With few exceptions, Tjon Sie Fat sees apanjaht consociationalism as a system by which elites garner and maintain political power, rather than an idealized process through which the needs of minority populations can be championed: "It is elite power-sharing through clientelism at the level of ethnically defined political parties; it does not involve group representation for disadvantaged segments who are striving for political equality" (2009, 11).[6] Quoting Joseph Rothschild (1981, 77), he maintains, "As in Malaysia and Guyana, 'organized ethnic political competition is for control of the (apparatus of) central government, which thus necessarily depends on fixed, predictable, but segmental ethnic support'" (Tjon Sie Fat 2009, 10).

While apanjaht consociationalism exerts strong pressures in favor of cultural compartmentalization and competition among ethnopolitical groups, Suriname's ideological discourse celebrates cultural plurality, peaceful coexistence, inclusivity, and intermixture. In general, intercultural relations are conceptualized either in terms of integration (an emerging cultural synthesis that is essentially Surinamese) or of fraternity (involving peaceful relations among ethnic groups without any expectation that they will merge or alter drastically). Both nationalist concepts took shape in the mid-twentieth century, in the decades leading up to Suriname's independence. Eddie Bruma, front man for the Netherlands-based social organization Wie Eegie Sanie (our own thing) championed an integrationist approach, whereas the Surinamese Hindustani political figures Jñan Hansdew Adhin and Jaggernath Lachmon promoted fraternity.[7] Both positions suggested ways in which a multicultural population could unify, yet both came under criticism for representing the political interests of one particular ethnic group. Wie Eegie Sanie tried to promote itself as being without ethnic affiliation, but its membership roster and the abundance of Afro-Surinamese imagery it employed in its Surinamese cultural synthesis led many to believe it promoted Creole political and social dominance (Oostindie 1996, 219). Lachmon and Adhin were both thought to be protective of Hindustani interests, attempting to consolidate the political power of this large and growing population and reacting against an integrationist vision that left many Hindustanis feeling alienated (Bakboord 2012, 12).

By and large, the concepts of integration and fraternity are well-worn models of social interrelation in a multicultural system, common to many nations beyond Suriname. They articulate in broad terms the dilemma of what roles cultural synthesis and miscegenation are to play in the national imaginary. They can be localized and given more focus through particular nationalist tropes, which identify aspects of diversity and modes of cultural interrelationship as sites of value. However, verbal political discourse does not shed much light on "how it is here" as Ganga described—how individuals perform identity and mobilize as ethnopolitical actors. Staged nationalist ensembles like Suriname's Alakondre Dron make audible and visible the expectations and social formations that the national rhetoric implies but dares not state directly. This chapter makes the argument that Alakondre Dron's nationalistic performances do not simply expound upon nationalist discourse: they manifest a more comprehensive expression of multicultural concepts that are only partially verbal in the first place. By providing its audiences with cultural representatives and scenarios with which they can identify, nationalistic performance makes a trope's meaning, function, and ideal application locally relevant and socially soluble. Performances focus on each model's unifying potential, but the social limitations of each are replicated as well—including tendencies to highlight and enforce social hierarchies; the persisting influence of ethnic clientelism; and above all the elusive nature of unity and genuine intercommunication, whether through synthesis or merging separate parts into a whole.

In donning clothing that didn't align with her ethnic identifications, Ganga expressed an integrationist stance, only to confront the unspoken but absolute expectation that participants would enforce their ethnic legibility above all else. She aligned herself with an accepted trope but performed at a time and in a way that was deemed unacceptable—to some, even distressing. Her experiences make clear the importance of considering how, when, and in what proportion one nationalistic message is promoted above others. In a similar vein, Alakondre Dron demonstrates civic ideals through both fraternalist and integrationist content but consistently places musical and visual emphasis on maintaining each performer's ethnic legibility. The true meaning and impact of the group's performances are best perceived by addressing the tropes they demonstrate as a collective and by paying particular attention to their signature piece, the mainstay of nearly every performance.

Adhin, Lachmon, and Bruma developed their cross- and intercultural models as Suriname confronted the prospect of its independence, but these ideas were tied to a particular political moment and issue. They have continued to circulate and exercise influence while Suriname's political climate has changed significantly. Most recently, the 2012 census indicates dramatic shifts within the population at large—a startling increase in the number of Maroons (from 14.7 percent of the population in 2004 to 21.7 percent in 2012), as well as the emergence of the category "mixed" (accounting for 13.4 percent of the population in 2012). Starting in 2004, a small but growing portion of the population identified as Afro-Surinamer, aligning with neither Maroon nor Creole identifications (Menke and Sno 2016, 90). These changes in the national demographic destabilize the ethnopolitical balance of Suriname's long-standing apanjaht consociationalist system. The "mixed" census category and the increasing social viability of claiming "Afro-Surinamer" ethnicity appear at odds with the representational logic on which Alakondre Dron was founded. Suriname's multicultural discourse, like the ensemble most frequently tasked with representing it, is increasingly seen as being insufficient for addressing a new generation of Surinamers who grew up in a postcolonial environment and who are effectively asserting identities that confuse and transcend independence-era narratives.

ALAKONDRE DRON

For over forty years, Alakondre Dron has played a prominent role in promoting Suriname's cultural richness. The ensemble was founded in 1971 by the playwright and director Henk Tjon, who remained its artistic director until his death in 2009. Though not officially recognized or sponsored by the Surinamese government, this ensemble has been commissioned to perform at nearly every event requiring a large-scale depiction of national culture since the 1970s. While it is familiar and recognizable to a popular audience, its target audiences are national elites and foreigners, whether businesspeople or tourists. While many national ensembles (for instance, the Ghana Dance Company [Schramm 2000] and the Ballet Folklorico de Mexico [Shay 2002]) train their performers in all the styles featured in their repertoire, Alakondre Dron recruits performers from preexisting cultural groups in Paramaribo to act as representatives of a singular ethnic group and musical tradition. In other words, the ensemble is composed of minigroups, each representing one cultural "ingredient" for the duration of the performance, rather than embodying and representing traditions from multiple ethnic groups. The number and variety of genres and minigroups featured in performance can change to some degree, but each Alakondre Dron performance necessarily includes contributions from people of Maroon, Hindustani, Javanese, Creole, and Amerindian ethnic groups—the five major ethnic groups in the country, described as the five children of Mama Sranan (Mother Suriname) in nationalist discourse (see figure 5.1).[8] Kifoko has represented Maroon culture in Alakondre Dron since the ensemble's earliest years.[9] Alakondre Dron performers broadcast their ethnic affiliations from start to finish through their attire, the instruments they play, and their grouping and interactions with other performers on stage—much as the Surinamese delegates at Carifesta did in Ganga's recollection that opened this chapter.

Generally, the meaning of the Sranantongo word *alakondre* is glossed as "all nations" or "all countries," thus making the ensemble's name "all countries' drum." A striped pattern of cloth that incorporates many colors

FIGURE 5.1 *Mama Sranan*, sculpted by Jozef Klas and erected on Kleine Waterstraat in downtown Paramaribo in 1965, depicts "Mother Suriname" and her five children, representing Suriname's primary ethnic groups. Photo by the author.

might be referred to as *alakondre koosi* (alakondre cloth), and a soup or rice dish that incorporates many contrasting ingredients can be called alakondre—the term always describes something that incorporates many parts, and it almost always bears national connotations. The dancer and actor Alida Neslo has theorized the term most extensively, positing that "Alakondrism" is a social and creative practice born out of constant exposure to and engagement with diverse sources—a disposition that is deeply linked to Surinamese circumstances and modes of socialization. She explains: "If one recognizes and/or acknowledges the *authenticity* of a phenomenon, it is not difficult to put your own imagination to work in order to make the 'strange' familiar. Alakondre . . . is difficult to translate but means something like 'the search for the other, for whatever differs from your own opinions, your own looks, your own vision of reality'" (2011, 110).

Neslo and Ganga, among others, credit Alakondre Dron with making a bold statement in its formative years. The group performed at elite theatrical and concert venues that had previously featured Euro-American works nearly exclusively, and Alakondre Dron saturated its productions with sounds and movements associated with the country's largest ethnic groups. As Annika Ockhorst put it, "In Surinamese Theater, the focus on Surinamese society was still a relatively new phenomenon" (2014, 297). Like its theatrical counterpart, the Doe-Theater Company, Alakondre Dron "was an exponent of this reorientation in Surinamese cultural life from Europe to Suriname" (ibid.).[10] On the eve of national independence, performers' showcasing their traditions openly and in contrast to Dutch conventions, without fear of censure or open ridicule, was a new and powerful phenomenon.

Of equal importance to Alakondre Dron's musical director, Wilgo Baarn, was the fact that musicians shared a stage with one another: "Earlier, when we held a cultural night, an event . . . then, the Hindustani come, they do their thing, they leave; the Amerindians come, do their thing, they leave; the Javanese come, do their thing and go; the Maroons come, do their things, and leave. But that is not how people are living in Sranan. We're not living that way, we're living together" (pers. comm., 2 December 2008). Baarn characterized Alakondre Dron's ensemble dynamic as being broadly reflective of Surinamese social life, but the message could be considered instructive as well: if these performers of diverse backgrounds can work together while maintaining mutual respect, average Surinamers ought to be able to do the same in their daily interactions. In fact, as a nationalistic expression, the group implies that the capacity to do so is essentially Surinamese.

PERFORMANCE ANALYSIS

Alakondre Dron has one hallmark piece that is featured in nearly every performance. This piece, the cornerstone of its repertoire, provides a textbook example of what Ganga characterizes as a formula for Surinamese nationalist performance. As she sees it, the formula is as follows: "The central theme is a display of the wealth of ethnicities; each group is depicted separately through cultural demonstrations; the event ends in a show of unity; the elements may be linked by a story line, codified in a rudimentary script. In the events that link ethnicity to multiculturalism, collective ethnic identity (and associated gender identities) is reiterated and the audience is shown how and where to place their life scripts" (quoted in Tjon Sie Fat 2009, 30).[11]

Although group and individual members in the ensemble have varied over time, the piece has maintained the same structure for decades. It begins with the whole ensemble playing together, fitting each of the parts together in relation to a unified pulse at a moderate tempo. Following a cue by the conductor, the entire ensemble plays a rhythmic break in unison (example 5.1).

Example 5.1: Alakondre Dron break rhythm.

After this, each of the subgroups in the ensemble is featured in turn. The featured group begins by responding to the break pattern with four pulses of improvisation. The entire ensemble and soloing group trade phrases three times. After these short solos ("trading fours," in jazz terminology), the featured small group has an extended solo that lasts roughly a minute, concluding with the rhythmic break once again. Between the groups' solos, the entire ensemble briefly resumes playing (see example 5.2). When Alakondre Dron performs with dancers, the dancers make their entrance after all the subgroups of

[X] [A]_____ [X] [B] [X] [B] [X] [B] [X] [C]_____

Repeated with every small group in turn.

X=Alakondre Dron break (example 5.1 above)

A=Alakondre Dron whole ensemble

B=Small group short solo

C=Small group extended solo

Example 5.2: Small group solo structure contribution, in dialogue with the larger Alakondre Dron ensemble. The long lines indicate the longer duration of sections A and C.

Alakondre Dron **145**

percussionists have been featured. The dancers affiliated with each subgroup typically perform once or twice, depending on time constraints. Alakondre Dron performances end with a song or song and dance number in which all the performers take part.

This structure provides a tidy and uniform framework, ensuring that each group is featured for roughly the same amount of time as all the others. Because each cultural group's contribution is relatively self-contained, groups can be extracted or added with minimal disturbance to the larger ensemble and its overall presentational structure: uniformity causes the groups to present musical modules that are unique in content but structurally interchangeable. Arguably, the consistent framework draws attention to the distinctive attributes of each group, in that its structural predictability allows listeners to focus more closely on what each group does with its allotted time.

For every group that is featured, the ensemble plays the rhythmic break (example 5.1) five times. With a minimum of five groups within the ensemble, by the conclusion of the piece the audience is thoroughly familiar with the break rhythm. The break has become so emblematic of the ensemble that on more than one occasion I have heard people refer to the group not by name but by this short but ever-present rhythm. In a way, calling the ensemble by its signature rhythm sums up a more general critique: rather than developing new content, it constantly reiterates the same material.

TROPES

Alakondre Dron performances tended to use minimal verbal exchanges, yet a number of the performance tropes that drive nationalist rhetoric are clearly discernible.[12] Each one activates certain structural relationships, and as cultural groups embody them and enact them in real time, the groups reveal fundamental elements of each trope's function.

Trope 1: To Each his Own

The most basic premise behind the name Alakondre Dron is that each *kondre* (nation or group) has its own drum. The drum stands as a symbol for a form of expression that unites community in each culture, and the existence of these drum traditions underscores the idea that despite surface differences between people, they have fundamental commonalities. By affirming their common bonds, Surinamers can recognize and appreciate the differences among themselves while honoring a shared humanity and a shared nationality.

This "to each his own" framework has been reinforced through theatrical elements that directors have incorporated into Alakondre Dron shows. In Carifesta X in Guyana, for instance, each minigroup within the Alakondre Dron ensemble provided an interlude, demonstrating aspects of religious practice associated with the given cultural group. The groups might have religious differences, but the fact that each community seeks connection with the spiritual world remains a constant.[13] At the 2014 Fiesta del Fuego in Santiago de Cuba, the group's narrative involved concocting a magical stew to which every group added one ingredient. The narrative depicted all the various ethnic groups working together in harmony until some members became greedy and took some of the concoction for themselves, throwing its delicate balance into disequilibrium as a result. Much as in *Peter Pan* when the audience is urged to clap if they believe in fairies, here the audience was directed to laugh, alongside the members of the ensemble, for only laughter would restore the magical properties of the concoction. This performance drew on a shared and presumably universal capacity to laugh to bond people together, regardless of their differences.

This same trope appears outside of Alakondre Dron as well—for instance, in a 2010 ad campaign that marketed Paramaribo as "the City of Smiles."[14] The message implied that the residents of Paramaribo may differ in outward appearance, but they are united by the capacity (and, purportedly, the inclination) to smile. All these cases imply an egalitarian framework, with no drum, laugh, or smile being inherently better or more valued than any other. The efficacy of these messages lies in the composite: the greater the variety of people or musical styles sampled, the more convincing and profound their commonalities.

In its efforts to accentuate the commonalities across disparate traditions, Alakondre Dron does narrow community representation in pronounced ways. Drumming is a gendered activity in almost every one of the musical practices the group samples. The ensemble's core group has represented Suriname's cultural output with a predominantly (and often exclusively) male cast. In its larger productions, the group swells in size with the addition of dancers and singers. These larger versions of the ensemble are designated Alakondre Dron Plus or Prisiri (celebration in Sranan Tongo). When the larger ensembles perform, it is the dancers who garner the lion's share of the audience's attention and praise. Nevertheless, the premise of the group and its structure of leadership frame dance and the role of women as supplementary.

The musical traditions that Alakondre Dron samples are also molded by the project's overall framework and narrative. Using the drum as a focal point risks depicting drummers' contributions as of paramount importance, whether or not the drum is given pride of place in a particular tradition. This may not be much of a stretch for the Amerindian and Afro-Surinamese ensembles, which feature drums almost exclusively, but it works less well for the Hindustani genres, in which the focus is more evenly shared among the tabla, *dantal* (a metal rod widely used in the Indo-Caribbean as percussive accompaniment), and harmonium players. The same could be said for the Javanese musicians; their ensemble includes a *kendang* drummer, but also several instruments that are not drums, including *angklung* rattles and various metallophones and gongs. In these cases, the search for common ground takes priority over maintaining accuracy in describing a drummer's communicative role within each of the traditions depicted.

In the same way that primordialist national narratives establish a sense of destiny or a bond with the land that belies a more recent history (Smith 2010, 55), drums are depicted as connecting with people on a primal, fundamental level that is ancient and wise and unites people despite their differences. As Baarn puts it, "Culture has one language, and above all it goes with the drum. This one drum is played, and you can be Hindustani, you can be Bushkondre [Maroon], you can be Chinese . . . the drum is speaking to you. You have direct contact with the drum. Communication is always there" (pers. comm., 2 December 2008). Baarn presents the ability to understand people through percussion (whether in relation to specific messages or in a more general spiritual way) as effortless and universal—a direct spiritual or psychic line that connects us all. At the same time, the group's capacity to absorb so many cultural influences is the result of something specific—even miraculous.

Trope 2: The Miracle of Multiculturalism, the National Sublime

Adhin begins his influential essay "Eenheid in verscheidenheid [unity and diversity]" by declaring: "The pulse of Surinamese life is of multiple origins and is sometimes confusing, because the different rhythms do not always correspond. The big challenge now is to align these various rhythms to create a harmonious and uninterrupted whole" (1998, 34). From these disparate "rhythms," Adhin expounds upon the notion of unity in diversity, in which the objective is not to cause shifts in the content of cultural practice, but rather to align each distinctive contribution in a way that creates a sense of order and unity while maintaining difference.

Alakondre Dron was established fifteen years after Adhin's essay was first published, but his analogy appears to be nearly tailor-made for the group. For many people, the convergence of such an array of musical traditions results in something mesmerizing. The journalist René Gompers recalled being "overcome" by the group's "multi-ethnic drum manifestation" at a performance in Santiago de Cuba.[15] Likewise, the American bassist Paul Beaudry was blown away upon hearing the group while on tour in Suriname in 2010. As he wrote in his blog, "When [Alakondre Dron starts] a piece you can hear that there are 6 distinct rhythmic traditions playing together at the same time, and it works! Myself having a background in percussion I have never seen nor heard anything quite like this before."[16] In a subsequent conversation we had on the topic, Beaudry elaborated on his reaction. While his response was uniquely rich in technical and musical detail, it contains the hallmark ingredients of what I consider the national sublime, and as such, it is worth discussing at length. The national sublime in a Surinamese context is most readily achieved through boggling the mind with a barrage of highly varied sonic and/or visual information, coupled with a sense that the work accomplishes something that eludes explanation and analysis altogether—an ineffable spirit shared among performers.

By "it works!," Beaudry meant a couple of things. One important component was achieving a sonic balance within the group as a whole, allowing a listener to identify rhythmic contributions from each minigroup. As he put it, "It was amazing to me to sit there and listen, and to be able to distinctly hear each influence, and yet it all came together" (pers. comm., 12 May 2018).[17] With so much going on, the sonic field of the ensemble sections of an Alakondre Dron performance can feel completely saturated, but Beaudry insists that part of the "genius" of the ensemble is the ways that each instrumentalist creates space for other performers' contributions. He explains:

> If you take African drumming, and it's extremely busy, you're not going to be able to add another influence that has a different concept of groove. And so the only way that those rhythms are able to work together is that every single rhythm has to have enough space for the other rhythms to go inside of it. . . . And I'm absolutely certain when they first put that Alakondre Dron ensemble together it did not work. . . . The reason why it works is because they still play together with a sense of space so that you can allow for the other

Alakondre Dron 149

instruments to come in. Because not everybody's playing with the same eighth note—I mean, not everybody's playing with the same quarter note! Some of those quarter notes are dead on, some of them are pushed, some of them are pulled and the eighth notes are all over the place!

A third component of how the ensemble "works" involves discipline—specifically the ensemble's willingness to respect the structure of the music's format and the authority of the ensemble leader (who was Baarn at the time of Beaudry's visit). Performers had to show restraint by allowing space for other musicians' input, and their willingness to limit their improvisations to the few minutes allotted to each minigroup was a way of demonstrating respect for the ensemble and the project of creating a musical representation of the nation.

Whereas many of Alakondre Dron's critics have expressed frustration with the ensemble's musical stasis on a macro level (and it's true that neither the overall structure, nor the rhythms that the minigroups contribute to the tutti sections seem to have changed much over the years), Beaudry points out that performers have to demonstrate perpetual dynamism and musical awareness in terms of their own rhythmic placement: "You all have to do this constant adjustment. Almost like airplanes going through the sky and there's all these little wind currents going by, and you have to constantly readjust to make sure that everything's gonna work out and the plane is gonna land exactly where you want it to land." While criticism of the group tends to concern the fixed and predictable nature of its content, Beaudry's admiration was on a more experiential level, focusing instead on tasteful execution and the kind of social attunement required of performers.

Alakondre Dron ensemble members—musicians and dancers alike—model many aspects of idealized citizenship: they must make space for one another's contributions, strive for a balanced dynamic level so that no one cultural "voice" is drowned out by any other, and demonstrate respect not just for fellow ensemble members but for the structure of the piece and the ensemble's conductor and musical director. In addition, Beaudry insists that to see a piece to fruition requires dedication to the cause: "I'm sure it took them a pile of time to figure that out. They were probably butting heads for quite some time and they said, 'you know what we're going to do, we're gonna keep working on this until we figure it out.'" The conductor, too, presents an idealized image of leadership by exercising authority while working judiciously to make sure that no one ensemble dominates the musical mix. The fact that these are not just musical but political dispositions was not lost on Beaudry. His expressed admiration for Alakondre

Dron aligns perfectly with the Adhinian rhetoric of unity in diversity while presenting a nonmajoritarian consociational political model as the structure that makes such a musical phenomenon possible:

> I think the thing that I was most blown away by was that somehow they were able to foster a sense of respect for other cultures and a sense of how to put this all together. And how do you come up with any kind of a national sense of being Suriname citizens and yet still be able to keep your individual cultures without expecting anyone to be . . . to somehow go into some kind of dominant Suriname culture the same way you would have with an immigrant [who] is coming to a country. It's like, you'd better acculturate or you're just not going to survive. You know, so they're able to keep their own individual culture and yet mix in with Suriname . . . and then, when you listen to the music, you hear that.

In performance as in social life, the miracle of "it working" is wielded as proof of its rightness, its undeniability—it represents a delicate balance and a closed system, an idealized state and a natural order. As with Neslo's interpretation of Alakondrism, Beaudry's language is saturated with the conviction of the specificity and specialness of this phenomenon and its inherent connection to Suriname and its people.

To find order and social harmony despite a bewildering number of musical and cultural referents and to hold these various contributions in balance in space and in one's consciousness as a listener or audience member—these are ways in which Surinamese multiculturalism approaches the national sublime. The musical manifestation as Beaudry describes it is a feat of technical virtuosity, but its transcendent quality stems from a social ethic: the true magic is rooted in Alakondrism.

Trope 3: The Mamio Quilt

> "Na mi de kari mamio: ting na ting yu abi fanowdu fu naai mi kong na wan [It's me they call mamio: piece by piece you have to stitch me together]."
>
> —Creole saying

Mamios are patchwork quilts of Creole origin that typically consist of multiple patches of relatively uniform size (see figure 5.2). Since at least the 1880s (Thompson 1983, 296), Creole women have assembled mamio quilts using scraps of cloth from worn garments or with cloth remnants left from various domestic tasks. Though any cloth could be used, the characteristic mamio quilt features multiple, contrasting striped patterns.[18] These quilts are a powerful testament to the resourcefulness of the Creole women, who are able to make something useful and beautiful out of relatively little—potentially, out of scraps. Beyond its utility as a symbol for personal identification (as in the above saying), the mamio is frequently used as a metaphor—or, as Peter Meel has termed it, a "myth"—for the nation. In this capacity, the multiple patterns in the quilt combine to symbolize "the unique variety of population groups and cultures inhabiting Suriname" (1998, 270).

Mamio quilts offer a vibrant visual display of color and pattern, avoiding chaos by virtue of the artful combination and placement of disparate segments and, typically, by the uniform shape and size of their patches. Constructing a nationalist performance piece in a manner similar to a mamio quilt typically involves both of these strategies: creating sections of uniform duration and use of space, and the artful arrangement of these relatively self-contained segments. As a whole these works can be an impressive display of variety, but each cultural

FIGURE 5.2 A mamio quilt.
Photo by the author.

contribution is treated as a patch—a small unit cut from a larger performance practice into a relatively uniform size, used primarily for color and texture but losing in the process much of the significance and coherence of the musical forms these minigroups reference.

Alakondre Dron groups performers representing a single ethnic tradition together into culturally homogeneous clusters, creating a visual display in which each ethnic group makes up a unit arranged in relation to others but for the most part without intermingling. Likewise, it imposes strict time and logistical constraints on performance. To ensure that all groups will have the opportunity to perform, the largest blocks of time for Kifoko and the other groups participating in Alakondre Dron to showcase their respective traditions seldom exceed two or three minutes. Ensemble portions of a performance include spotlight moments, often no longer than a few seconds, which are long enough to familiarize the audience with the sounds of the instruments in the ensemble and perhaps to establish a groove or provide a flashy drum break, but little else. As a matter of practice, cultural groups already truncate music and dance genres to retain the attention of less discerning audiences and to fit their performance program into a limited window of time, but when cinched into a mamio-style patch rather than a miniature representation of a performance genre, there simply isn't time to maintain some elements of context or of musical or choreographic development.

The cultural groups that participate in Alakondre Dron have to crop and compromise to function as a patch. The components of their performance that remain most accessible and durable are their visual impact (through their carved and painted drums, their colorful traditional clothing, their hair braiding and styling, and so on) and timbral particularities of their instruments. These aural and visual snapshots can give a vivid impression of tone color or rhythmic texture, but they leave little room for the compositional or communicative properties that distinguish a genre or demonstrate a performer's mastery.

Trope 4: Mee Doen

The Dutch phrase "mee doen" (or, as an imperative, "do mee") means joining in, participating. In the context of Alakondre Dron's performances, this concept asserts the importance of trying new things—going beyond one's comfort level, and specifically beyond the ethnic categories that render a person politically legible. Two examples demonstrate how Alakondre Dron has used this concept in its works.

The first comes from a performance that I witnessed at the elite Hotel Torarica in downtown Paramaribo in the spring of 2009. "Alakondre Dron Plus" (all the percussionists, with the addition of Amerindian and Maroon dancers) was one of several acts presenting light entertainment at a lavish reception for business executives. On this occasion, in addition to the standard performance for which Alakondre Dron is most widely known, the group presented a few short theatrical works, of which this choreographed piece was one:

Two young people—Herman Tojo from Kifoko and a young woman from the Amerindian group Paremuru—approach each other timidly in the middle of the dance space. They behave bashfully toward each other, giving a subtle implication of courtship or flirtation. Tojo appears to be at a loss as to how to communicate or what to say until he thinks to invite the young woman to dance with him. Backed by the Kifoko drummers, he demonstrates the basic step and posture for awasa. After his brief demonstration, he gestures toward the young woman, entreating her to join him. She shakes her head vigorously and hides her face in her hands. He is adamant, however, and repeats his demonstration. Again, though she watches with interest, when he asks her to join him she appears anxious and refuses. On his third attempt her refusal wavers, and finally on the fourth try she joins him, to the approval of the ensemble and the applause of the audience. The members of Paremuru and Kifoko embrace, and subsequently all members of Alakondre Dron reassemble for their next component of the performance.

By the first time the young woman from Paremuru refuses Tojo's invitation, the narrative arc of the choreography is clear to an audience familiar with Suriname's multicultural tropes. This piece promotes intercultural communication, and it is a near certainty that it will conclude with these two performers dancing together. As the piece progresses, the young woman's considerable discomfort and anxiety appear unnecessary—the audience is well aware that acceptance (theirs and that of the Alakondre Dron members) is required of them. With the main structure of the piece accounted for, the remaining questions that drive the routine become: What strategies will Tojo use to win over his dance partner—perseverance or creative problem solving? How long will this woman resist before acquiescing (as she inevitably will), and what will convince her to "do mee"? When at last the two performers dance together, they convey a satisfying feeling of inclusivity—"trying on" this dance indicates cultural receptivity among people of different backgrounds.

Whereas this piece was performed only once in the dozens of Alakondre Dron performances I have witnessed, the second example of "mee doen" is the most common way that Alakondre Dron concludes their "Alakondre Dron Prisiri" performances, involving both musicians and dancers from each represented tradition. Here, all the performers come together to sing and dance *sambura*, an Amerindian genre. They create a single line, each dancer placing their hands on the shoulders of the person in front of them as they would in a conga line (see figure 5.3). Following the movements of one of the Amerindian performers, participants step in time with a steady bass drum beat, rhythmically pulsing their shoulders and torsos forward as they snake in and around the performance space. In some instances, audience members join in. By doing so, they fully enter their role as ethnic performers: they may not be wearing traditional attire, but they too are "read" in terms of ethnicity, right alongside the ensemble members.

This routine is often the only point at which performers from each of the mini-groups that make up Alakondre Dron are thoroughly interspersed (rather than positioned in clusters corresponding to their minigroups) and also among the few segments in which the entire Alakondre Dron ensemble commits to performing in a singular musical tradition. While in other ways Tjon and subsequent leaders shied away from ordering the performance segments to imply a chronology or hierarchy (Ockhorst 2014, 306), concluding an evening's entertainment with a performance of an Amerindian genre provides an opportunity to acknowledge Amerindians as the original inhabitants of the land.

Both these routines end in triumphant, transcendent participation. They provide occasion for interaction and even a rare instance of physical contact among performers. Each supports the notion that to participate in a tradition with which you are unfamiliar is a way of communicating respect and galvanizing community. Sonically and visually, they express unity. As an ethic of good citizenship,

FIGURE 5.3 Members of Alakondre Dron close their performance at
the Suriname Independence Chess Tournament in November 2013.
Photo by the author.

Alakondre Dron **155**

participation serves to structure experience in a fundamentally different way than the previous three tropes. While "to each his own," mamio, and the miracle of multiculturalism stress positive interactions and inherent similarities among cultural units, "mee doen" joins participants in a singular practice.

The directive to "do mee" might seem simple enough, but in a culture-representational context there are some indications of the complexity of the issues involved. What, for instance, is the cause for the young Amerindian woman's reluctance to join Tojo's dancing, and why is it that such anxieties are not expressed when the entire ensemble performs sambura? How is it that to perform sambura at the end of a performance registers as unifying, even transformative, but Ganga's choice to don Amerindian rather than Hindustani apparel at the Carifesta ceremony was met with anxiety and disapproval?

The micropolitics of participation hint at how ethnic performativity occurs in intersectional space and that its effects have to account for differentials of privilege and mobility. Ganga articulates an extreme outcome of "mee doen" in relation to ethnic identity, recalling how in her youth she participated in a full range of cultural activities. She quips, "I was well on my way to washing myself of my Hindustani identity and becoming a real Surinamer—one who belonged to everything, and therefore nothing." Yet in the same article, Ganga complicates her own statement by indicating that she, too, wasn't able to "resist the straitjacket of being a Hindustani" (2014). For Tojo and his dance partner, as for Ganga, their physical features, gender, class, and a host of other factors prevent "belonging to nothing" in an environment so deeply invested in ethnic categories from being a viable option. That said, it is through a discourse of participation that Alakondre Dron comes closest to acknowledging the possibility of multiple or overlapping identifications. While the ensemble leaves no performance role that corresponds to an ethnically mixed identity, the celebration of participation and intercommunication provides one mode of presentation through which those who identify themselves as mixed could insert themselves into a national narrative.

Summary

With the exception of the ensemble's name, none of the above tropes are expressly verbalized by Alakondre Dron, yet all are immediately recognizable, owing to their proliferation through nationalistic and touristic initiatives. Especially given national expectations of ethnic performativity, most Surinamers are thoroughly adept at mobilizing for the sake of national representation: they see people modeling the nation on local television and on postcards, and they are asked to perform it in classrooms and group photos. Groups like Alakondre Dron do not, then, transfer verbal concepts to the realm of performance, since the concepts are already embodied and engrained. In turn, Alakondre Dron performances do not simply demonstrate nationalist ideals; they are processes of internalization, with each trope structuring and conveying different felt experiences of community. By deliberately (re)connecting the verbal discourse of the tropes to their performed manifestations, it becomes easier to discern what a given trope is asking of (or doing to) its citizens (see table 5.1).

TABLE 5.1. Comparison of tropes

Trope	Unique structural features	Shared structural features
1. To Each His Own	• Narrows comparison to specific parameters • Buried or emerging likenesses • Functional uniformity	• Equal representation • Collection of parts
2. The Miracle of Multiculturalism	• Saturation of a sonic or visual field	• Transcendent participation • Collection of parts • Aesthetic value of simultaneity and "fit" • Implied civic ideal
3. The Mamio Quilt	• Creating patches or samples • Spatial or temporal uniformity	• Equal representation • Collection of parts • Aesthetic value of simultaneity and "fit"
4. Mee Doen	• Extending beyond categorical limits • Social integration	• Transcendent participation • Implied civic ideal

Trope 1 ("To Each His Own") narrows the comparative frame to a single element that is shared among all representatives. The designated element is isolated—having a thing (be it a drum, a laugh, or a religious practice) takes precedence over what that thing might mean in a cultural context. The trope's basic premise is that there are fundamental likenesses among seemingly dissimilar people or things. The more obscured the connection is at first, the more satisfying it is to uncover, explore, and celebrate that connection. Trope 1 employs structural uniformity to underscore the similarity (or even sameness) of the designated feature and eliminate any appearance of bias.

Trope 2 ("The Miracle of Multiculturalism") and trope 3 ("The Mamio Quilt") both establish their impact by using a full sonic or visual palette. In trope 2, the sheer amount of audible or visible input is nearly overwhelming, yet somehow the cultural sources or representatives work together to establish order. This can be portrayed as virtuous and virtuosic sociality on the part of performer-citizens or by some more charmed or magical set of circumstances, such as destiny or luck at being a good fit.[19]

Trope 3 combines many of the aesthetic effects of trope 2 with the imperative of structural likeness inherent to trope 1. Yet whereas trope 1 isolates a single element and makes that the basis for comparison, trope 3 establishes some uniform field (of time, space, or something else) that cultural representatives can occupy however they please. These are then assembled in an artful way to create a whole greater than its parts. But for that to work, cultural forms must first be made into parts—chopped up in such a way that they cannot truly be appreciated or evaluated as whole or complete performances but rather give the *impression* of a genre of music or dance.

In contrast to the previous tropes, trope 4 ("Mee Doen") focuses on the transgression and transcendence of categorical divides. It does not create a performance or experience that belongs equally to everyone. In both of the examples I cited, a single genre of uncontested origin is performed. Others might join in, but they do so as invited guests rather than as collaborators. The multiethnic splendor that is so central to Suriname's national discourse is still in evidence, though the music and dance in these examples does not signify as multicultural or hybrid. Instead, the variety can be located in the performers as national subjects who demonstrate a willingness to venture beyond what may be familiar to them, transcending the subgroup to participate in something larger—the nation. It is not coincidental that trope 4 occurs so often at the conclusion of a performance, after the characteristics and categories of each group or performance style have been thoroughly established: the dramatic effect of transcending difference requires its prior enforcement.

CRITICISM

While many people enjoy Alakondre Dron's presentations and identify with its performance of *makandra libi* (living together or getting along, in Sranan Tongo), others, including Ganga, find that over the years these performances and their attendant social ideology have grown stale: "As a performer and member of the public, present at two consecutive Carifestas, I have found myself increasingly confused by the main part of the theatrical presentations, a disorientation that grew into weariness and dissatisfaction with each performance visited. . . . What exactly fuelled my displeasure? Simply put, it was the feeling that we were stuck artistically somewhere in the seventies, and that with each passing Festival, and each passing year, we were transgressing into a comatose state of repeating ourselves artistically over and over again" (2004). By claiming that these presentations of national culture are "stuck . . . in the seventies," Ganga calls attention to the fact that as times change, even nationalistic portrayals of ethnicity, invested in timeless and essential cultural qualities, must keep up. The presentational strategies that are used to stitch together traditional performance have to adapt so as not to collect the symbolic residue of the social and political moment in which they are crafted—in short, to avoid seeming dated. The cultural symbols and practices with which people can identify are useful in part because of their stability, yet without exhibiting some kind of dynamism or engagement with the contemporary moment, nationalistic performances can alienate those they claim to represent, appearing instead like little more than an animated tourist brochure. Ganga elaborates:

> Once upon a time exciting new things were happening with our theatre using exactly the same ingredients as described above. The form it took on was what [Judy S.] Stone called the ritual theatre, and it was viewed as perhaps the most exciting new voice coming out of the Caribbean theatre. . . . The interesting part of ritual theatre was that it abstracted meaning and form from different rituals and used them in a new construction, to tell our own stories, or to tell stories from everywhere in the world, through our own rituals. . . . But the great experiment of ritual seems to have fallen still, at least in Suriname, as we watch one performance after another being recycled into another, without even a[n] attempt at creating new repertoire. (Ibid.)

These thoughts came out of a conference paper that Ganga delivered in 2004, but Alakondre Dron's creative output has changed little since then. Meanwhile, the criticisms have persisted.

Baarn alluded to the ensemble's critics in 2009, but he framed the group's work not only in terms of aesthetic grounds but also in terms of message: "Many people love [the group]. Some people say they've heard Alakondre Dron already. But they don't take the message to heart. So long as people don't understand what we mean, we're going forward. 'I've heard this thing before' . . . But how are you living?!" (pers. comm., 2 December 2008). Here, Baarn equates finding fault in the group with not understanding or embracing a truly Surinamese, and truly alakondre, spirit. Framed in this way, Alakondre Dron has a clear civic objective: to spread a message of social cooperation as well as patriotic sentiment.

With Tjon's death in 2009, followed by Baarn's in 2017, Alakondre Dron is facing a pivotal change in leadership, and the ensemble's artistic direction appears unclear. Its members have an opportunity either to treat Tjon's and Baarn's output as a text that is central to the group's repertoire (and continue as Baarn indicated he would, performing this work until Surinamese people truly come to know and embrace its message), or to try to re-create for a new generation the kind of work that won them acclaim early on—work that helped to make visible counter-hegemonic cultural expressions of the present moment, in which the population could more fully recognize themselves and their present-day circumstances.[20]

Alakondre Dron's shift in leadership foreshadows a parallel political shift. There is a discernible absence of young leaders in the country's political arena, as Bouterse, Ronnie Brunswijk, Paul Somohardjo, and others maintain political authority as they have for decades. From the present vantage point, it is unclear what direction the country might take when these leaders eventually leave their posts. The ethnic clientelism inherent to apanjaht consociationalism might continue without much structural change, or the population's changing modes of identification—made evident in the 2012 census and the rise of political parties without overt ethnic affiliation—may foreshadow larger, structural changes in Suriname's political sphere in the years to come.

CHAPTER 6

The Avondvierdaagse

Civic Exercise in a Consumer Society

The AVD, or Avondvierdaagse, is one of the biggest sport events in
Suriname. Also for the participation of the people who are watching it.
It is a special Surinamese activity. They tell me that no place in the world
do they have something like this. The AVD is only in Suriname. That is very
important for our country, and that we can sell it as a tourist attraction.

—*Percy Oliviera (pers. comm, 5 October 2017)*

At the same time that Henk Tjon, the founder of Alakondre Dron, set to work
creating visions of the multicultural nation for the elite spaces of the stage
and concert hall, De Bedrijven Vereniging van Sport en Spel (the Association
for Sport and Leisure, hereafter BVSS) was busy developing a different kind of
national cultural expression, designed for the streets of Paramaribo. Whereas
Tjon pursued decidedly anticolonial content, the Avondvierdaagse (AVD)—also
known as Wandelmars—is derived from an event that is emphatically Dutch,
transplanted and adapted to suit a Surinamese context. Like Alakondre Dron's
performances, the AVD developed into a prominent expression of national culture
and sentiment, but it did so by overtaking public space, clustering together a
variety of seemingly disparate agendas, and appealing to Surinamese citizens
as consumers.

The AVD takes place over four consecutive evenings in early April. Each
evening, participants walk a different route through the streets of Paramaribo,

totaling as many as seventy kilometers over the duration of the event. People can register to take part as individuals; members of various social and political organizations or businesses; or members of performance collectives of numerous sorts, including cultural groups, brass bands, and even martial arts groups.[1] Participants who complete all four days of the event receive a medal, with additional prizes and trophies awarded to individuals and groups for outstanding performance in various categories.[2] Some people approach the AVD as a test of physical fitness, while others take part as a means of gaining public exposure, whether their motivation is political, commercial, cultural, or some combination thereof. The event is widely covered by the local TV and radio stations and newspapers, with specific places along each day's route designated as media "hot spots."

Attracting a large number of participants who represent a wide range of the country's population, the AVD provides a unique opportunity for city residents to consider the nation as an imagined community (Anderson 1983) larger than their immediate social networks. As the AVD closes streets, saturates the media, and interrupts the rhythms of daily life, it impacts and implicates a large portion of the city's population, no matter what their thoughts are about the event's social, aesthetic, or nationalistic merits. In contrast to Alakondre Dron's meticulously rehearsed and idealized depictions of the multicultural nation by designated cultural representatives, the AVD demarcates public space as a performative field and amplifies the representational potential of city residents, registered participants and bystanders alike.

The AVD exemplifies a truly popular nationalism in the sense that Shannon Dudley describes: "a nationalism that takes place in popular culture—a nationalism that is generated by interactions between diverse individuals and groups, and that is not easily controlled by a single constituency" (2008, 264). This event embraces multiplicity, saturating public space with what David Guss describes as a "superabundance of symbols and meanings" (2000, 13) that is characteristic of festivals and large-scale popular occasions. City residents are encouraged to model idealized behavior on a number of fronts: as individual citizens striving for self-improvement, ethnic representatives and cultural actors within a multiethnic national narrative, consumers supporting the local economy, and networked individuals with ties to organizations and neighborhoods within the city and beyond. I argue that the act of signifying from amid multiple and competing agendas is itself a way of embodying a Surinamese subjectivity, exercising a kind of political discourse that bears similarities to the country's ambivalent position vis-à-vis global networks and categories. Put more simply, it is fitting that a

Dutch-speaking South American country with a Hindustani informal majority that aligns culturally with the Caribbean would find national resonance in an event that is like an athletic event, a cultural showcase, a business fair, and a political rally but that cannot be fully understood as any one of these. Percy Oliviera, the director of the BVSS, referred to the event as being uniquely Surinamese. Here I'm suggesting that beyond the particular elements that converge to create this hybrid event, navigating that "superabundance of symbols and meanings" provides a unique opportunity to cultivate a Surinamese sensibility.

From among the various groups and messages a person can endorse, participants make careful selections that represent them as individuals, their talents, and their aesthetic preferences. They become aware that certain modes of identification and participation attract certain benefits, foremost among them greater media exposure and eligibility for various prizes. While all participants are subjected to being "read" in relation to ethnic identity, overt ethnic signification and demonstration of one's proficiency in an ethnically coded performance genre boost one's impact in the event—the images of such people are the ones that are circulated most widely, celebrated as the "most Surinamese," and gain the greatest attention and praise from onlookers. Here I consider the role of ethnic performativity in Wandelmars, first among people walking in support of political parties, and second within the cultural group Fiamba.

FROM COLONIAL EXERCISE TO "SPECIAL SURINAMESE ACTIVITY"

Suriname's AVD (four-evenings walk) is modeled after a Dutch tradition of Vierdaagse (four-days walks). The first such event was held in the Netherlands in 1909 and was intended primarily for the military as a way of promoting the troops' health and fitness.[3] Participants were charged with walking a total of 140 kilometers (approximately eighty-seven miles), or thirty-five kilometers (twenty-two miles) per day. As the Vierdaagse became more established, its participants became diversified—first to include civilian men, then women beginning in 1925, and later walkers from other countries. At present, participation in the Dutch Vierdaagse is capped at 47,000 participants. Each day's walking concludes in a different town within the Netherlands, but since 1925 the event starts and ends in Nijmegen, the oldest city in the country. Successful completion of all four days entitles participants to a *vierdaagsekruis*, a medal of distinction approved by the Dutch monarchy. The Vierdaagse, then, is thoroughly national in character, affirming and celebrating the Dutch armed forces, monarchy, and countryside.

The first Surinamese event styled after the Dutch Vierdaagse took place in 1964. Oliviera explained that in its early years the AVD was a part of the Koninkrijkspelen, a Dutch colonial project aimed at developing solidarity with and among its colonies through a youth-oriented, friendly athletic competition. The AVD was later dropped from the Koninkrijkspelen, but as Oliviera put it, "When they dropped it, the BVSS caught it" (pers. comm., 5 October 2017). While the AVD retained many of the characteristic features of the Vierdaagse—including its promotion of physical fitness, the four-day structure, and the award of a medal to successful participants—the BVSS also made several significant adaptations. Mercifully, in Wandelmars the walking commences in the late afternoon, thereby avoiding most of Suriname's intense afternoon heat. With fewer hours of the day devoted to walking, the distances covered are significantly shorter than those of the Vierdaagse. In 2017, the shortest day was estimated at eleven kilometers, and the estimated total distance walked by participants was fifty kilometers.

The two most influential alterations involved the increasingly prominent roles of advertising and cultural display. Paul B. Tjon Sie Fat suggested that the AVD has "gradually succumbed to commercial interests and the influence of cultural NGOs and become a sales promotion show and folklore manifestation with wide spectator appeal all rolled into one" (2009, 239). In fact, rather than functioning as external pressures to which the BVSS succumbed, businesses and cultural organizations were sought out and were precisely the mechanisms that enabled the AVD to distance itself from its colonial origins and emerge as its own distinct nationalist project—reflecting a political structure fueled by ethnic clientelism rather than appealing to loyalty to the crown.

In lieu of Dutch financial support, the BVSS reached out to local businesses to help cover event costs. These commercial partnerships exercised a tremendous impact, to the point that by the 2000s advertising not only facilitated the event but had become integral to its mission, structure, and entertainment value.[4] The AVD's most prominent sponsor has been the Fernandes Company, a local manufacturer of multiple goods including soda, ice cream, and bread. Fernandes has long shared official name sponsorship alongside the BVSS, and Fernandes ice cream vendors and advertisements are omnipresent along each day's walking route (see figure 6.1). Although the BVSS pursued international as well as national business partnerships (with McDonald's becoming a name partner in 2018), the prominence of local industries gives the impression that the event champions local businesses and national economic growth. In many ways, the promotion of economic health dovetails nicely with the AVD's long-standing goal of encouraging physical health and wellness. However, the abundant advertisements for Fernandes sodas and ice creams do lead to occasional cognitive dissonance with a given year's designated health-related theme, such as reducing one's sugar intake, fighting obesity, or choosing to eat healthy snacks.

The role of advertising extends well beyond business interests. With the involvement of such a wide cross section of the population, the AVD provides an unparalleled forum through which groups representing any number of organizations can take maximum advantage of that most valuable consumer resource—attention. It prompts participants to enact exactly the kinds of self-marketing strategies by which Zygmunt Bauman characterizes a society of consumers: "[Members of a consumer society] are simultaneously, *promoters of commodities* and the *commodities they promote*. They are, at the same time, the merchandise and their marketing agents, the goods and their traveling salespeople. . . . The test they need to pass in order to be admitted to the social prizes they covet

FIGURE 6.1 A Fernandes ice cream vendor approaches
bystanders during the 2014 AVD.
Photo by the author.

demands them to *recast themselves as commodities*: that is, as products capable of catching . . . attention and attracting *demand* and *customers*" (2007, 6). As a citywide and national spectacle, Wandelmars frames the consumer as both object and subject. Whether political, commercial, or cultural in nature, participating groups petition for the continued support of their existing networks while hoping to attract the attention of new audiences as well. A person can support a business or organization by walking as a member of that group, while in the same gesture becoming a source of entertainment to be consumed by spectators who support their preferred organizations and acquaintances from the sidelines.

Groups participating in the AVD use a number of strategies to convey the robustness of their organization. Beyond the obvious demonstrations of their members' physical fitness and resilience, groups can indicate strength through the number of people who march under their banner and the amount of physical and sonic space they can occupy once the event is under way. The financial health of an organization can be made evident through elaborate uniforms or by having different coordinating outfits for each day of the event. The more impressive a group's presence, the more memorable it will be, leading to increased visibility in the media and name recognition among bystanders.

Against the backdrop of pervasive advertising and the hypervisibility of corporate sponsors, some participating social and cultural groups have adopted practices that make them more closely resemble businesses, with an increased focus on their creative output, organization, and public image as "professionals." The cultural group Fiamba serves as a good example. As a well-documented and adjudicated event, the AVD gave Fiamba members a point of comparison by which they could measure their progress as a group: each year's performance was created with the goal of being a better show than that of the previous year. The group created new musical content, choreography, and uniforms with the expressed purpose of group promotion and satisfying audience expectations for new material in the AVD. In anticipation of their participation in the 2018 AVD, the group's leading members' planning meeting addressed finding businesses to sponsor them, creating an official group logo, and instituting audition and registration procedures aimed at streamlining their organizational efforts and selecting the strongest participants. Their attempts to enhance the group's official profile, operate more efficiently, and produce new material were all expressed in relation to the AVD.

By taking part in the AVD, groups and individuals also tacitly endorse the given year's theme. Each group marches with a banner announcing the name of the organization, its starting number in the event's lineup, and the designated theme for that year. In general, themes endorse a message pertaining to health or physical fitness, yet they can also promote civic responsibilities or social ethics of various sorts. Sometimes the lines between these categories blur. For example, the 2014 theme was "Een gezond levensstijl is matig zijn voor altijd [A healthy lifestyle is to be moderate in all things, always]," and the 2018 theme was, "Do mee met de AVD: fit zijn is oké! [Join in with the AVD: it's okay to be fit!]." Both practicing moderation and joining the AVD can improve health, but they also enforce social ethics and ideals of good citizenship.

All told, the AVD involves a tremendous amount of signification and promotional messaging. This cluster of agendas and motivations make the event as a whole difficult to describe or categorize: it is like a parade, a fitness event, a political rally, and an advertising fair, but it is not entirely any of these. Likewise, individual participants become complex signifiers, linked to products, groups, neighborhoods, the city, and the nation—all while promoting an array of ideas pertaining to social, economic, and physical health. Whereas the Alakondre Dron performances discussed in chapter 5 placed deliberate emphasis on specific nationalistic ideals, the cluster of available significations in Wandelmars allows for multiple and varied interpretations, both of what transpires and what it means.

Cultural Representation, Ethnic Performativity

Tjon Sie Fat categorizes the AVD as a "national and basically non-ethnic event," in contrast to events like talent competitions and beauty pageants that target particular subgroups (2009, 239). It is true that the health and wellness agenda, as well as the AVD's advertising objectives, do not make an explicit target of any particular ethnic group. Nonetheless, performances of ethnic and cultural affiliation are in evidence everywhere. Political parties and cultural groups use ethnic performativity in different ways, but each demonstrates the degree to which cultural and political representation are intertwined.

Political parties taking part in the AVD make habitual use of ethnic identifiers to represent their constituency. A political group can utilize traditional dress or performance to express affiliation with one ethnic group; alternatively, by having participants show a range of ethnic affiliations within a single group, a party can provide evidence that its support cuts across ethnic categories. In 2014 the AVD groups representing the Algemene Bevrijdings en Ontwikkelings Partij (the General Liberation and Development Party, hereafter ABOP) and the NDP in 2014 illustrate these two strategies. The ABOP has a long-standing affiliation with the Maroons, whereas the NDP represents itself as aligning with no particular ethnic group. All those who walked with the ABOP sported the party colors, yellow and black. Instead of or in addition to wearing T-shirts with the party name, participants were free to fashion an outfit for themselves using a designated pattern of black-and-yellow striped cloth. Through accessories, hairstyles, and creative manipulation of both the T-shirts and the striped cloth, many participants expressed their combined Maroon and political affiliation (see figures 6.2 and 6.3). Some of their stylistic choices did not refer to Maroon culture explicitly but nonetheless implied ethnic ties. The T-shirts shown in figure 6.2 provide a good example: these women's creative manipulations of their party T-shirts were not of themselves considered Maroon but rather used contemporary fashion trends that had gained particular traction within the Maroon community and that resonated with long-standing practices of textile manipulation (see, for example, S. Price and R. Price 1999, 81–113).

FIGURE 6.2 Women marching with ABOP demonstrate
their creativity in personalizing their T-shirts.
Photo by the author.

FIGURE 6.3 A young ABOP supporter sporting head and wristbands and a pangi.
Note that her shirt specifies her affiliation with the Maroon village of Santigron.
Photo by the author.

Despite the fact that the NDP declares no ethnic affiliation, many participants who walked the AVD as NDP supporters chose to perform aspects of their ethnic identity. Like people walking with the ABOP, all those walking with an NDP group wore their party colors (in this case, purple and white) and could exercise considerable expressive freedom in their self-styling. By wearing clothing associated with various ethnic groups (as with the Amerindian fashions NDP supporters donned in figure 6.4 and the Creole koto misis worn in figure 6.5), participants collectively conveyed the point that NDP supporters hail from a variety of ethnic backgrounds.[5]

Not all members of either the ABOP or the NDP chose to don apparel that would indicate affiliation with a particular ethnic group. Many walkers opted instead for the unaltered T-shirt and a plain pair of pants or shorts, or to accessorize their outfit in ways that did not signal a specific ethnic identity. As citizens of a country in which ethnic categorization is a constant preoccupation, these participants are not exempt from being "read" by others for clues as to their ethnic

FIGURE 6.4 NDP supporters representing their Amerindian heritage.
Photo by the author.

FIGURE 6.5 Participants in the junior category walking in Creole
*kotomisi*s (traditional Creole attire) in NDP purple and white.
Photo by the author.

affiliations: this is a consequence of what Tjon Sie Fat terms the inevitability of ethnic performing (2009, 30–31). However, the incorporation of cultural referents magnifies a person's presence in this street pageant, entering them in a different system of risks and rewards. Participants become hypervisible and thereby risk becoming a lightning rod for different kinds of social bias, but they also garner a far greater share of the public's attention and praise. For none is this more true than for members of cultural groups. Through music and dance they make known their ongoing, embodied practices of cultural engagement. Their performances signal difference and mark a departure from Eurocentric conceptions of modernity.

As a socially and politically marginalized group, Maroon participants are particularly susceptible to negative ethnic stereotyping, including allegations that they are primitive, uneducated, or out of pace with urban and cosmopolitan life in one way or another (Campbell 2012b, 59–60; van Stipriaan 2009, 148). This creates a paradox. Ethnic performativity in the sense that Tjon Sie Fat describes is a requisite of a political structure and the national, multiculturalist narrative that is emphatically city-based and city-focused, but to demonstrate a deep cultural familiarity with one's (non-European) heritage is to risk appearing at odds with a version of modernity and social progress that privileges urban, Christian, and predominantly Euro-American practices and ideals: it both fulfills and is used as a counterindication of metropolitan and cosmopolitan expectations.

Cultural groups proclaim no overt political agenda, but the choice to perform an ethnic affiliation further instills the logic of apanjaht consociationalism (discussed in chapter 5) and the ethnic categories through which it operates. To be considered for a prize in the "cultural" category, a group has to present itself as representative of a particular ethnicity—marching bands, for instance, are not eligible for prizes in that category, even though they certainly participate in a cultural practice. In this way, the AVD's prize categories (general, business, cultural, and junior) further entrench the notion that cultural performance is ethnic performance.

Fiamba and the Wandelmars Experience

In the remainder of the chapter, I focus on the cultural group Fiamba's ongoing participation in the AVD. I use my own participation, walking in the AVD with Fiamba in 2009, and conversations with other group members to do three things: give an experiential account of participating in the AVD with a cultural group; discuss the ways in which overcoming this challenging physical task links personal feelings of accomplishment to identifications with a group and the broader community; and illustrate how group members extrapolate meaning from their interactions with strangers during the event, using these interactions to inform their ideas about ethnic performativity and its various risks and rewards.

Ever since its members first took part in the AVD in 2007, Fiamba has made it the culminating event of its annual performance calendar. As mentioned in chapter 3, preparations for the event begin months in advance. These include recruiting new members, developing new material, and planning what to wear. With so many people watching from the roadside and following the event through the media, these four days present an unparalleled opportunity for cultural groups to show off their individual and collective skills and enjoy a moment in the spotlight. As Oliviera said, "The AVD is the only place where they can show what they can" (pers. comm., 5 October 2017). Clearly, given that the group doubles in size in preparation for the AVD, participation in a cultural group for its own sake is not the only (or even the primary) factor motivating people to join Fiamba: many new recruits join Fiamba primarily as a means of participating in a major citywide event, even if their preference is to do so while representing Maroon culture.[6]

Having rehearsed and occasionally performed with Fiamba for a number of months, I was an early target of their recruitment efforts—by the end of 2008, members of Fiamba had started asking me if I would walk in Wandelmars with them in 2009. Knowing little about the event other than that it was like a parade and that the previous year's participants were enthusiastic about returning, I agreed to take part, figuring that if group members were so excited about this event, I really ought to see what it was about. For me, the four days of Wandelmars were filled with emotional highs and lows, some having to do with my own astonishment at the magnitude of the event and bewilderment and dismay at finding myself (as a white foreigner performing with a cultural group) the focus of a tremendous amount of media attention. Beyond the particularities of my situation, however, there were numerous ways in which the physical challenge of performing in this endurance event created an emotional trajectory for the group as a whole.

As groups assembled in the afternoons on each day of the AVD, the energy and anticipation were palpable. Group members arrived at the sports field well rested, meticulously styled, and wearing a fresh set of clothes. Reporters, photographers, relatives, and friends milled about, interacting with and snapping photos of participants. Once the AVD was under way, the group's mood clearly shifted as we moved along the parade route. Morale flagged in the moments when nobody was there to watch or cheer, but it inevitably picked back up as we approached neighborhoods where group members anticipated seeing friends and relatives. Every media hot spot presented an opportunity for the group to put on a minishow that lasted only a couple of minutes. For these brief performances, group members dug deep, giving such a demonstration of energy or enthusiasm that it seemed everyone had forgotten whatever fatigue they may have felt even a short while earlier. As we neared the end of the event, exhaustion set in. At one point in the last few kilometers before the finish line on the fourth and final day, one of Fiamba's singers improvised a song in which he listed everything that was tired from the day's walk, from his head to his feet. Not long after, when Fiamba passed the finish line for the last time, performers relished their achievement, singing, dancing, and playing drums with renewed vitality alongside reveling participants from other groups.

The physical and emotional challenges of the AVD contribute substantially to its affective power. More than other participants, performers' stamina is put to the test, as they are expected not only to complete each day's parade route but to do so while singing, dancing, and playing instruments—sometimes in constricting or impractical attire. Successful completion of this self-imposed challenge creates a positive orientation toward the various social ideals the AVD promotes both implicitly and explicitly. The associations a person makes and the kinds of belonging they feel most acutely are bound to vary, but attitudes toward the group, the nation, and the general public all interlace with the positive feelings of self-proving, personal accomplishment, and support.

Dorinne Kondo describes experiencing a similar phenomenon at an ethics retreat in Japan, in which the positive feeling of overcoming a physical obstacle led to larger shifts in self-perception (both for her and others who attended the retreat) and people's relationship with their immediate communities. The culminating event of the retreat was a 7.5 kilometer "marathon," intended to instill in workers a number of ethical notions: "(1) you can do it if you try; (2) life is not a competition with others, but a battle with yourself; and (3) the road to success is through consistent, constant effort" (1990, 102). Like this culminating event, the AVD presents a daunting task, with the distance covered on a given day often exceeding ten kilometers. At the same time, it is low-intensity in that participants are walking rather than running and, owing to intermittent performances, groups generally proceed at a slow pace. The result is an event that is accessible (if challenging) to everyday people, not just those with significant athletic ability. The physical burden may be substantial for some, but typically it can be overcome through socially affirmed ideals similar to those Kondo describes, including personal resolve and consistent effort. Each successive day requires participants to renew their commitment to completing the event, resolving to come back and subject themselves to more walking.

These personal challenges take place in a profoundly social environment. Group participants bond with each other as they experience the full emotional span of the event as a team. A group member can rest assured that their presence or absence will be noticed, linking their personal commitment to complete the AVD with group accountability. Especially in moments when fatigue sets in, they rely on collective support and determination to keep going. To give a concrete example, Fiamba members marched while carrying various instruments and accessories—drums and shakers for the percussionists, and small paddles and baskets containing sugar cane and other items for the dancers. As the participants carrying the heavier loads grew fatigued, they would switch with other group members; every exchange entailed taking on more weight for another member of the group or giving a heavier burden to someone else. This fostered a constant awareness of an individual's level of fatigue in relation to that of others and encouraged people to do their best, not simply for their own sake but for that of the group as a whole.

Bystanders, too, have a role to play. Beyond cheering for performers and commending the efforts of walkers of all ages and levels of fitness, many onlookers make sure to wait and watch for friends and relatives who they know will be participating. As the media hot spots illustrate, a high density of bystanders is crucial to the event as a whole. Accordingly, onlookers get frustrated and disheartened when they show up along a parade route only to watch a group of dancers or musicians walk by in silence, conserving their energy for bigger crowds. Intermittent cheers of "show time" and complaints that onlookers did their part in showing up to see a group perform indicate that some people feel they are owed a performance by virtue of helping constitute an audience. In these ways and others, people have occasion to consider their roles in relation to the community—in particular, what kinds of interaction, accountability, and support one can anticipate from acquaintances and strangers.

PERSONAL NARRATIVES

Unlike Alakondre Dron performances, in which performers' actions and interactions are meticulously planned, the interactions along a parade route are informal and unpredictable. These unscripted encounters allow participants to formulate and test ideas about the nature of Surinamese society and their place within it. Fiamba members' observations after the 2009 AVD demonstrate how aspects of ethnic performativity are intensified through this event, as people are categorized not simply in relation to ethnic legibility, but also in terms of the manner and degree of their cultural engagement.

Mano Deel, one of Fiamba's drummers, confronted his fear of ridicule as he prepared to take part in his first AVD. At the conclusion of the last rehearsal before Wandelmars was to begin, Clifton Asongo, the group's leader, relayed instructions for the next day's activities. All members of the group were to arrive at the athletic field that was the starting and ending point for each day of the parade in their performance clothes, since there was no space to change and minimal storage space at the field where the group was to assemble. Deel balked at the idea of stepping out in public alone, wearing a *kamisa* loincloth. While women could wear a pangi in public without attracting much notice, men hardly ever wore kamisas in the city.[7] While kamisas are strong identifying markers of Maroon identity, many men feel self-conscious wearing a kamisa outside of a village setting, in part because it exposes their upper thighs. At first Deel protested, telling Asongo he would not do it—if he had to leave his house ready to perform, he would simply wear his *putukele* (cape) and a pair of jeans. Asongo, however, remained adamant—wear your kamisa or don't march. Taking this moment to address the group as a whole, he insisted that Fiamba members should not internalize the idea that to wear their traditional attire in public is shameful or indecent. He exhorted group members to be proud to wear Maroon clothing, just as they should be proud of what they have accomplished as performers and proud of their heritage in general. Once it was clear that he would not get his way, Deel acquiesced.

Arriving at the gathering point on the first day, Deel's trepidation seemed to have vanished. In place of the criticism that he had feared, Deel reported receiving praise and encouragement from others, many of whom were also Maroons and took heart at seeing a young man embracing this aspect of his heritage. Rather than feeling isolated, Deel found that wearing a kamisa helped affirm community.[8] In subsequent years, he has relayed this story to other young men in Fiamba, whose ambivalence about venturing out of the home in a kamisa might mirror his own initial concerns. Confronting this social risk became a meaningful lesson about public acceptance and cultural pride for him—one he then used to encourage a younger generation of participants.

Deel's interactions demonstrate an unexpected positive response where he feared ridicule. In contrast, Sandrine Akombe, one of the more heavyset members of Fiamba, had a negative experience of body shaming that she then cast in a positive light as a moment that tested her personal resolve. Months after the AVD had concluded, Akombe recalled with passion the jeers she had withstood and her response to them: "When I walked Wandelmars, the city folk said, 'With all that fat, you're dancing?!' But then I told them, 'Fat isn't anything, fat is nothing. You must know what you're doing.' When someone says, 'With all that fat, you're dancing?,' we don't know what is fat. When we see fat, what will we call it? How you are, you're not too small, you're not too big, you're not too fat, you're not too skinny, you're not anything. Something that you love, when you do it, learn it well, then you'll do it. With what God gave you, right?" (pers. comm., 27 July 2009; my translation from Okanisi).[9] The intensified visibility of the AVD exposed her to greater public scrutiny and social vulnerability, but through her successful completion of the event she was able to prove what she was capable of achieving and that she would not let negative commentary get the better of her.

Through her reflections, Akombe drew distinctions that situate her within a broader social context. She referred to those who criticized her as "city folk" (my translation of the Okanisi term "fotosama"), contrasting them with "we" who share her convictions that people can do anything they set their mind to and agree that dancing as an inclusive activity. As discussed in chapter 2, "fotosama" calls to mind long-standing terminological distinctions made between Creoles (Fotonengee, meaning City Negro in many Afro-Surinamese dialects) and Maroons (Businengee, or Bush Negro) that hinge on their relationship to the city. Even though she has lived in Paramaribo all her life, Sandrine identifies herself in contrast to a notion of city people, in the process reinscribing her experiences and group identifications as marginal within the city. In her case, the AVD was both the forum in which she encountered criticism and a proving ground where she was able to overcome it.

Both Akombe and Deel described experiences in which their performance in this citywide event affirmed their Maroon cultural affiliations, but in different ways. The support and encouragement that Deel received—in large part from fellow Maroons—emboldened him to demonstrate publicly his cultural affiliations without fear of mockery or reproach. Conversely, Akombe experienced the ridicule of "fotosama"—city folk, ostensibly not Maroon cultural practitioners— that affirmed her Maroon cultural affiliations by way of contrast. Their experiences created powerful social narratives in part because they required Deel and Akombe to go beyond the mundane and expected sociopolitical conventions of ethnic legibility to demonstrations of active engagement with cultural practices in unscripted interactions within a multiethnic environment.

Rather than affirming a specifically Maroon affiliation, Asongo's reflections concerned what he saw as an increasing willingness among Surinamers of diverse ethnic backgrounds to engage with one another's traditions. As he told me, "For the year 2009, the thing that was really unique for me, different from other years, was the fact that you as a not-Okans [non-Maroon], that you walked with us as part of the group. That was a really extraordinary thing for me. Up to now. For all of Sranan [Suriname] it was an exceptional thing. I feel that, so long as I'm playing music or something, I'll never forget that" (pers. comm., 17 September 2009).

My participation was not universally well received, and I certainly look back on my experiences during the AVD with ambivalence.[10] I was the only individual that year to perform in a cultural group who was so obviously outside of the ethnic category the group represented. Separated from the others by age, height, and white skin, my presence was a source of curiosity and widespread interest. Though my intention in taking part was to better understand an event that was the high point of Fiamba's social calendar, my involvement had the effect of drawing the public's eye toward me and away from the (often more virtuosic or nuanced) performances of Fiamba's regular members and from the ensemble as a whole. The media flocked to me as a curiosity, but without providing any opportunity to clarify my relationship to the group or my motivations for taking part. The public at large was left to speculate broadly about what my participation represented. This was a source of frustration for me and hard feelings on the part of some members of Kifoko and Saisa, who were displeased that I became so publicly affiliated with a competing cultural group, that media curiosity resulted in more publicity for Fiamba, and that there was no occasion for me to credit them as well for all they had taught me.

Asongo's experiences, motivations, and interpretations of the event differed from mine. He had been adamant that I take part for reasons that had to do with the possibilities for breaking out of rigid patterns of cultural performance. The AVD allowed him as a group leader to make a statement to "all of Sranan" and subsequently to speak of national reception with such confidence. Like Akombe,

Asongo developed a narrative that posited inclusivity as a social ideal, and in particular as a priority within Fiamba. Again referring to my participation, Asongo said: "Always I had something in me that felt, I really wanted to see something like that. Because . . . I think it's good for us to learn from each other. That is an important thing in life. And, just as I said already, Fiamba is open. And it doesn't matter who, so long as you feel that you want to learn, always Fiamba is ready to help, and to teach also" (pers. comm., 17 September 2009). Taking time to learn another group's tradition is something that he viewed as extremely positive, a step toward becoming a more inclusive and tolerant society.

My presence was not only that of a "not-Maroon" but also that of a white "not-Surinamer," which had an undeniable impact on the representational politics at work. Nonetheless, Asongo viewed my participation as a statement that people can enjoy and celebrate traditions other than those into which they were born. He spoke on multiple occasions about one woman he saw who danced alongside the group as it passed, trying to get us to dance more at a point in the route without a crowd or media presence large enough to guarantee a performance. His hope was that other non-Maroons would be encouraged to participate, going beyond the traditions that align with their ethnopolitical identifiers. He told me he saw my participation as something that emboldened others, like the woman bystander, to try for herself, to "do mee."[11]

The AVD garners a citywide audience in an unparalleled way. Widespread civic attention and participation creates abundant opportunities for formulating ideas about the self and/in the community and nation. Deel, Akombe, and Asongo all drew from unscripted interactions with people outside their immediate networks, arriving at very different conclusions that helped bring order to their social environment and chart how they intended to move through it. Deel felt more confident in displaying his cultural affiliations in public and multiethnic spaces, at least on holidays. Akombe's negative experiences caused her to identify strongly with a social subgroup (perhaps not exclusively Maroon, but certainly containing Maroon cultural group members) that she articulated in opposition to "fotosama". And taking a national perspective, Clifton focused instead on how cultural groups could promote and explore the potential for Surinamers to participate more actively in each other's traditions. The process of extrapolating personal and social meanings from the AVD constitutes one way that Fiamba members "managed" their cultural and social relations in the sense that Paul Schauert describes: "harnessing the resources at hand not only to accomplish objectives but also to construct satisfying lives" (2015, 8). Participants in the AVD are united by a common objective, completing the four-day walking course through Paramaribo's streets. Their motivations can vary and overlap, but in the process of completing the established task they also engage with the city in a different, personalized way. By submitting themselves to extended contact with the city and its residents and participating in the AVD in a way that is both promotional and performative on so many levels, participants construct a relationship with the city, creating signifying spaces and roles within its citizenry that help them manage their social interactions—the effects of which linger long after they have crossed the finish line.

CHAPTER 7

Subversive Choreographies

Strategic Impositions on an Archetypal Image

Not long ago, I was commissioned by a colleague to write a letter attesting to the cultural uniqueness of a group of performers from a "developing" country whose members were trying to obtain US visas for an upcoming tour. The lawyer who was processing the paperwork for this endeavor summed up what was expected of me: "We need evidence that what they do does not exist in the West because it is so weird." Granted, this lawyer was speaking off the cuff, and I doubt that she spent more than a couple of seconds considering her word choice. Even so, the statement reveals a pervasive sentiment, if one that is seldom articulated so baldly. Despite having no point of reference for the group in question, the lawyer was confident not only that this group would offer something unlike other kinds of performance, but that this difference would strike audiences as odd, uncanny, strange—in a word, weird. Furthermore, she emphasized that it was precisely this quality that the State Department officials would need to be able to recognize for my letter to be effective: "weirdness" generated cultural value. Through her use of the word "because" she implied that successful applicants are admitted for doing things that "we" not only don't do but wouldn't do. This rejection ("we" in the United States would not do this) then became the precondition for the group's perceived value and provisional admission into the country. In sum, while the official language of the visa application stressed uniqueness, the lawyer's unofficial language specified an attitude toward this uniqueness that emphasized both social difference and distance.

The lawyer's comment drives home an important point: while in the humanities, sheer novelty is considered a weak justification for researching a social or performative practice, outside of academia, performances of difference (that is, weirdness or uniqueness) continue to be imbued with a particular type of value, especially for artists in the global south.[1] More readily than exceptional talent or poetic sensibility, politically or economically marginal performers' "weirdness" mobilizes resources: it facilitates travel and garners interest, attention, and mobility.

The use of cultural uniqueness to assess value presumes that the rareness of a performance enriches the lives of those who witness it. Yet experiencing difference does not necessarily require people to rethink their position or beliefs, nor does it by itself guarantee personal growth. It is when people maneuver through new situations and remain comfortable and largely unmoved that the concept of weirdness enters discourse. Weirdness occurs when a person encounters difference and denies that encounter any relevance to their social or ideological landscape. Objectified, that experience becomes akin to a curio, whose features can be appreciated but whose identity is fundamentally intertwined with its lack of fit or immediate applicability. Despite the diversity of material or viewpoints that difference presupposes, valuing "weirdness" as a form of cultural uniqueness leads to a homogenization of experience, limiting both content (only the unusual is valued) and function (emphasizing alienness discourages contextualization or practical application).

This chapter features three choreographies from the cultural group Saisa's repertoire that create alternative sources of interest and cultural value through a politics of recognition. Recognition provides a counterbalance to the alienation inherent to weirdness because it admits a connection, memory, and context. Recognition *of* an action or object (as opposed to recognition *as*, which assigns the thing in question to an established category) is largely involuntary, eliciting a response that is closer in character to a reflex than to a deliberate act or premeditated decision: it is a personal and embodied manifestation of connection over which a person has minimal control. In this sense, choreographies that are designed to play on recognition are inherently provocative. When paired with themes of vulnerability, trust, and disclosure, recognition presents ideal conditions for the formation of affective communities (Gandhi 2006). Recognizing another individual's embodied experience makes it harder not to feel a personal involvement, the metaphysical proxemics of the performance drawing the audience and performers ever closer to each other.

For one in a position of sociopolitical privilege, celebrating "cultural unique-ness" as a way of attaining "knowledge of the world" can at times be used in constructing fallacies of the superiority of one's own station within it. Recognition of commonality from this cosmopolitan vantage point (identifying *with* perform-ers instead of *against* them) compels resistance to the "othering" processes that make "cultural uniqueness" socially edifying, yet this resistance is confined within the framework of its domination. It enacts the relational dynamics that Michel Foucault outlines in his claim, "Where there is power, there is resistance, and yet, or rather consequently, this resistance is never in a position of exteriority in relation to power" (1978, 95–96). The historian Jonathan Schneer sums up well the paradoxical relationship between cosmopolitanism (here with reference to a metropolitan center) and imperialist power: "Because London was an imperial metropolis it was cosmopolitan and because it was cosmopolitan it contained anti-imperialists and critics of empire. These men and women did not attain the influence of their imperial counterparts, but neither were they a negligible force. Moreover, just as the champions of empire helped to shape the imperial metropolis, so too did they" (2001, 162, cited in Gandhi 2006, 1). Likewise, in the present case, encountering recognition in the face of a desire for cultural uniqueness introduces a form of subversion, but it remains situated firmly in conditions of inequality and domination characteristic of folkloric projects.

CLAIMING DIFFERENCE

Pressures to emphasize cultural difference may be amplified in cases involving international travel or audiences, but they are by no means exclusive to these settings. In the Surinamese context, nationalist discourse has tended to delineate the country's ethnic categories with a particular fervor. As discussed in chapter 5, the ethnic clientelism that forms the base of Surinamese politics has a strong correlate in nationalist music and dance conglomerates like Alakondre Dron, in which each performer is taken as a representative of a single self-contained and easily discernible ethnic identity.

A clear delineation between cultures can be politically advantageous for Ma-roon performance collectives as well, albeit for different reasons. Maroon cultural groups may choose to celebrate distinctiveness in a spirit of cultural pride or solidarity—for example, the group Kifoko has at various times encouraged its members to sport only traditional hairstyles or talk exclusively in Maroon dia-lects during performances, even if these members may act or present themselves differently outside of a performance context. Beyond cultural pride, however, demonstrating the enduring nature of their traditions can help Maroons argue for social continuity and, by extension, the continuing viability of treaties dating back to 1760 that ensure their rights to land and self-governance.[2] The dissolution of the Maroons' semiautonomous status under the auspices of a united country with equal citizenship would help the Surinamese government ensure that Maroon land claims do not interfere with the mining and lumber concessions that have been granted without the input or approval of Maroon authorities.

This situation uncovers additional paradoxes—one at the national level and the other within a cultural group. Clear delineation of ethnic groups, including the Maroons, helps promote the national theme of unity in diversity, yet it also strengthens the justification for Maroons' autonomous action. For a cultural group, defining and emphasizing the distinctive performance practices of Maroons as a people can, in fact, have a homogenizing effect on performance, resulting in fewer opportunities to exhibit stylistic difference on a group or individual level.

To be clear, Maroon performance practice has a long history of incorporating a breadth of social and cultural references. In *Maroon Arts*, Sally Price and Richard Price cite numerous examples of Maroons borrowing widely in their artistic practices, concluding: "We have seen that Maroons enjoy artistic innovation, play, and creativity in every domain of life. . . . [They] display a recurrent inventiveness and irrepressible dynamism that provide a telling contrast to the popular image of 'traditional' artists in non-industrial societies" (1999, 308). While this may be the case, it is also true that trends toward conservatism in cultural representation and pressures for group members to demonstrate the depth of their knowledge restrict the type of references one is likely to see in performance. In a relationship that Michael Herzfeld (2004) analogizes as that between the pedestal and the tethering post, the adulation that accompanies traditional performance practice (the pedestal) also engages more stringent parameters, limiting the kind and degree of change that is deemed acceptable (the tethering post). The esteem accorded these performances is functionally linked to the restrictions placed upon it.

All this leaves cultural groups with a representational dilemma: how might they demonstrate their cultural distinctiveness and benefit from the exposure and resources that folkloric performance opportunities can offer, without having their social and political acuity undermined or their creative efforts interpreted as corrupting or distracting from tradition? Put differently, how can performers create works that generate interest and demonstrate cultural value, while steering clear of the tropes of weirdness and isolation too often taken by outsider audiences as an assurance of their relative superiority and modernity? One possible approach entails upsetting the relational dynamics between performers, iconic images of Maroon culture and cultural practitioners, and the audiences for whom cultural groups perform.

Here I investigate strategies performers can use to represent music and dance genres that have strong cultural associations without suppressing or omitting from performance those parts of their life experiences that do not directly affirm their authority as bearers of a singular tradition. Specifically, I introduce three choreographies from the cultural group Saisa's repertoire that in one way or another direct audiences' attention and expectations away from abstracted notions of Maroon culture and toward the personal narratives and narrations of Maroon individuals. I call these strategic impositions on an archetypal image because these references interrupt well-rehearsed cultural-historical narratives and stock images, creating opportunities to consider how abstracted notions of Maroon cultural practice might compare to the experiences of specific Maroons in a contemporary age, or to reflect on the performance conventions of cultural representation. Especially given the emphasis on remote settlements in Maroon history and the urban base of Saisa's membership, such impositions afford group members a chance to present their lived experiences as being constituent of Maroon culture, rather than peripheral to it.

The following routines draw from different kinds of social alliances and intimacies. All three engage in a politics of recognition, sometimes in ways that are inclusive (using references with which most audiences will be familiar) and other times in ways that accentuate differentiated levels of access (such as familiarity with Maroon languages or with certain environments or experiences, or a personal connection with Saisa and its members). Occasionally intimacy of a different sort is established by creating a behind-the-scenes effect, using meta-theatrical practices in which dancers perform as though they were in private or informal situations. The first strategy engages the audience's subjective experience, whereas the second depicts rather than establishes intimacy, recasting the audience as undifferentiated and invisible in the process. In each case, audience interest is decoupled from the articulation of cultural difference determined along purely ethnic lines.

These performances are therefore effective as a mode of critique, as described by Homi Bhabha:

The language of critique is effective not because it keeps forever separate the terms of the master and the slave, the mercantilist and the Marxist, but to the extent to which it overcomes the given grounds of opposition and opens up a space of translation: a place of hybridity, figuratively speaking, where the construction of a political object that is new, *neither the one nor the other*, properly alienates our political expectations, and changes, as it must, the very forms of our recognition of the moment of politics. . . . The challenge lies in conceiving of the time of political action and understanding as opening up a space that can accept and regulate the differential structure of the moment of intervention without rushing to produce a unity of the social antagonism or contradiction. (1994, 37)

By dissolving the categorical dichotomies of performer and audience or insider and outsider, new opportunities for communication and appreciation are made possible. Bhabha suggests that such dissolutions allow individuals to interpret the political moment with greater clarity. In the case of folkloric performance, it has the added benefit of reestablishing coevalness (Fabian 1983)—audiences become aware of the contemporary moment not in contrast to a staid and time-less veneer on cultural spectacle, but by noting how enduring social scenarios and current cultural references engage performers and audiences alike—with shared experience reflecting the present moment and crosscutting categorical divides. Recognition, then, becomes a crucial ingredient in creating this "third space." To be sure, it can divide as much as it unites, but the affiliations and differentiations it creates carve out affective alliances that are far more nuanced than an audience and performer binary.

Furthermore, the existence of multiple possible points of recognition enables the same choreographed routine to generate different but overlapping fields of interest and meaning as it is performed for contrasting crowds. In some cases, these differentiated points of recognition—understood by a subsection of the audience—create a narrative subtext or can otherwise inflect the way the overall narrative is understood. Relevant to this phenomenon is James Scott's conceptualization of public and hidden transcripts. Scott defines the hidden transcript as part of "a discourse that takes place 'offstage,' beyond direct observation by powerholders," whereas the term "public transcript" describes "the open, public interactions between dominators and oppressed" (1990, 4). Between these two frames exists a politics of disguise, which "takes place in public view but is designed to have a double meaning or to shield the identity of the actors." Scott explains: "Rumor, gossip, folktales, jokes, songs, rituals, codes, and euphemisms—a good part of the folk culture of subordinate groups—fit this description. [Through a politics of disguise] a partly sanitized, ambiguous, and coded version of the hidden transcript is always present in the public discourse of subordinate groups" (ibid., 19).

The choreographies I discuss here share with Scott's politics of disguise the delineation of new audiences, subsections of the entire audience whose members glean from performances meanings to which the rest of the audience or event participants have limited access. Yet these examples differ from Scott's model in a few key respects. First, the knowledge that is privileged in these choreographies does not always delineate between clearly established dominant and subordinate groups; rather, the choreographies make use of constellations of connection that perpetually redefine the categories of insider and outsider. Second, instead of operating by virtue of various degrees of concealment, all three choreographies can be more accurately described as selectively counteracting a politics of concealment that has become standard fare for folkloric performance. In this light, performances activate processes of disclosure more than they do concealment. Finally, while Scott notes that the processes in this third category can create anonymity, therefore diminishing the speaker's accountability for the message (1990, 19), in this instance the points at which dancers emphasize personalization and social specificity are at the root of their subversive potential. For groups involved in cultural representation, anonymity can be a controlling force, rather than a means through which critiques of domination can be aired more freely. The pressure to act as spokespeople for a broader collective can alienate performers from their own vantage points as cultural practitioners. In a performance environment in which distinctions between personal experience and a general narrative can be a liability, getting audiences to focus on a specific performance group or individual performer (rather than on Maroons more generally) is one way for groups like Saisa to avoid being trapped in a discourse of ethnic essentialism that discredits Maroons' urban and cosmopolitan experiences.

While many of the examples Scott uses to ground his theories involve direct subordination, power is decentralized in the context of these performance groups. Although there are several political and economic structures that enforce it, domination is most clearly presented in public discourse—in habitual ways of talking about culture, tradition, power, and social and political mobility. It is through everyday discourse (in which they, too, take part) that urban Maroons are most likely to have their cultural ties challenged. I agree with Scott in his assertion that "to the degree structures of domination can be demonstrated to operate in comparable ways, they will, other things being equal, elicit reactions and patterns of resistance that are also broadly comparable" (1990, xi). These three choreographies, then, can help us identify and better understand specific tools by which people combine public and hidden transcripts in socially poetic processes more generally. Ultimately, this is a politics of recognition and affirmation of shared elements, through which the interest in the performance no longer hinges on cultural exclusivity but on overlapping spheres of intimacy with which individual audience members and participants forge their own unique connections.

THREE CHOREOGRAPHIES

The majority of Saisa's choreographies had no explicit story line. More often, the drama of the performance took the form of improvised interactions between and among singers, dancers, and drummers, or an audience's interest would be sustained by the shifting geometrical configurations that dancers created as they circulated within a dance space. (These complex patterns are part of the group's trademark style.) However, in those choreographed routines that featured an implicit narrative, the dancers in Saisa created especially playful and sophisticated ways of asserting commonalities and differences between themselves and their audiences, no matter whether the audience was a group of tourists or friends and relatives at a funerary rite or a neighborhood birthday party.

All three of the choreographies in question are rooted in the awasa genre, yet in each example, the narratives are sustained through pantomimed body movements that refer to a range of mundane acts in daily life. Theatrical elements combine with virtuosic dance sequences in a characteristic awasa style, while the music remains more or less representative of the genre throughout. Danced portions of each routine are punctuated by signature moves that relate to the story line of the specific piece, thereby creating continuity within the piece as a whole.

The first two examples are solo segments from one of Saisa's standard pieces— a sequence of male solo dances. This piece starts off much like most others in Saisa's repertoire, with a short, introductory phrase by the lead drum, followed by an unaccompanied lead singer performing the opening verse of a song. After the chorus and the drummers establish the musical framework of the piece, the featured dancers enter the dance space with a characteristic shuffling step (waka kon). Once the soloists have formed a line, facing away from the drummers, the dancing stops, thus marking a change from Saisa's standard performance practice. The singers, too, stop swaying in time to the music. Surrounded by this unusual stillness, each dancer steps forward from the line to present his solo, with the attention of onlookers and fellow performers firmly upon him. Once he has completed his performance he resumes his place in the line of dancers, thereafter nudging the next performer in line as though that touch was bringing the next dancer to life. This pattern continues until all the dancers have completed their solos, at which point they turn and, with a shuffling step, return to the perimeter as a group.

Although the number of performers featured in this routine varied depending on who was able to attend a specific gig, the approach each dancer took in his solo remained consistent from one performance to the next. Some of these solos were largely improvisational, although the group members who chose to perform in an improvisational style did so in every performance, and they used the same manner of audience interaction or the same distinctive moves so often that these improvisations, too, had their own signature style. Interspersed with these nonprogrammatic segments were Eduard and Benny Fonkel's solos—each distinct in character and subject matter but using similar modes of reference and playful banter with the audience.

Eduard Fonkel's Solo

Wearing his putukele *(cape) and* kamisa, *Eduard stands in the center of the dance clearing. He pantomimes the act of unbuttoning a shirt and pants, hanging them on an imaginary peg. After brushing his teeth, he takes a shower, lathering himself with soap and toweling off once he's finished. Next he applies deodorant and puts on slacks and a button-up shirt. He finishes the sequence by spritzing himself with cologne (first his neck and wrists, then his private parts for comic affect).[3] Freshly showered and ready to go, he admires himself in a mirror. Satisfied with his reflection and feeling good, Eduard finishes his routine with an energetic solo awasa dance.*

The first few times I witnessed this solo, it did not register to me as an explicitly cultural or political statement. I found the most immediate surprise was when, with no prior indication as to the content of the solo, Eduard's pantomime transformed the dance space into a bathroom. I was startled by the intimacy of the scenario, the man in front of me—the leader of the group, no less—symbolically naked, performing an especially private aspect of a daily routine. In the care with which he prepared his toilette, his actions and facial expressions as he faced his viewers as though facing a mirror, the myriad of gendered social ideals conveyed through this theatrical canvas, Eduard's routine seemed to be a playful and intimate character study above all else. It was only after several more performances that I started taking note of the sophisticated mixture of associative frames at play between the man, the character, and the various references to place and culture.

While the narrative of Eduard's performance is quite clear (a man washes, changes clothes, prepares to go out, feels good about looking and smelling good, and dances to express his confidence and satisfaction), as a continuous sequence of events, it presents a few logistical wrinkles. After washing, preparing for the day, wearing his slacks and his button-up shirt, chances are he would not then *poolo* (show off) with his energetic dance moves. This strenuous dancing would get him sweaty and wrinkle his slacks, assuming that they could accommodate his deep knee bends in the first place. Clearly, his character is not dressing in preparation for dancing awasa but for some other purpose. There is little indication where, if anywhere, we are supposed to imagine this character might be when he begins to dance. He makes no gesture that indicates a change in location, leaving the bathroom scene to dissolve during the course of his dancing, or with his audiences imagining a freshly coiffed man dancing awasa in a bathroom, with cramped quarters and a wet floor.

As with the ambiguous relationship between performer and character, this solo resists a definitive reading of time and place. When Eduard dances awasa after the pantomimed portion of his routine, it is unclear whether the audience is to continue his established narrative, imagining that it is the character dancing, or rather dispense with the story line and return to the present setting, watching a man dressed in traditional attire performing an awasa dance in a conventional style. Do we continue to "see" the various pantomimed elements he introduced—the formal Western attire, bathroom sink, shower, and mirror?

These logistical puzzles complicate any notion of Maroon cultural purity and isolation. Before Eduard begins his dancing, there is no element of his skit that signals a Maroon lifestyle. His character takes a shower as opposed to washing himself in a river or with a bucket and calabash; and the clothes his character dons are not the traditional Maroon clothes Eduard wears to perform, but rather a button-up shirt and slacks. In his grooming regimen, he spends a significant amount of time unscrewing caps and wielding imagined products that can be easily identified by Maroon and non-Maroon audiences alike.

The choreography derives its interest not only from its combination of culturally specific and generally shared practices, but also from the manner in which they are combined. Eduard's dance would read differently, for instance, if he performed the act of dressing in a cape and loincloth while wearing slacks and a button-up shirt. Rather than relegating the Maroon aspects of this double persona to an unnamed place and time, it is the more outwardly cosmopolitan character who floats in spectators' imaginations, without any context beyond the bathroom door; it is Eduard, dressed in his traditional Maroon attire, who most fully occupies the here and now. The interplay of traditional and cosmopolitan signifiers is further nuanced in the juxtaposition of habitual actions (portrayed with the said cosmopolitan signifiers) and his emotional and expressive state, which is manifested most directly through his dancing.

Even with its various perplexities, the routine as a whole goes down easily. After the initial moment (often eliciting surprise and chuckles) in which the audience recognizes the setting and theme of Eduard's skit, the psychological continuity overshadows logistical incongruities. The question of whether the performer is imagined to be wearing the clothes he just pantomimed donning or the traditional attire on his actual physical person might even seem beside the point, for the audience acknowledges both of them, and the routine does not depend on the negation of one or the other to be successful.

It is easy to imagine Eduard's performance as a reenactment of his own morning routine, all the more so for those individuals who know of his life and work outside a performance context.[4] Eduard is one of few Maroons in Paramaribo to secure employment as a police officer, a highly coveted well-paying and stable job. Due to his occupation, his regular dress code is more formal than that of the general population, including button-up shirts and trousers and a general emphasis on appearing clean and well groomed. In performance, Eduard does not make specific reference to his work attire—he does not don a policeman's cap, for instance, or strap on his gun and holster. Yet even without such explicit cues, Eduard's solo highlights life practices that share a particular affinity with his profession. Thus, for people who know Eduard, the choreography is likely not to seem arbitrary but rather an affirmation and reinforcement of elements of his personality and social position. Their ability to recognize these resonances between character and performer form a kind of insider knowledge that changes not only the meaning of Eduard's performance but also their relation to it and other audience members.

Regardless of the degree to which the performance is interpreted as autobiographical, it is undergirded by evidence of familiarity with the various external points of reference, thus placing elements of the narrative squarely within the realm of the dancer's personal experience. Eduard's motions when he holds an imaginary bottle of cologne or tube of toothpaste are so convincing because they indicate the physical fluency and muscle memory that comes from repeated interaction with those objects.

This analysis does leave lingering questions about Eduard's compositional intentions. When I asked Eduard to comment on the degree to which this solo is autobiographical, the responses he gave to my inquiries varied.[5] In some instances, his answers supported the interpretation that this choreography was created in a way that emphasizes parts of a daily routine that coincide with specific features of Eduard's daily routine as a police officer, yet at other points he stressed that this solo did not contain references that were unique to him, but rather experiences that are quite common among Maroons and non-Maroons alike. Questions about place and spatial context prompted similar responses. He summarized the overall narrative of the solo as a man washing, changing clothes, and then going "na staati," which translates literally as "going to the street" but can be glossed as going out. To follow up I asked if, by saying "street," he imagined the solo to take place in a city or town rather than a village or camp. He replied by bringing the conversation back to activities rather than geographic locations, stating that what he depicted were cultural practices exercised by Maroons everywhere, and that these actions—shaving, brushing one's teeth, and wearing Western clothes—were entirely normal for Maroons in the interior as well as in cities and towns. In fact, he said, they are part of Maroon culture.[6] Our discussion lasted nearly twenty minutes, during which time Eduard consistently both affirmed and problematized interpretations of this choreography related to location and autobiography, refuting any statement that could place Maroon cultural signifiers in opposition to other practices or objects referred to.

While our conversation did little to clarify a fixed meaning of his choreography, it was a compelling demonstration of the discursive tensions between group representation and personal expression, and between the aesthetic forms that characterize a performance practice and the practices that characterize daily life. Returning to Bhabha, this conversation with Eduard reiterates the same mode of critique that is fundamental to his solo—it "overcomes the given grounds of opposition and opens up a space of translation: a place of hybridity, figuratively speaking, where the construction of a political object that is new, *neither the one nor the other*, properly alienates our political expectations, and changes, as it must, the very forms of our recognition of the moment of politics." This space of translation might confound efforts to establish facts, but it can also clarify experiential truths and realities. In essence, Eduard's solo and our subsequent discussion provide a prime example of the kind of signification from an ambivalent position discussed in chapter 2. Both demonstrate presentational or argumentative skills that can help a social actor overcome categories when no single category sufficiently honors the experience or position it would describe.

Benny Fonkel's Solo

The sequence of male solos that Eduard initiates goes on for several more minutes, with successive dancers occupying the center of the performance space. One of the final soloists in the routine is Benny Fonkel, who likewise choreographed his own narrative. In Benny's performance, the recognition of locally specific cues adds a touch of humor and irony to his piece that is accessible only to a select few. Whereas Eduard's solo emphasizes social commonalities by highlighting the translocal nature of cosmopolitanism, the wit and humor of Benny's solo derives largely from cultural and geographic specificities:

Benny limps forward from the line of soloists into the center of the performance space. He then bends down and examines the bottom of his foot, picking at something that is buried in the skin. Standing upright once again, he holds his hands in fists above his head with his thumbs touching, and then rotates his hands toward each other, as though bending or breaking something with his thumbs. After repeating the same move a few more times, Benny begins dancing, maintaining a slight limp. His dancing gains in intensity and his limping movements lessen until, in the culminating move, Benny holds the foot on which he had been limping in his opposite hand while jumping through the circular shape thereby created with his standing leg. Having completed the signature move of his short routine, Benny returns to his place in the line of male soloists, resuming his character's limping gait as he does so.

Even without knowing the specific references Benny makes, his solo is enjoyable for the clever way that the tender foot evolves from being an (imagined) impediment into a feature of its most impressive stunt. Benny, one of the group's older members, did not perform with the explosive energy that some of the younger soloists could generate. This short narrative plays to his strengths, creating interest in a way that complements his more subdued style.

Benny told me he developed this routine at home, incorporating it into the compilation of solos once it was essentially finished. The "something" he pretends is lodged in his foot in his solo is not a splinter but a sand tick (*sika*, also known locally as *chika*), a foot parasite commonly found along Suriname's coastal areas and riverways. He told me he used to pretend to pick lice out of his hair and then squash them, but now that he's shaving his head, this part of the routine no longer makes sense. He said he borrowed the idea for his signature move from a loketo performance he saw on a DVD. Throughout our conversation, Benny emphasized that awasa is a free dance that accommodates a performer's creativity. To emphasize his point, he recalled how he had incorporated some Michael Jackson moves from *Thriller* into other routines, exclaiming, "Try it and just see how the people will cheer!" (pers. comm., 12 November 2009).[7]

Especially considering this solo in light of the one it replaced, Benny's explanation highlights his particular brand of humor and the comedic character he aimed to contribute to this collection of solos, complete with a certain "gross-out" factor. It also makes clear the many ways in which Benny combines influences from a range of non-Maroon and non-Surinamese sources with elements that are expressly local and particular to the Maroons.

Before Benny explained the story line to me, I did not catch the reference, even though I had had an experience with the parasite in question some months before. This was not only a performance of an understanding of what sikas do and how it feels to be an unfortunate host to them, but a performance of a response to these circumstances as well. I might have missed the reference because I wasn't expecting to find it in the dance solo, because the way his character managed this inconvenience differed from my own (I went to a doctor's office to have them removed),[8] or because one experience was simply not enough to make the accompanying behaviors immediately recognizable to me.

In addition to its use of local referents, Benny's solo draws from loketo, a Congolese-inspired popular music and dance genre that came to Suriname through a series of transnational circuits (Bilby 1999, 286). Audiences might therefore recognize in this performance their shared connections to an internationally circulating popular art form, in place of or in combination with local references to sikas. The result is a choreography that has more nuanced meanings beyond the immediately accessible, connecting both to local and transnational aspects of lived experience.

Like Eduard's solo, Benny's performance calls attention to aspects of life that are likely to be excluded from portrayals of Maroon daily life or culture. To be sure, Benny acted out a scenario that highlights a decidedly unglamorous dimension of daily life in many Maroon villages. Sikas tend to be found in the sandy soil of paths and waterside areas on the coast and extend further inland to many northern Maroon camps and villages. They burrow into the skin, most often in a person's foot and in particular between the toes. Without knowing specifically what is lodged in Benny's character's foot, a lay audience can still follow the general trajectory of this solo with little difficulty. Yet the deeper significance unites a local community by referring to situations and practices that are culturally intimate.

Herzfeld describes cultural intimacy as "the recognition of those aspects of a cultural identity that are considered a source of external embarrassment but that nevertheless provide insiders with their assurance of common sociality" (2005, 3). We might consider Benny's crude method of extraction and extermination of a common parasite a performance of cultural intimacy, uniting as it does those onlookers who have not only experienced the parasite but can identify with Benny's character's strategy of removal. To clarify, becoming a host to sikas is considered an unsavory aspect of living or working in certain areas, but in everyday social situations it seldom elicits shame or embarrassment. People will tend to sikas in the open air or even ask friends or family members to aid in their extraction. The embarrassment that I see (or the potential for embarrassment) derives from the formality of the performance occasion and perhaps in some ways from the capacity to represent a culture that cultural groups like Saisa often serve.

In contrast, Eduard's performance certainly does evoke an intimate situation, with the audience acting as interlopers on a man's solitary grooming routine. The actions his character takes are, I find, endearingly self-conscious—the way he leans forward holding his chin, as if to inspect the closeness of his shave or, perhaps most obviously, the way he pauses after spritzing his neck and wrists with cologne, and then gives a quick spritz to his private parts. Through attention to these details, we gain a sense of who this character is. But while this performance is certainly intimate, it cannot be considered culturally intimate in a Herzfeldian sense. The part of his performance that registers as the most vulnerable and private is precisely the part that blurs the social or cultural points of reference.

The culturally intimate scenario that Benny refers to in his performance draws together in a rather humorous way those individuals who recognize its local references. But for cultural insiders, this humor is potentially magnified when performed for audiences of tourists and cultural outsiders. When faced with the pressure to depict exotic and romanticized notions of Maroon culture and an insatiable curiosity about the "weird" features of Maroons' daily lives, Benny depicts a decidedly unromantic, uncomfortable side of daily life, without these cultural outsiders fully recognizing the allusion. By missing these local references, uninformed audiences inadvertently perform the limits of their understanding, thus strengthening the bonds between those who are "in the know."

Instead of putting differences on display for the entertainment or education of others as a type of "weirdness," this routine empowers audiences who share with the performer certain experiences and points of reference. Recognition grants these individuals the ability to delineate themselves from others who miss the reference, discern the significance of that distinction, and respond to the performance and the audience as a differentiating subsection of a differentiated crowd.

In both Benny's and Eduard's solos, the performer's body functions as a semantic pivot point, on the one hand playing upon sensate experiences to which audiences can relate as physical beings, and on the other hand conveying mannerisms and reactions that are learned within a particular social fabric and through experiences that are linked to specific locations or circumstances. It is through these coexisting facets of bodily experience that both Eduard's and Benny's solos are rendered generally comprehensible to most audiences, yet also saturated with personal and culturally specific nuances. These demonstrations of multiple culturally informed physical fluencies are especially effective in subverting stereotypes because they are embodied demonstrations of competence born of practice.

Debora Fonkel, Cheke Pinas, and Nicholas Banjo's Trio

My third example comes from a separate choreographed routine from Saisa's repertoire. In the winter of 2008, Saisa began developing a new move that involved a deep knee bend and gradual rise while bringing the hands to one's head, coordinated with a specific pattern played by the lead drum. This move was difficult for dancers to learn, due to several small departures from their standard practice that, when combined, proved challenging to coordinate. Group members were in the process of learning this move when I left Paramaribo for a month-long trip. Shortly after my return to the city, I attended an event at which they performed a new piece based on this move. This dance featured two of the group's youngest and most virtuosic male dancers (Nicholas Banjo and Cheke Pinas) and Debora Fonkel, a talented young singer and dancer who had been instrumental in developing the step:[9]

Arriving in the center of the performance space, the drummer cues Nicholas and Cheke to begin their soloistic dancing, but both dancers appear confused by the move and look at each other, baffled. Debora approaches from the sidelines. Pushing the two men out of her way, she demonstrates how the movement is supposed to go. After watching her dance solo for several moments, Nicholas and Cheke join in, enthusiastically performing and embellishing the movement, following her example.

This choreography serves as a convenient and clever way of masking the difficult transition into the solo dance move that had given dancers so much trouble in rehearsal. The risk of coming in wrong is mitigated by the story line of the routine. For Cheke and Nicholas, both of whom had struggled with the move initially, mistakes no longer matter, so long as they catch on eventually. Their confusion is recast as intentional, yet it is open to speculation whether, even in these later performances, they would be able to master the movement's timing and coordination on the first try. Only Debora has to get the timing right for the choreography to be effective, and she is the dancer who developed the move and introduced it to the group—showing mastery over the requisite timing and coordination from the outset.

Beyond the pragmatic benefits of the choreography, the trio's most striking feature is the way it replays the circumstances under which the group first learned this particular movement. It acts as a kind of collective autobiography, in that all three dancers are essentially playing themselves, dramatizing for an audience the events that had taken place in these early rehearsals. Lived experiences—ones that might otherwise discredit individuals—become the featured points of interest, thus complicating an impression of innate ability while also prioritizing group members' experiences above abstracted, archetypal portrayals of Maroons and Maroon culture.

The ability to recognize the choreography as self-referential, however, is predicated on a person's access to the rehearsals from which the routine drew inspiration. As described in chapter 3, Saisa rehearsals were semiprivate events, taking place in back of the house of Dansi Waterberg, the group leader, and the music and commotion from rehearsals were audible within a considerably large radius.

Neighborhood youngsters and friends of performers often came to watch and socialize as a rehearsal took place. Group members and the various onlookers who were present when the move and subsequent choreography were introduced would have no trouble recognizing the event portrayed in performance as being related to actual events in a rehearsal. In contrast, audiences without access to this backstory have no way of determining whether the scenario is autobiographical or wholly fabricated.

Yet even without knowledge of the routine's historical valence, the very fact that learning a dance step is the focal point of the choreography lends this routine a behind-the-scenes quality. As Saisa recreates the events that took place behind Waterberg's house, an audience at a formal performance comes to resemble the initial, informal audience of onlookers at these rehearsals. Dancers act as though they are allowing the audience a glimpse of them with their guard down, and, arguably, in the process the dynamic between spectators and performers takes on a veneer of familiarity and trust. The crucial difference is that whatever vulnerability and frustration Saisa dancers felt as they attempted to learn this new move in rehearsal are replaced by a controlled situation in which the work of learning had already taken place, and whatever social risks may have accompanied mistakes in the initial rehearsals have been mitigated by the performance frame of the finished routine.

Just as the dancers are both playing themselves and characters in a narrative, the audience at a performance comes to stand in for the audience at Saisa rehearsals. They are positioned as though they have a kind of insider status, regardless of whatever social or cultural distance separates them from performers. It is easy to imagine why this affectation of intimacy might appeal to tourists in particular. The manicured performances and scripted interactions that prevail in cultural tourism can lead to ambivalent feelings and uncomfortable reminders of the transactional nature of their experiences. The social intimacy of this routine, however predetermined and controlled, may act as a palliative to these ambivalences, even giving the impression of a more realistic and genuine cultural experience.

When the routine was performed for Maroon audiences, a different kind of imaginative practice was possible. In such instances, nonmembers of the group often emerged from the sidelines to join in the dancing. This particular routine tended to generate more lively participation than many of Saisa's other choreographies. Some of the reasons for this are purely pragmatic—a number of Saisa's routines discourage participation because they feature constantly shifting geometric formations that only work with a certain number of performers who understand the routine's formal logic. This choreography, in contrast, does not require the precise placement or circulation of dancers within the performance space. Beyond its structural features, however, the routine's subject matter served to amplify its participatory potential.

Within the routine resides the potential for the situation it depicts to be actualized by those in attendance. The choreography begins with two performers expressing their confusion about a particular move. Debora's role is a pedagogical one, directed at Cheke and Nicholas, but it serves a similar function for onlookers: She demonstrates the move in a clear and exaggerated fashion, repeating it until the other dancers catch on. Audience members can join in, adding their own mistakes, confusions, and successes to the given narrative. The story line and Saisa's presentational role both seem to evaporate as portrayals of learning intermingle with the audience's or participants' experiences of learning. The signature move that is featured in this choreography is disseminated in the process—it becomes available for audiences to remember and re-create in future contexts, all while retaining its associative link to Saisa. With audience participation, the choreography has the capacity to project and anticipate future performances, even while maintaining its historical and autobiographical aspect.

In sum, different reactions to this choreography engage different kinds of intimacy between Saisa and its audience. By embracing its behind-the-scenes character, the audience gets drawn into the established metanarrative; by learning the featured move and dancing alongside the trio of Saisa dancers, audiences can transform a depiction of a learning situation into an immediate context in which they are among the main actors. Both responses have the potential to reconfigure the relational dynamics between and among performers and audiences, albeit in very different ways.

Geographic and social nearness are pivotal elements in creating these relational possibilities. In a subtle way, this choreography changes the projected location of culture (Bhabha 1994). It depicts a scenario that did not take place in a village context, performed by people who might more neatly fit the idyllic images of the Maroon cultural practitioner. In contrast, the "source" of this text was what occurred in a fenced-in backyard in Ramgoe, a neighborhood on the outskirts of Paramaribo. Its narrative draws attention to performers' fallibility, refuting any notion that the cultural practitioner is always already deft at any musical or choreographic gesture rendered in "their" aesthetic language. Instead, this trio highlights the fact that the learning process continues well into adulthood, even for accomplished dancers. It serves as a reminder that innovation is no less important for cultural groups than is preservation: introducing new material—and the sometimes arduous process of learning it—is a crucial part of this living tradition.

SUMMARY

To state outright that these performances are about power relations is a viewpoint that I think many Saisa members would reject. Yet open play with stereotypes and audience expectations is a crucial ingredient in the satisfaction these choreographies generate, and those expectations are indeed born of a series of unequal power relations. Accordingly, while I do not consider any of these choreographies as existing in opposition to a specific organization or person, I do consider the dancers to be engaged in a play of oppositions that nonetheless has political resonance.

Scott describes the public transcript as, "to put it crudely, the *self*-portrait of dominant elites as they would have themselves seen. . . . It is designed to be impressive, to affirm and naturalize the power of dominant elites, and to conceal or euphemize the dirty linen of their rule" (1990, 18). Some characteristics of the expected public transcript of a cultural group were laid out in the anecdote at the start of this chapter. To value a group's cultural uniqueness, or to delight in weirdness, is to invest in the distance between performer and audience. The greater degree of formality in a performance event, the easier it becomes for an audience to appreciate the performance as an isolated occurrence, dissociated from acts and people encountered in day-to-day life. Yet while a performance might be experienced as singular, at least to some extent, performers are framed as generic: a group that is billed in a representative capacity encourages audiences to look for the forest rather than the trees.

This chapter has detailed a number of interpretive moves (Feld 1984, 8) that are both agentive and disruptive to dominant performance tropes. I have argued that through portraying themselves and their own life stories, Saisa members are able to delineate a cultural frame that they can inhabit more completely. While the featured choreographies are infused with broadly recognizable markers of Maroon performance aesthetics, they avoid essentialism by their practices of disclosure, drawing from experiences that are both personal and undeniably the members' own. In so doing, they provide alternatives to more distanced and reified archetypes of Maroon social and cultural practice. Their strategic references to a wide array of actions and objects disrupt folkloricizing impulses that functionally alienate performers from their audiences. Through the choreographies' intimate and recognizable subject matter, audiences are drawn into close social proxemics with performers, making it difficult to proclaim mutual (in)difference and distance.

While all three choreographies use a politics of recognition, what in particular an audience member will recognize can vary considerably, thus affirming an individualized set of social and cultural connections. Beyond basic story lines that are accessible to all, each piece contains deeper narratives to which access is limited. Restricted access is not granted exclusively to those with the deepest knowledge of Maroon culture. Instead, additional layers of significance are available to onlookers who know the individuals involved, live in certain locations, or have witnessed the group's rehearsal processes, and even to those who share the same cosmopolitan sensibilities and interests. All these connections have the potential to form critical affective alliances that cut through discursive binaries (Gandhi 2006). Such alliances do as much to disprove the myth of a uniform, undifferentiated audience as they do to disprove the myth of performers who represent absolute cultural uniqueness, untainted by outside influence.

Cultural stereotypes and iconic imagery are subjected to multiple subtle subversions, but within a standard Saisa performance they remain largely intact. Presented amid a dense musical texture over the span of only a few minutes, each of these three pieces contains far more information than a casual spectator is likely to notice. In the moment of performance, an audience is unlikely to consider in any depth the source of their humor or the ways in which performers undermine distant and reified depictions of Maroon culture. Furthermore, these routines are clear anomalies in Saisa's repertoire, far outnumbered by nonnarrative pieces that stick to more conventional imagery. However, their modest scale should not be taken as a constraint to their success; on the contrary, it is crucially related to their social function. After all, archetypal images retain symbolic and commercial value, and strategic essentialisms (Spivak 1990, 11) remain instrumental in navigating Suriname's ethnically coded social and political networks. There is little to be gained in overthrowing or denying cultural images that continue to have symbolic and rhetorical value. It is far better to present these in combination with images that are individualized and immediate, privileging multiple potential points of access and interaction.

As Saisa members recalibrate the location of culture, away from caricature and toward a dynamic practice that acknowledges other points of reference and contexts (from backyard to bathroom), they simultaneously redesignate what might be considered "weird." The intimacies that gratify as social affirmations and points of interest also draw attention to the strangeness of being observed, in particular to having one's actions interpreted in relation to cultural value. Within a performance scenario that has an audience primed for a public transcript (complete with a certain level of detachment), it becomes "weird" to see Eduard's mundane actions of showering and getting dressed, see a dancer tend to an issue that might not make for polite conversation, and witness performers working out a step on a stage (where it's expected that all the working out has already happened). The level of closeness appears at odds with the mode of presentation. Because audiences both recognize these general activities and recognize them as being private or intimate in nature, these routines invite a degree of reflexivity. In all of these ways, Saisa demonstrates that cultural groups are capable of much more than a simple repackaging of traditional genres using formal and cosmopolitan aesthetic conventions. These choreographies are critical and sophisticated, and they exhibit the potential to change people's perceptions about Maroon culture and touristic practices of cultural consumption.

RETURNING TO THE ADMINISTRATION
OF CULTURAL UNIQUENESS

Ultimately, and owing in part to the help of the lawyer who so frustrated me, the group that my colleague wished to invite to the United States was granted the appropriate authorization, reportedly putting on a successful performance some months later. In the end I imagine I was a passable but not an ideal recommender—my letter attesting to the group's cultural uniqueness went through multiple revisions before gaining the lawyer's approval. To our mounting frustration, my attempts to articulate the projected value of the group's performance clashed repeatedly with her demand for weirdness. I added my signature to the final copy with a fair amount of disillusionment. I wished that the contents of the letter more accurately reflected what was, after all, supposed to be my expert opinion, but I was determined that my principles should not jeopardize a musical and cultural exchange that I believed would be an enriching experience for those involved.

I can't help but wonder what I would say, if I were called upon to write a similar letter attesting to Saisa's cultural uniqueness. Despite the significant amount of time that I have spent with the group, my fondness for its members, and my deep respect for their craft (or perhaps because of these things), the idea of the task makes me profoundly wary. Would I recognize the group in my letter by the time all was said and done?

Conceptually engaged and brimming with creativity, the three choreographies at the center of this chapter are among my favorites in Saisa's repertoire, but I doubt they would do much to help the group gain entry into the United States. The recognition on which they draw is peripheral to the State Department's objective. And even if they were not peripheral, it would take too long to explain how they relate to cultural uniqueness. The reviewers of these applications are not looking for puzzles, ambiguity, or features that require explanation to be understood properly. Nobody—performers included—is interested in slowing down the application process. For simplicity's sake it seems advisable to note Eduard's cape and loincloth but not his pantomimed slacks and shirt; Benny's flashy move without the story line or the links to loketo and Michael Jackson; and the enthusiasm with which Debora, Cheke, and Nicholas dance but not the struggle that contextualizes it. What truly constitutes the group's uniqueness becomes at best inconsequential, and at worst an impediment to a successful review. In dozens of ways, the resurrection of cultural archetypes becomes the price of the visa.

Saisa did in fact perform in the United States in 2007, a year before I became involved with the group. By all accounts, the high point of the visit was performing for an event in New York City sponsored by the United Nations that marked the two hundredth anniversary of the abolition of the transatlantic slave trade. I have watched some footage from the occasion and seen that Saisa puts on a typically energetic and engaging performance and the audience gives them an enthusiastic reception. But I wonder if the spectators are cheering and clapping out of appreciation for Saisa's cultural uniqueness. I have to admit to hoping that any audience, but this gathering of politically empowered individuals in particular, would go beyond titillation at encountering difference and notice the aspects of the performance that eschew cultural estrangement—using recognition as a road map that points to more meaningful dialogue and the possibility of shared narratives.

CHAPTER 8

Closing the Night

Invitations to Participation

It's a familiar folkloric convention, one that appears dependably as a cultural group nears the end of its performance: one at a time or in small groups, dancers leave the performance area and walk among the audience members. Approaching someone from the audience with a smile and an outstretched hand, the dancers motion for the chosen person to join them on stage for a dance (see figure 8.1). Like many other elements of a cultural group's program, this gesture is premeditated (even formulaic), but it finds unique resonance in dialogue with the place, purpose, and interactive dynamic of a given performance. Fundamentally, it broadens the possibilities for inclusion and dialogue, transcending the structural division between audiences and performers and whatever social differences that structure might accentuate. As with so many other aspects of groups' operation, however, this common gesture does (and requires) different kinds of work, depending on its application and context. The following three instances demonstrate just how wide a single choreographic strategy's application can be.

APRIL 2009—LAETITIA TOJO'S BIGI YALI

André Mosis, Kifoko's founder; his wife, Laetitia Tojo; and their children have come back from Holland to Suriname to celebrate Tojo's bigi yali ("big birthday"—in this case, her fiftieth birthday). They have rented Broki, a restaurant along the waterfront in downtown Paramaribo, and are treating their large list of

FIGURE 8.1 Nicholas Banjo (a former Saisa member, now a Tangiba member) approaches a reluctant audience member, requesting his participation. Photo by the author.

esteemed guests to an evening of food and entertainment. Tojo's children deliver short speeches and performances, Mosis narrates a PowerPoint slideshow that depicts the couple's history together, and a steady line of DJs and musicians keep the party going until well into the night. Intermittently, Tojo and her twin daughters disappear and reemerge wearing different outfits, marking the progression of the night with wardrobe changes from formal dresses to Maroon-inspired fashion and evening wear. And of course there is a performance by Kifoko, the group that got its start in her backyard and that her whole family helped build during the tumultuous years after Suriname's independence and civil war.

Kifoko has been preparing for this performance with special care, its members anxious to demonstrate to the group's founders that it has remained strong in their absence. For many Kifoko members, this performance is personal. Among the performers are several who have been in the group since its earliest years and a number of people who are part of Tojo's family. They have extended their regular lineup to include theatrical interludes—a series of short monologues, rendered in Dutch and specially prepared for the event, that focus on the beauty and grace of the African woman; the presentation of a pangi as a gift to Tojo from the group; and a brief skit that features Maria Dewinie, the group's leader, and Tiomara, the youngest dancer in the group.

After a Kifoko member delivers a particularly sentimental line or dances especially well, the guest of honor springs up from her chair and hurries over to the performer as quickly as her narrow dress and high heels will allow. Exclaiming "*a doo*" or "baaya ee," Tojo and the performer *baasa* (embrace) warmly—a common demonstration of affection and an acknowledgment of a job well done. Tojo is so pleased by Tiomara's dancing that she runs across the dancing space, chasing after the young girl so she can give her a hug. The performance concludes with a very brief rendition of a circular dance called "Uman Daguwe," for which they usher Tojo back on stage one last time to sing and dance in their midst. Kifoko members take their bows to warm applause, and Tojo and Mosis give the group a standing ovation.

Through commissioning Kifoko's performance, Tojo and Mosis were able to demonstrate a style of patronage while showcasing an ensemble that is part of their legacy of perpetuating Maroon traditions in a spirit of cultural preservation and pride. The elements that Kifoko had prepared especially for this event—the monologues (in Dutch) and theatrical interludes—highlighted many of the features that set Kifoko apart from other groups in the city, alluding to their training and involvement with Alakondre Dron and various other cultural institutions through which they expanded their stagecraft. During their performance, Kifoko's members focused their attention squarely on Tojo—no other individuals were sought out from the audience, although those present included many notable personalities and former Kifoko members. Tojo was fully aware of her performative role as host and patron: the social script required her to lavish praise and approval in ways that could be clearly interpreted by all, and she appeared to be happy to oblige. Kifoko's monologues and theatrical elements gave the performance a "modern" touch, but the group members retained enough familiar material that, when scheduled alongside formal speeches and a PowerPoint presentation and followed by popular music and dancing, their folkloric rendering had the overall effect of demonstrating cultural connectedness—meaningful and lasting bonds to both culture and community.

Tojo's bigi yali was a high-class event, showcasing the host family as one that was thriving financially and had a robust and elite network within Suriname. Significantly, the family had continued to embrace their Maroon cultural heritage as they had ascended to their current status, rather than downplaying Maroon traits for the sake of fitting in. Kifoko provides a ready complement to this narritive.

Beyond the key roles that Tojo and Mosis played as founders, the group enacts a parallel kind of social trajectory, having achieved access to travel, training, and elite public spaces through their investment in Maroon performance culture. Like their founding family, group members were able to demonstrate social and expressive mobility without calling into question the centrality of their Maroon heritage to their identities.

The gesture of inclusion in Kifoko's closing number demonstrated social codes that marked the event's focus on an individual. Tojo and her family were consummate hosts, attentive to their many guests and eager for them to enjoy themselves. But this was Tojo's day. Performative decisions like Kifoko's use of participatory gestures helped keep the spotlight squarely on her.

JUNE 2014—FIAMBA PERFORMS AT ZUS EN ZO

Fiamba sets up on a small stage and dirt clearing at Zus en Zo, an open-air restaurant. This venue, which also houses a bike rental shop, guesthouse, and travel agency, caters unambiguously to tourists and foreigners, although a few upper-class Surinamers are there as well. The group performs amid the quiet but constant chatter of dinnertime conversation and the sounds of the kitchen and wait staff as they contend with a full house. When Fiamba nears the end of its set, the dancers fan out, searching for people at the tables who don't appear to be in rapt conversation or in the middle of their meal. After receiving one or two polite refusals to participate in the performance, two dancers approach a group of Dutch vacationers seated at the table next to me. A man and a woman from their party obligingly stand up and follow the Fiamba members to the dance clearing. The woman smiles and laughs nervously as she tries to follow the movements of the girl opposite her, who smiles back as they dance until the end of the song. The man is a good deal taller than the group's dancers—a feature that further magnifies the evident difference in appearance and skill. He scoops his head and waves his arms, making movements that bear little similarity to anything Fiamba has performed. Paying little attention to the dancer opposite him, he dances vigorously, glancing up rather often to smile over at his friends, who are chuckling at his efforts. I'm inclined to agree with his friends—he looks goofy. Whether that is by design or in spite of his intentions is open to interpretation.

Fiamba's performance at Zus en Zo—and the concluding number in particular—highlights the social "working out" that happens through a direct engagement with difference. In a touristic context, the gesture of inviting an audience member to dance offers an opportunity to dissolve the boundary that separates performers from audience members, appealing to all who join in to imagine themselves as part of a shared community, however temporary. This resonates with the reflections about the Avondvierdaagse (chapter 6) of Clifton Asongo, the group's leader, and his idealistic view that through "mee doen" (participation), people will recognize and honor their shared humanity. In other words, perhaps in the process of "trying out" a dance from another culture, audience members' physical efforts will give them insights into the difficulty of the feats they have just witnessed and additional respect for performers. Or, more simply, perhaps this gesture will allow two strangers to share a moment together. But for a performance to produce those sentiments requires specific actions and reactions from the audience. When performers' and audiences' intenions seem out of alignment with these goals and each other, the result can be deflating, leaving a group or its members with lingering questions about their overall success.

Taken as a whole, Fiamba's "cultural show" at Zus en Zo served a clear function. It was one event that helped round out the venue's entertainment calendar, which also featured a weekly rotation of live bands and movie nights. While some diners looked on with attention and interest for the duration of their show, the venue and context set some particular constraints for performance: the group should be engaging but not intrusive, catering to the sentiments of the room of paying customers. The group's final number involved an invitation that several people refused, prompting a situation that put pressure on the dancers because although no one audience member was obliged to take part, the success of the group's final number requires participation from someone in the audience. Each declined invitation drew out this final number and added a sense of anxiousness to the encounter.

Yet when an audience member's intended affect is ambiguous, one source of anxiety can give way to a different kind of uncertainty. Personally, I found the male vacationer's performance to register ambivalence: it seemed to ride a fine line between a joyful and good-natured way in which a member of the crowd did "his own thing" when in the company of an unfamiliar practice and goofing off (whether as a reaction to performance anxiety or out of irreverence), ignoring the invitation to connect and join with the group in favor of putting on his own show for his friends. Ambivalent and ambiguous encounters like this are common features of folkloric performance, and in practice they are rarely clarified.

They leave individuals to their own resources as they make sense of cultural encounters through their own narrations of self and community within shifting social constellations.

DECEMBER 2009—SAISA PERFORMS AT A POLITICAL RALLY IN SANTIGRON

On this night, following a series of rousing political speeches, Saisa performs for a large and lively crowd. At several points before the end of the group members' performance, Maroons from the community rush into the dance clearing to dance with them, usually for only a minute or so at a time. This has provided some minor complications in rendering Saisa's choreographies: for instance, when Benny Fonkel performed his solo (described in chapter 7), two women began dancing with him early on, making it impossible for him to convey his pantomimed story line or execute the dance's culminating move. Yet on the whole, Saisa members receive these interruptions good-naturedly; they seem happy to be performing in their hometown for a full and enthusiastic crowd.

The very last choreographed routine of the night begins with a man and woman dancing awasa opposite each other. After a few seconds, another member of the group steps into the middle of the performance space, interrupting either the male or female dancer to take his or her place. Another person and then another do the same, so that there is a steady rotation of dancers coming into and out of the performance space. These interruptions provide much of the fun of this choreography, giving group members a chance to express their own theatrical flair. Usually, after several Saisa members have cycled through the dance space, some people from the crowd will catch on and interject themselves in a similar fashion, cutting in somehow—effectively nudging a dancer out of the way and assuming his or her place. Nobody is surprised when members of this particular audience begin to join in.

However, one man's participation stands out. He enters the dance space, as several nonmembers of the group have done already. But instead of following the protocol established in the routine and giving way to the exaggerated "hook" of the next performer, this man continues to dance for a long time (nearly three minutes instead of the roughly thirty seconds that other performers have taken). Some Saisa members attempt to give him clues that he should leave the space, but to no avail. The dancer Nicholas Banjo stands next to him and looks at him pointedly, gesturing as though pointing to a wristwatch to indicate it's time to go. The man waves him off and keeps dancing until, finally, he staggers off of his own free will. In essence, the hypothetical scenario upon which the choreography was based comes quite close to what is actually happening on stage—here is a man who can't be made to leave. The subtle and unsubtle hints he's been given by Saisa's dancers makes it clear that more drastic measures would in fact be necessary to interrupt his performance.

The drummers conclude this piece shortly after this man's exit, and Carlos Pinas initiates the final song. Instead of selecting performers from the audience at large, dancers head to the stage in back of where they have been performing, where the BEP party members are seated and have been looking on. Dutifully, they descend from the stage to the clearing below and dance among their constituents. The crowd cheers as these political figures demonstrate that they are willing and capable of joining in. Michel Felisie, minister of regional development, is received especially warmly, as he nimbly assumes the deep bends and angles of mannengeefutu. After all, Carmen Ajerie of Kifoko reminds me later, Felisie had been a member of the group for a number of years.

In thinking about what happened in Saisa's penultimate number, I wonder what is at stake in whether the man from the audience stayed in the performance space or left it. Logistically, it doesn't really matter how long the performance lasts. The politicians have already spoken, and the local pop band that will finish the evening's festivities won't go on for quite some time, regardless of when Saisa ends. All that is left is a quick bow, a song announcing that Saisa is wrapping up, and then opening up the floor and inviting the political leaders to dance among Saisa members and their supporters. (Incidentally, the politicians' participation in the final dance was in no way optional—to refuse to perform would be read as disinterest and arrogance and lead to mistrust or social alienation, especially as they are running on an explicitly Maroon political platform.) So if the issue isn't logistical, what is it? The longer this man stays, the more the dance's structure and narrative form are threatened. What is at stake, it seems to me, is the notion that the performer and audience are working together to achieve the same thing—the idea that Saisa's members and their audience agree as to what will make the performance satisfying. It demonstrates the precariousness and contingent nature of a cultural group's control over the space and what transpires therein. In this case, the nature of the event is overtly political, with BEP representatives and their constituents endeavoring to articulate their shared struggles and visions for collective mobilization—all from the categorically ambiguous "suburban" village of Santigron.

These closing gestures reiterate many of the themes that interweave through-out the book. Once more, comparison helps draw attention to matters of function and form. A cursory glance reveals a familiar folkloric trope—one that all three groups employ in an inclusive and interactive spirit—yet the contexts and effects of these performances are starkly different. At Tojo's bigi yali, the gesture singles out the guest of honor and asserts her connection to Kifoko, not just as a performance collective but also as a community in its own right. In their invitation to participation, Fiamba's members extend to their audience of tourists and expatriates the chance to do mee—to experience something that they might be unlikely to try otherwise and potentially to connect with people across social and cultural differences in the process. Finally, at the political rally, Saisa first blurs the distinction between performers and audience members, allowing the latter to share in a dance style familiar to nearly everyone who is present but to experience it within a choreographic framework that might offer a different perspective. Then they invite politicians who ostensibly represent Maroons and Maroon interests to perform (in a literal sense) their cultural ties to community. In each instance, this gesture is mobilized to suit a communicative objective particular to the event at hand. On another night, at another event, the same choreographed strategies might do different cultural and interactive work.

APPENDIX A

Maroon Genres and a Comparative Table of the Cultural Groups Kifoko, Saisa, and Fiamba

COMPARATIVE TABLE OF THE CULTURAL GROUPS KIFOKO, SAISA, AND FIAMBA DURING FIELDWORK (2008–2009)·

	Kifoko	Saisa	Fiamba
Founding (Date, founder)	1983 André Mosis	1991 George Lazo	1995 Louise Wondel
Leadership in 2008–9	Eddy Lante and Saiwinie "Maria" Dewinie	Dansi Waterberg and Eduard Fonkel	Clifton Asongo
Rehearsal location	Downtown Paramaribo, in the historic district Suriname Culture Center (CCS)	A private residence in the Ramgoe neighborhood	A private residence in the Hanna's Lust neighborhood

	Kifoko	Saisa	Fiamba
Founding (Date, founder)	1983 André Mosis	1991 George Lazo	1995 Louise Wondel
Repertoire (Short descriptions below)	Awasa Songe Susa Mato Aleke[b] Uman Daguwe[b] Loonsei[b] "Kikri" ("Kifoko Creations," original compositions)[b]	Awasa Songe Susa Bandámmba Kumanti Awawa[b] Tuka[b]	Awasa Bandámmba Aleke Loketo[a]
Rehearsals	Twice weekly (on Thursdays and Sundays)	Once weekly (on Thursdays)	Once weekly (on Fridays)
Number of regular members in 2008–9	30	25	18
Predominant ethnicities or Maroon subgroups	Pamaka and Ndyuka	Saamaka	Ndyuka
Gender distribution[c]	More women than men	Roughly even	Slightly more men than women
Age	Wide age range, though core dancers were older in comparison to dancers in other groups active at the time (in their late thirties and early forties)	Predominantly ranging from late teens to early thirties	Majority in their teens

	Kifoko	Saisa	Fiamba
Founding (Date, founder)	1983 André Mosis	1991 George Lazo	1995 Louise Wondel
Dancers' roles in performance	Most performances used 8–12 dancers, selected by Lante or Dewinie. Typically these were dancers of senior standing and/or exceptional talent. Younger dancers were included at the request of patrons.	Typically, all regular members performed at gigs, though each choreography used 1–9 dancers at a time. The strongest dancers performed in several numbers, while newer or less experienced members performed less often. Choreographies (as well as songs) became associated with specific group members.	All members were included in most performances. Female dancers were "on stage," arranged in rows, for the duration of the performance, with male dancers standing near the drummers when not soloing. Dancers stepped into the foreground to perform a solo and then returned to their starting place. The structure was "een voor een" (one after another), with each female dancer performing a brief solo in succession. Nearly all dancers spent an equal amount of time dancing or soloing, regardless of skill.

	Kifoko	Saisa	Fiamba
Founding (Date, founder)	1983 André Mosis	1991 George Lazo	1995 Louise Wondel
Ethnographer's roles in performance	Mostly observing or documenting. Performed with the group five times over the course of two years.	Performed regularly, 1–2 pieces, and included in the concluding piece described in chapter 8. Sang in the koor on the group's fourth CD (Saisa 2009).	Performed regularly, dancing and singing in the koor. Undifferentiated from other group members (treated like other group members) within the structure of performance.

[a] Since 2009, Fiamba has expanded its repertoire to include songe and mato.

[b] Performed occasionally.

[c] During the time of research, none of the members identified themselves as nonbinary.

GLOSSARY OF MAROON GENRES FEATURED IN THE CULTURAL GROUPS KIFOKO, SAISA, AND FIAMBA

Aleke (Ndyuka origin): Popular music genre (see Bilby 2001a, Campbell 2012a).

Awasa (Ndyuka origin): Discussed at length in chapter 4. Last dance featured in the gaansamapee (the sequence of genres traditionally performed on special occasions).

Awawa (Saamaka origin): A singing genre in which two singers carry out a conversation using clever, often competitive wordplay or light insults. Saisa's performances of awawa were enacted as a battle of the sexes between the group's two primary singers, Silvana Pinas and Carlos Pinas. Does not feature dance.

Bandámmba (Saamaka origin): A celebratory dance featuring women's skillful manipulations of their waists, hips, and buttocks (see Campbell 2018).

"Kikri" ("Kifoko creation"): The name by which Kifoko referred to its original compositions that existed outside of (or drew on a combination of) established Maroon genres. "Kikri" often involved elements of theater or oratory. Kifoko referred to these pieces as though they were a genre of their own.

Kumanti (Ndyuka and Saamaka origin): Warrior spirits and music associated with them.

Loketo: Popular music genre developed in eastern Suriname as an adaptation of Congolese soukous (see Bilby 1999, 286).

Loonsei (Ndyuka origin): A style popular in the mid-twentieth century, considered a precursor to aleke.

Mato (Ndyuka origin): A genre (the first included in the gaansamapee) featuring storytelling and riddling, often in combination with song and dance (see chapter 3).

Songe (Ndyuka origin): Typically the third genre performed in the gaansamapee. The fundamental movements recall the natural landscape and fishing practices of the rain forest interior. This dance is named after *agankoi* (*Geophagus harreri*, or Maroni eartheater), a freshwater fish that swims from side to side as it guards its eggs. The steps and postures that women use to dance songe replicate this side-to-side motion, and the men often make as though they are drawing a bow, as the agankoi is typically fished using a bow and arrow.

Susa (Ndyuka origin): A dance framed as a competition (or battle) between two opponents. The competitive element requires fast footwork and lightning-quick reflexes as the dancers attempt to mirror or counter each other's foot movements. A separate version of susa is sometimes played in kumanti music, which does not involve two opponents facing off. The former version was performed by Kifoko, the latter by Saisa.

Tuka (Ndyuka and Saamaka origin): Funerary music played shortly following a person's death (see chapter 1).

Uman Daguwe (Ndyuka origin): A genre that is played at the conclusion of an event in which the Papa or Vodu snake gods have been invoked. It functions to bring both levity and closure to the event. It is danced in a circle.

APPENDIX B

List of Group Members
Mentioned in the Text

Within each group, individuals are listed alphabetically by first name. The individual's Maroon nation affiliation (Ndyuka, Saamaka, Pamaka, Aluku, Matawai, or Kwinti), where it is known, is the first descriptor in each listing.

KIFOKO

André Mosis

Ndyuka. Residence: The Hague, the Netherlands. Role in the group: founder, former artistic director, and drummer.

For a biography of André in relation to his founding years, see Mosis 2012; Campbell 2012b, appendix B. Trained in ethnographic methods by Terry Agerkop at the Ministry of Culture Studies.

Carmen Ajerie

Cottica Ndyuka, from Saa Kiiki. Residence: Sunny Point. Role in the group: core dancer.

During 2008–9, Carmen had just started working as a housekeeper at Torarica, an elite hotel in downtown Paramaribo. Carmen and her husband, Eddy Lante, have two daughters who were also regular members of Kifoko.

Eddy Lante

Ndyuka. Residence: Sunny Point. Role in the group: artistic director, coleader, drummer, core member.

Eddy led rehearsals on a regular basis. Previously employed in a clerical capacity at the regional airport (which offered several small, commercial flights to the interior regions on Blue Wing Airlines), Eddy had retired by 2017. Eddy and his wife, Carmen Ajerie (also a longstanding Kifoko member), have two daughters who were also regular members of Kifoko.

Fabian Asidjan

Role in the group: drummer.

Fabian was an occasional participant in Kifoko in 2008–9.

Georgio Mosis

Ndyuka. Residence: Shanghai, China. Role in the group: former member, drummer.

Eldest son of André Mosis and Laetitia Tojo. After moving to the Netherlands with his family in 1990, Georgio and his siblings maintained their involvement in performance as they grew into adulthood. Georgio's career interests in digital technologies have led him to relocate to China.

Graciella Dewinie

Pamaka. Residence: Sunny Point. Role in the group: dancer, core member, often took the lead in training young dancers and developing choreography.

Graciella was trying to start up a day care in her home. In 2008–9 she had one infant child, Dikembe, whom she would bring to rehearsals. Ten years later, he continues to go to rehearsals, along with his younger sister.

Henny Tojo

Pamaka. Residence: Sunny Point. Role in the group: drummer.

The father of Minio and Herman Tojo, Henny worked as a tour operator for MaYeDu Tours. He participated in Kifoko rehearsals and performances sporadically.

Herman Tojo

Pamaka. Residence: Sunny Point. Role in the group: drummer (gaan doon), occasional dancer.

Herman had been a member of Kifoko since he was a young boy. Intermittently, he functioned as an officer (treasurer or communications liaison) for Kifoko. Herman achieved multiple certifications in digital media technologies. Along with his mother, Irma Dabenta, and brother Minio, Herman left the group for Gadoe Talentie. Currently, Herman works at the Ministry for Regional Development.

Irma Dabenta

Residence: Sunny Point. Role in the group: lead singer.

Irma has left the group for Gadoe Talentie, a Christian group. She is the mother of the drummers Minio and Herman Tojo.

John Binta

Residence: Sunny Point. Role in group: dancer, drummer.

John was known as an exceptional dancer. An active member of the group in previous years, he stopped attending rehearsals in 2009.

José Tojo

Residence: The Hague, the Netherlands. Role in the group: former drummer, dancer.

Tojo, a former member of Kifoko, now directs his own Maroon dance initiative, Kula Skoro, geared toward cultural enrichment for Maroon youth in the Netherlands. He has traveled and taken on a range of theatrical and educational projects, including holding awasa training sessions with Kifoko for Maroon youth in Paramaribo.

Laetitia Tojo

Residence: The Hague, the Netherlands. Role in the group: wife of Kifoko's founder, André Mosis.

As Mosis describes events (2012), Laetitia and her family connections were influential in the group's founding.

Lucia Alankoi

Residence: District Centrum, Paramaribo. Role in the group: dancer, koor singer. A long-standing member of Kifoko.

Minio Tojo

Pamaka. Residence: Sunny Point. Role in the group: drummer, occasional dancer.

In 2008–9 Minio was increasingly playing a leadership role in Kifoko. He frequently led warm-ups and developed training exercises for dancers. He and his brother Herman were very active in collaborative and theatrical projects throughout Paramaribo, and in 2009 Minio led his own dance workshop for small children, independently of any initiative that Kifoko had. Toward the end of 2009 he was employed as a bodyguard for Michel Felisie, the minister of regional development. Along with his brother Herman and their mother, Irma Dabenta, Minio left Kifoko to join Gadoe Talentie.

Saiwinie "Maria" Dewinie

Pamaka. Residence: Sunny Point. Role in the group: president, co-leader, koor singer, core member.

Maria led rehearsals on a regular basis. A member of Kifoko since its founding, she also worked as a primary school teacher.

Tiomara

Kifoko's youngest dancer and regular member in 2008–9 (when she was approximately 8–9 years old). Tiomara lived roughly a half mile from ccs, where Kifoko rehearsed at the time. She would walk to rehearsal along with several members of her household, including the established group members Liento Day (the only male member of Kifoko at the time who participated primarily as a dancer, rather than a percussionist) and Marguerite Deel. Owing to her diminutive size and dancing talent, Tiomara was a crowd favorite at Kifoko's public performances.

Vera Pansa

Saamaka. Among the group's most long-standing members. Role in group: dancer, occasional singer.

FIAMBA

Clifton Asongo

Ndyuka. Residence: Hanna's Lust. Role in the group: leader, drummer.

Clifton took over leadership from his aunt, Louise Wondel, in 2006, after she became ill. Rehearsals were held at his house, in spaces that he built specially for the group and maintained meticulously. Clifton had no musical training before joining the group, but he gradually acquired skills—first by playing the shakers and then graduating to the drum parts.

Errel van Dijk

Ndyuka. Residence: moved from Paramaribo to Diitabiki in 2009. Role in the group: drummer.

Errel has assumed increasing leadership roles in the group and influenced its creative direction, including its expanded repertoire that in 2017 also included mato and songe.

Erwin Alexander Tolin

Ndyuka. Role in the group: former member of Fiamba, with some leadership responsibilities. Playwright.

Erwin is the artistic director of the Ministry of Culture in Suriname. He also directs a youth afterschool theater program in Paramaribo.

Faizel Pinas

Role in the group: singer.

Faizel left Fiamba for the cultural group Tangiba.

Jemi Sikanar

Residence: Hanna's Lust. Role in the group: group affiliate, former Fiamba member.

Louise Wondel

Cottica Ndyuka mother, Saamaka father. Residence: Hanna's Lust. Role in the group: founder.

Louise's health was failing during 2008–9 and she was unable to work. Although she was too ill to take part, she would often look on from the porch of her family house as the group rehearsed in her front yard.

Louise was widely known as a poet and cultural activist as well as a dancer. She got her start performing publicly after winning the Miss Pompololi dance competition, the prize for which was to be featured on a music video and in an international tour with the aleke band Sukru Sani. Before founding Fiamba, Louise rehearsed with the cultural groups Kifoko, Maswa, and Kifangu. She passed away in 2017.

Mano Deel

Ndyuka. Role in the group: drummer.

Mano learned how to drum from his father. In 2017, according to Clifton Asongo, Mano still maintained his connection with the group and performed with them on occasion, though he had moved away from Paramaribo.

Maranjaw

Role in the group: singer, song composer.

A former member of Fiamba, Maranjaw was active in the group under Louise Wondel's leadership.

Norma Sante

Ndyuka. Role in the group: singer, dancer.

Former member of Fiamba and a singer of enduring popularity with the kaskawi group, Naks Kaseko Loco, Norma was "scouted" as a singer for the latter group while performing with Fiamba.

Sandrine Akombe

Saamaka. Role in the group: dancer.

A student, Sandrine joined Fiamba in 2008, alongside her friend Sheryl Tesa. During my fieldwork in 2014, Sandrine was still with the group and had taken on some leadership responsibilities, in particular regarding recruiting new members. She had left the group by 2017.

Sheryl Tesa

Ndyuka. Role in the group: singer.

A student, Sheryl joined Fiamba in 2008, alongside her friend Sandrine Akombe. She started rehearsing as a dancer, but her singing talents led to a gradual shift in her performance role over time. She had left the group by 2011.

SAISA

Benny Fonkel

Saamaka. Role in the group: dancer.

Carlos Josimba Corason Pinas

Saamaka. Role in the group: lead singer.

After Saisa disbanded, Carlos performed occasionally with the cultural group Oséle.

Cheke Pinas

Saamaka. Role in the group: dancer.

A crowd favorite for his signature high jumps.

Dansi Waterberg

Samaka. Residence: Ramgoe. Role in the group: leader, former drummer.

Saisa rehearsals were held at Dansi's house. Dansi rarely performed with the group, but he was instrumental as a group coordinator and advisor. He was a talented wood carver and had made the group's drums.

Debora Fonkel

Saamaka. Role in the group: singer, dancer.

In 2009, Debora had recently joined Saisa. She composed the trio choreography discussed in chapter 7 and sings the song "Jang jou njang," discussed in chapters 3 and 4.

Delia Waterberg

Saamaka. Role in the group: dancer.

After Saisa disbanded in 2011, Delia joined the cultural group Oséle.

Eduard Fonkel

Saamaka. Residence: Commisarisweg, Paramaribo. Role in the group: leader, dancer; typically directed rehearsals.

Eduard worked as a police officer. He also played trumpet in a local kaseko band.

Jill Triesie

Long-standing member of Saisa. Role in the group: dancer, occasional singer; occasional leadership role in rehearsal.

George Lazo

Role in the group: founder, supporter.

Though he was never a regularly participating member, Lazo played a crucial role in the establishment of the group, as discussed in chapters 2 and 3. He was also the founder of Arinze Tours, a Santigron-based tourist operation where many Saisa members first began performing publicly.

Nicholas Banjo

Saamaka. Role in group: dancer.

Nicholas was a student in 2008–9. After leaving Saisa, he joined the cultural group Tangiba.

Silvana Pinas

Saamaka. Commisarisweg, Paramaribo. Role in group: lead singer.

NOTES

1. Introduction

1. The literal translation is, "It's work we're working here."

2. These names were most commonly articulated in Dutch (*cultureelgroep, dansgroep, sociaal-cultureel vereniging,* and *awasagroep,* respectively). The Kifoko leaders, Eddy Lante and Maria Dewinie, both expressed a preference for the term "social-cultural association," a phrase that Fiamba also employed in an official capacity. This name highlights the significance of what the groups accomplished for Maroon audiences and group members, above all in the more private space of rehearsal. However, the title proved unwieldy for the purposes of advertising performances, and thus the other names circulated more freely in the public sphere. I do not ascribe a particular Afro-Surinamese referent to the general use of this term, because other groups within Suriname representing other ethnicities were also described by it. However, the word *kulturu* in Sranan Tongo has a more complex usage: it can sometimes refer to spiritual or medicinal treatments or activities, "glossing over any references to healing and witchcraft" (Cunha 2018, 270), in addition to its more general meaning, similar to the English word "culture."

3. Estimates are from "Trans-Atlantic Slave Trade—Estimates," accessed June 2019, https://slavevoyages.org/assessment/estimates). The precise number listed is 340,988. Of those shipped, only 294,652 disembarked. The slaves brought to Suriname were taken from many locations throughout West and Central Africa, shipped from ports in three broad African regions—the Bight of Benin (or "Slave Coast"), the Loango-Angola Coast in Central Africa, and the Gold Coast (R. Price 2008, 291–93).

4. Maroon societies developed throughout the New World—for instance, in Colombia, Brazil, and Jamaica. In this book I use "Maroon" to refer to the Maroons in Suriname and French Guiana, unless otherwise specified.

5. Spanish explorers had ventured to Suriname in the early seventeenth century, but it was Francis Willoughby, Earl of Parham and governor of Barbados, who first established a European presence in the region. The territory was transferred to Dutch jurisdiction in the Treaty of Breda (1667) in exchange for Manhattan.

6. Earlier scholarship uses alternative spellings (Saramaka for Saamaka and Paramaka for Pamaka). Richard and Sally Price indicate that "Saamakas have asked to have the 'r' dropped since their language doesn't have an 'r' sound" (pers. comm., May 2019). See R. Price (1996) for a comparative study of Maroon societies by geographic area.

7. See Stedman's influential firsthand account (1796) from his vantage point as a colonial officer in Suriname from 1773 to 1777. See also R. and S. Price (1983) for further colonial accounts of these conditions, and R. Price (1983) for oral history accounts as preserved by the Saamaka Maroons. Mintz and Price (1992) offer a compelling discussion of social and cultural formations in this New World context.

8. An earlier treaty was established between the Saamaka Maroons of central Suriname and the colonial government under Governor Jan Jacob Mauricius, but the terms of the treaty were violated shortly thereafter. The 1760 treaty with the Ndyuka (Okanisi) Maroons was the first one to prove durable.

9. See Bilby 2001a, 31; Counter and Evans, 1981. Richard Price points out that the striking Africanness of Afro-Surinamese societies was in part related to the high slave-to-planter ratio on the plantations—at times as high as 65:1 in plantation districts. Creolization, he argues, involved the merging of many African languages and customs with "far less input from European and Amerindian sources" (2011, 10).

10. See R. Price 1983 for an extended discussion, including oral history accounts.

11. As stated, all of these phrases and words are part of regular, everyday speech. The frequency with which such phrases occur in everyday conversation is difficult to overstate. All of them have been expounded upon in Louise Wondel's poetry. Maranjaw's song "A mi dugudugu" (see chapter 2) provides one representative use of the sentiment that slavery still exists in a person's work situation. The precise phrasing, "u komoto katibo, u á de a keti moo," comes from the recorded mock interview between Errel van Dijk and Mano Deel referred to in chapter 2 (10 October, 2009). I've included phrases in the Okanisi language, yet similar sentiments are commonly expressed in the other Maroon languages as well.

12. The concept of *marronage* (flight from slavery) and its relationship to freedom have attracted increased contemporary interest, often separated from the Maroon populations that resulted from marronage's historical occurrence. Examples include Roberts (2015) and Melyon-Reinette (2012), as well as the recent theorizations of the musician and music critic Greg Tate (see Russonello 2015). While these conceptual directions can offer new and valuable perspectives, I maintain that it is important to keep in mind that those whose societies were founded by marronage are also engaged in such theorizations, and much could be gained by including their experiential vantage points in such works. Contemporary Maroon populations may not have experienced the marronage that led to their founding, but flight from slavery undoubtedly shapes many aspects of their experiences and identifications in a distinctive and definitive way.

13. The Suriname Maroons have in common a three-tiered religious structure. The top tier is occupied by the god of all creation, Masaa Gadu (also known in the Kumanti language as Anana Keduaman Keduampon), followed by his assistants in the second tier and by minor deities in the third tier—including ancestor spirits (*yooka*), reptile spirits (*papagadu* or *vodu*), forest spirits (*ampuku*), and "warrior spirits residing in celestial phenomena such as thunder and lightning, carrion birds, and other animals of prey," called *kumanti* (Thoden van Velzen and van Wetering 2004, 25). Typically, the spirits in the second or third tier can intervene in human affairs.

14. For a more thorough discussion of the civil war, see Dew 1994 and 1996.

15. While *The Myth of the Negro Past* is Herskovits's most influential book that draws from his research in Suriname, this research was first published in two works coauthored with his wife, Frances Herskovits (Herskovits and Herskovits 1934 and 1936). For a discussion of the nature and character of their research, see also R. Price and S. Price (2003). Thompson's earlier article, "An Aesthetic of the Cool" (1973), has likewise been influential—in particular in scholarship concerning African Diasporic performance.

16. To this category also belong a handful of recording compilations, featuring traditional genres and comprised primarily of field recordings. These include the following items in the discography: R. Price and S. Price (1977), Bilby (2011), and Pakosie (2002). Although I'm not aware of any formal academic publications that he has produced, André Mosis circulates aspects of his research and knowledge informally and through his website (kingbotho.com).

17. Maroon women's contributions to Maroon performance culture are underrepresented. Here I present accounts of the mixed-gender spaces of rehearsal and performance. I do not focus exclusively or even primarily on women, aiming instead to achieve a balance in gender representation. Even so, this breaks from the norm. With a few exceptions (S. Price and R. Price 1999; Campbell 2012b and 2018), a focus on the traditionally male realm of drumming and on popular genres in which men predominate has led to the diminished visibility and audibility of women's contributions to music and dance, above all in a popular idiom. There are many Maroon and Afro-Surinamese women who have exercised considerable influence, even in the male-dominated sphere of popular music—including the Maroon performers Norma Sante, Sa Wowi, and Zus Mien. A discussion of genres including gospel, spoken poetry, and Suripop (see Campbell 2012a) would reveal the very active roles of women in popular music production, as performers and taste makers.

18. As discussed in the chapter 2, mining and lumber operations, from small-scale ventures to government-sanctioned contracts with multinational corporations, are a conspicuous presence in the region, leaving Suriname's Maroon and Amerindian populations struggling to maintain control over the land on which they depend.

19. Technically, the territory occupied by the Cottica Ndyuka can be considered part of this coastal region—one of several examples complicating a strict division between the coast and interior.

20. The 2012 census estimated that 66 percent of the country's population resided in the neighboring districts of Paramaribo and Wanica (Sno and Ritfeld 2016, 54).

21. The first shipment of Chinese laborers (nearly 3,000 people) came to Suriname via Java in 1853 (Meagher 2008, 260).

22. Indentured workers shipped from Indonesia were not exclusively Javanese, yet the population of Indonesian descent is referred to as Javanese both in official census data and in most conversations concerning Suriname's demographics. I follow Stuart Strange's use of the word "Hindustani" to refer to "all Sarnami [a Surinamese dialect of Bhojpuri] speaking Surinamese of South Asian descent, regardless of religion" (2016, 1).

23. The cause for the drastic increase in the Maroon population as represented by the census has attracted much speculation. Richard Price provides a useful analysis of the situation, as well as estimates of the size of the Suriname Maroon population as a whole—including those living in French Guiana and the African Diaspora (2018). He suggests that previous reports (his own and those provided by the Suriname Bureau of Statistics [Algemeen Bureau voor de Statistiek in Suriname]) severely underestimated the population size. The birth rate of Maroons increased substantially between the 2004 and 2012 censuses (raising concerns among many about the availability of contraceptives and sex education to Maroon women and girls), but this alone cannot account for the radical change. Among the additional factors under consideration is the potential for an increased willingness for those represented in census statistics to identify themselves as Maroon. (See chapter 5 and Tjon Sie Fat [2009] for a discussion of social factors encouraging Surinamers of mixed ancestry to identify and be identified in relation to a single ethnic group.) Not reflected in the national statistics are the numerous Brazilians, Suriname's southern neighbors, who travel up along Suriname's rivers to engage in small-scale gold mining and a recent influx of Haitian refugees. Neither are culturally influential populations such as the Lebanese (who first came to Suriname as traders in the late nineteenth century [see de Bruijne 1979]) and the Portuguese Jews (among the nation's first colonial inhabitants, who founded the Jodensavanne sugar plantations).

24. See Carlin et. al. (2014) for a general overview of the languages common in Suriname and Migge (2018) for a discussion of Maroon languages in particular.

25. Guntis Smidchens has made a similar distinction in describing folklorism as the "conscious recognition and repetition of tradition" (1999, 56). Nahachewsky states: "Reflectiveness . . . refers to the perceptions of the members of the subject culture themselves. It deals with self-consciousness WITHIN the emic worldview of the participants; inside the tradition before an outside ethnographer even arrives" (2001, 20).

26. For influential early theorizations of cultural brokerage, see Geertz (1960) and Paine (1971). See also White (2000), Steiner (1994), and Kurin (1997).

27. My understanding of these titles is informed by Turino (2000, 51–52). However, my work with Maroon cultural groups (and Kifoko in particular) has led me to consider

professional status as something that is not based exclusively on the group's capacity to generate income. In its usage by Kifoko members, the term indicated not only that their labors warranted compensation, but also that they had acquired modes of comportment on and off the stage that allowed them to maneuver in cosmopolitan networks and spaces with relative ease and with minimal strain on the part of their host or patron.

28. Shay's notion of "parallel traditions" (1999) and the influential concepts of first and second existence folk dance (Hoerburger 1968; Nahachewsky 2001) and participatory versus presentational performance (Turino 2000 and 2008) are examples of theories that have sought to define or categorize folkloric performance along these parameters. See chapter 2 for an extended critique.

29. For further critique, see Feldman (2006, 128), Hagedorn (2001, 4 and 19–20), and Hellier-Tinoco (2011, 240–58). The term "folklore" is credited to William John Thoms, who coined the term in the British literary journal *The Atheneaum* in 1846.

30. Kifoko was the only one of the three groups I studied in depth (Kifoko, Saisa, and Fiamba) that compensated individuals on a regular basis for their performances. Incidentally, they were also the most selective as to who among them was invited to perform, and they had access to a larger number of more lucrative or high-profile gigs, owing to their extensive network that they had built up over the years (see chapter 3).

31. As examples, Tangiba performed as an interlude for Paramaribo's 2008 Awasa Contest, and the drummers from Kifoko performed as accompaniment for the SaDumaa Multi-Talent Contest in 2009.

32. Bilby describes loketo as a fusion of soukous and Surinamese kaseko music (1999, 286). For a more detailed discussion of aleke, see Bilby (2001a). For a further discussion of the social contextualization of popular musical forms, see Waterman (1990).

33. The Ndyuka Maroon Paul Abena established Radio Koyeba in 1997.

34. See M. Herskovits and F. Herskovits (1936) and Wekker (2006). In both sources, birthday parties are discussed together with women's homosexual *mati* relationships (as described in M. Herskovits and F. Herskovits 1936, 32). While adult women were more likely than men to have a *fuuyali oso*, I did not witness any of the performative greetings or ritualized gift exchanges mentioned in these sources as being characteristic of birthday celebrations among matis. I offer this comment with the caveat that in many of these performances, the cultural groups that I accompanied tended to stay for only a portion of the festivities. Further research would be necessary to determine if, how, and to what extent the Maroon festivities derive from their function among these earlier Creole festivities.

35. This excerpt from my fieldwork resonates with Tomie Hahn's discussion of the methods and impacts of modes of dance transmission in *nihon buyo* (2007). Graciella delivered her commentary in Paamaka; the translation is mine.

36. Likewise, the directive "kibii i kulturu" or "kibii i sani" (keep your things") is invoked in the Kibii Foundation, a community art and culture organization located in

Moengo, a municipality between Paramaribo and Suriname's eastern border. The foundation is directed by Marcel Pinas, a renowned Maroon visual artist.

37. See appendix A for a comparative table of what genres were featured by what group. The "traditional" genres featured regularly in cultural groups' routines included awasa, songe, mato, susa, *bandámmba, awawa, kumanti, uman daguwe*, and tuka (see below in this chapter for a further discussion of groups' varying interpretations of tuka's role in performance). More "popular" or contemporary forms included *loonsei*, aleke, and loketo. Finally, Kifoko created its own classification of "Kikri" (short for "Kifoko creations"), consisting of original works that usually involve theater or oratory. Notably absent from this list is the Saamaka genre *sêkêti*. This is one of the best-known music and dance genres of the Maroons, but none of the groups included it in their regular lineups. Vera Pansa (a Saamaka member of Kifoko) did on occasion perform a short sêkêti song, but I never witnessed rehearsal time being devoted to learning sêkêti.

38. My translation from Okanisi, excerpted from a group interview I had with Kifoko on 12 October 2017.

39. I had conducted short-term fieldwork in Ghana as an undergraduate and a master's student, and I wondered about the nature of Suriname's cultural connection to West Africa in general, but also with Ghana in particular.

40. I agree with Kofi Agawu (2003, 42–43) that the amount of time spent in a country, while crucial to conduct various kinds of research, does not in and of itself grant any kind of authority to a researcher. I provide this information in an effort to represent myself accurately and to help the reader contextualize my narrative voice and observations.

41. To supplement the knowledge of the percussive traditions that I experienced in rehearsal and performance as a dancer, I took drumming lessons with Clifton Asongo from Fiamba and with Ernie Wolf, who specialized in Maroon and Creole ritual percussion music. Subsequent visits to Suriname (ranging from one and a half to eight months in duration) have built upon the relationships and routines I established with each group.

42. To give a few examples, Rumya Putcha has addressed white women's appropriation of yoga (2018), and numerous essays and journal articles have critiqued "white women's tears"— public performances of white women's vulnerability and/or grief that silence or distract from the greater suffering of people of color, and women of color in particular. See Hamad (2018).

43. In all three cultural groups membership was generally free, but given my position in relationship to them I made donations, bought materials for them (including skins for broken drum heads or other instruments, cloth for matching group outfits, technological gear, drinks and snacks) and provided whatever additional compensation they requested. The needs and requests from the three groups differed in kind, but I attempted to compensate each group to an equivalent degree.

44. Influential case studies include Hahn (2006 and 2007), Browning (1995), Blanco-Borelli (2016), and Rahaim (2012).

2. *Ambivalent Forms*

Epigraph for the section titled "Political Ambivalence: Maroons in the Surinamese Nation-State," between notes 4 and 5: Quoted in R. Price 2011, 201.

1. "Ambivalence," *Oxford Etymology Dictionary*, accessed 27 June 2018, https://www.etymonline.com/word/ambivalence.

2. As discussed in chapter 1, this is an oversimplification: the Dutch officially assumed colonial control over Suriname in 1667 in the Treaty of Breda.

3. Now, over fifteen years later and thanks to consistent efforts to boost the tourist economy, the Guianas are included more frequently, if only with a couple pages about each of them.

4. See, for example, Francois Taglioni and Romain Cruse, "Is Suriname a Caribbean Island Like the Others?," in Caribbean Atlas, edited by Francois Taglioni and Romain Cruse, 2013, http://www.caribbean-atlas.com/en/themes/what-is-the-caribbean/is-suriname-a-caribbean-island-like-the-others.html. Examples of scholarly and literary inclusion of Suriname in a Caribbean purview include Arnold (2001) and Higman (1999).

5. The relevant Inter-American Court on Human Rights (IACHR) cases are Case No. 10.150 (Aloeboetoe et. al. v. the Government of Suriname), decided on 10 September 1993, and Case No. 12.338 (Twelve Saramaka Clans [Los] v. Suriname), decided on 15 June 2007. The relevant UN Committee on the Elimination of Racial Discrimination (CERD) rulings include "General Recommendation XXIII (41) Concerning Indigenous Peoples," adopted 18 August 1997; "Prevention of Racial Discrimination, Including Early Warning Measures and Urgent Action Procedures, Suriname, Decision 3(62)," CERD/C/62/CO/Dec.3, 21 March 2003; "Tenth Periodic Report of Suriname," CERD/C/446/Add.1, 31 July 2003; "Concluding Observations/Comments, Suriname," CERD/C/64/CO/9, 12 March 2004; "Follow-Up Procedure Decision 3(66) Suriname," CERD/C/66/SUR/Dec.3, 9 March 2005; and "Prevention of Racial Discrimination, Including Early Warning Measures and Urgent Action Procedures Decision 1 (67) Suriname," CERD/C/Dec/Sur/2, 18 August 2005.

6. Groot (2009, 23). In *Rainforest Warriors* (2011, 72) Richard Price includes an excerpt from the testimony of Suriname's Judge Advocate General Ramón de Frietas at the 1992 Inter-American Court of Human Rights proceedings, which attributes the desire and benefit for increased travel to the coast exclusively to the Maroons, ignoring well-documented aspects of colonial strategy.

7. Fifty-four meters high and two kilometers long (R. Price 2011, 244), the dam also drowned untold numbers of rare and endangered species of flora and fauna. For an account of wildlife rescue efforts, see Walsh and Gannon (1967).

8. Less common, but also problematic for the Maroons, is the designation of some of their areas as protected rain forest, which entails restrictions on how populations are able to utilize their own lands. See Kambel 2006.

9. Bouterse's dictatorial leadership was unequivocally asserted in 1982 in what is now known as the December Murders. On 7–9 December 1982, fifteen public figures who had voiced opposition to the military government were taken to the military headquarters at Fort Zeelandia, where they were tortured and executed. On 29 November 2019, a military court in Suriname found Bouterse guilty of their murder and sentenced him to twenty years in prison. At the time of writing, the verdict is under appeal.

10. The Dutch, who had been contributing sizable amounts of money to the country in the wake of its independence, withdrew their financial support in opposition to the military coup and Bouterse's leadership.

11. Connell also observes that state entryism potentially has several additional benefits, including more direct involvement of women in political affairs and opportunities for Maroon leaders to benefit from a more nuanced knowledge of the projects and concessions proposed in areas that fall under their jurisdiction. In the latter case, Connell suggests that this would help leaders identify and safeguard against misleading information or coercive tactics in negotiations.

12. Kambel (2006) enumerates many ways in which the government magnifies preexisting challenges owing to the remoteness of Maroon and Amerindian villages through lack of funding and resource allocation.

13. See R. Price (2011, 230–33). While Price's comments apply primarily to those living in the interior, there is likewise a strong case to be made that this ability of Maroons to use their ancestral lands in accordance with their traditions impacts Maroons living in Paramaribo in numerous and important ways. Even for those whose firsthand experiences of the interior are limited, their engagement with indigenous religious practice, tribal authority, and the availability of traditional foods and medicines are all mediated to some extent by the perpetuation of cultural practices and land use in the interior.

14. R. Price estimated the total number of Maroons residing in Paramaribo as 83,050 in 2018—exceeding the number of Maroons living in the interior of French Guiana and Suriname by nearly 3,000 (2018, 282).

15. Based on the 2018 population estimates in R. Price (2018).

16. In my experience, in the Ndyuka language Okanisi (and, I imagine, in other Maroon and Afro-Surinamese languages, "foto" can be used in the general sense McLeod describes or to mean Paramaribo specifically—the level of generality is determined in large part based on context. If, for instance, one were to encounter a Maroon traveling downriver toward the coastal area, the statement "Mi e go na foto" ("I'm going to foto" in Okanisi) would be an unambiguous statement that the traveler is going to Paramaribo—another urban coastal location would be specified by name, such as Soolan (Saint-Laurent-du-Maroni), Albina, or Cayenne.

17. Among the numerous Maroons who consider themselves Rastafarians, the notion of their capital city as a site of Babylonian corruption and moral decline maps easily onto preexisting ideas and sentiments about urban life. See Bibly (1999); Jaffe and Sanderse (2008).

18. Though close in spelling and pronunciation to a word the Okanisi Maroons use to identify themselves (Ndyuka, alternatively spelled Ndjuka), "Djuka" is used as a derogatory term.

19. Sally Price and Richard Price have commented on these or similar dynamics regarding Maroon visual art (S. Price 1989; S. Price and R. Price 1994a, 1999).

20. As with the previous song, these lyrics demonstrate the kinds of linguistic transformations that Okanisi can undergo, in particular in city populations. Here, Maranjaw's song (in this case sung by Pinas, as in the previous example) uses the Sranan-ized *wroko* instead of the Okanisi *wooko* and *slaafu* instead of *saafu*. These word choices could be as intended by Maranjaw, who had left Fiamba before my fieldwork began, or it could be indicative of the linguistic fluencies and preferences of Pinas as lead singer.

21. The choreography in question appears at 9:03.

22. As I discuss in chapter 8, there is, in fact, a well-established practice in folkloric performance of inviting selected audience members to accompany performers onstage, but typically these invitations are cloaked in formality—here, the male dancers' interactions encroach and demand engagement, functioning more as provocation than invitation. Significantly, while inviting audience members to participate (see chapter 5 on "mee doen" as a performance trope) blurs distinctions between group members and spectators, if anything the interactions by these members of Tangiba seem to enforce these divisions.

3. *Cultural Groups as Interpretive Communities*

1. The ways in which these groups structured their shows bore many similarities, which included progressing through a predetermined succession of genres and presenting choreographed works that each tended to last three minutes or so. All three groups included at least one piece, typically toward the end of a performance, during which dancers would circulate within the audience, inviting selected audience members to join them in the performance area for a dance, as described in chapter 8. These are among the features of their public performances that make unfamiliar material more digestible for audiences with little or no previous exposure to Maroon music and dance and that make cultural group performances aesthetically and operationally aligned with a cosmopolitan folkloric aesthetic.

2. For a more exhaustive discussion and comparison of the salient features of these three groups and their operation, see Campbell 2012b.

3. Fish writes: "The concept is simply the rigorous and disinterested asking of the question, what does this word, phrase, sentence, paragraph, chapter, novel, play, poem, [and here we might add performance genre or traditional form] *do*?" (1980, 26).

4. Weber 1947, 110. See Bauman (2007, 27) for additional commentary.

5. The term can also be used to mean a corner in a more general sense (Kenneth Bilby, pers. comm., 2011).

6. For commentary on African Diasporic experiences of longing and loss, see Hartman (2008) and Marschall (2015).

7. Mosis received substantial training as a research assistant under the direction of the ethnomusicologist Terry Agerkop at the Ministry of Culture Studies during this same period. Among the places where Kifoko members conducted research are Santigron, Marchall Creek, Brokopondo, Alasabaka, and Langetabbetje.

8. The nature guide Giovanni Courtar identifies the bird as the plain-crowned spinetail (*Synallaxis gujanensis*).

9. As noted in chapter 1, loketo is a local adaptation of Congolese soukous. By including loketo in its repertoire, Fiamba places Maroon cultural and expressive traditions in direct dialogue with broader African and African Diasporic genres and sets the project of the cultural group as extending beyond the practice and preservation of Maroon traditional styles from past generations.

10. Interestingly, with the exception of André Mosis, the other two groups discussed here had few or no examples of people who as individuals outside of their respective groups achieved a similar kind of public recognition as performers.

11. Lante alleges that initially Saisa was to be called Kifoko of Santigron, but Kifoko insisted the new group choose another name. To my knowledge, Saisa is the only Maroon cultural group operating during my study period that used an acronym. Eduard Fonkel and Dansi Waterberg, the group's leaders, gave no indication that this name was influenced directly by governmental or NGO programs that make frequent use of acronyms.

12. The historical information that follows comes primarily from interviews by me and the unpublished writings of anthropologist and Santigron resident, Salomon Emanuels.

13. I have received conflicting information about the precise year of Santigron's founding. However, it is clear that the village was established by 1900, and possibly by the late 1800s.

14. For a discussion of the changing attitudes toward Afro-Surinamese religion and cultural expression in the twentieth century, see Lamur (2001).

15. Cyriel Eersteling, pers. comm., 10 October 2009. The majority of Santigron's residents are Catholic, yet the village has a long tradition of peaceable coexistence between practitioners of different religions.

16. Venetiaan is a Creole, not a Maroon, but he is connected to Santigron through marriage.

17. As mentioned in chapter 1 in Eddy Lante's discussion of apinti drumming and in the volatile nature of tuka funerary music, drumming has an important and powerful place in Maroon spiritual practice. Playing songs and drum rhythms associated with lesser deities in the Maroon pantheon and other spirits—even out of ritual context—can risk attracting those spirits, leading to the possibility that a person would become possessed and a spirit would need to be placated.

18. This essay is the primary source for the following historical information about the group's founding and early activities. A translated version of this text is included as an appendix in Campbell 2012b. Here is the Dutch original of the quote: "Op 3 juni 1983 werd een nieuwe ontwikkeling ingezet met het bezoek van een aantal jonge muzikanten van de Alekeband Clemencia, die ruim twee jaar non actief was. Dit bezoek leidde tot een nauwe betrokkenheid van de zangers Abélé Albert Malon, alias Bote, Rudolf Anaje en de percussionist Atiye Balimoi bij Kifoko. Sindsdien hadden er regelmatig 'jamsessies' plaatsgevonden, waarbij er al vroeg een muziekgroep ontstond, 'Kifoko House Band.' Op onregelmatige basis kwam de groep op zondagen bij elkaar, waarbij Aleke muziek werd beoefend. Kifoko House Band kreeg steeds meer vaste vorm. Er werd overgegaan tot de registratie van jonge Marron muzikanten, zangers en dansers.

"Begin augustus 1983 betrok ik samen met mijn echtgenote Laetitia Tojo en onze vijf kinderen het huis aan de Christoffel Kerstenstraat nr.26, dus naast het atelier. Op het erf stond ook een onbewoond bouwvallig huisjes. Dit krotje heb ik samen met Cognac en Tjofoni omgetimmerd tot activiteiten ruimte. . . . Deze ruimte kreeg gauw de naam 'Kifoko Garden.' De muziekoefeningen en discussies die plaatsvonden in het atelier werden voortaan in Kifoko Garden gehouden."

19. Kifoko has participated in Carifesta on multiple occasions, in locations including Suriname, Guyana, Barbados, and Trinidad and Tobago.

20. For a thorough discussion of the role of various senses in the transition of bodily knowledge, see Hahn (2007).

21. The change in status was informal. Age, skill, ties to other core members of the group, consistent attendance, and length of time in the group were all factors that could help a person become a core member. Acceptance as a core member was demonstrated through invitations to participate in public performances; acquiring leadership responsibilities within the group; and, for dancers, being placed among other accomplished dancers and core members in rehearsal.

22. My own early research efforts demonstrate this point. While it was relatively easy to make contact with Kifoko, seeing that it had well-established ties to larger cultural institutions throughout Paramaribo (including the Ministry of Culture Studies, where Mosis got his ethnographic training in the 1980s; the CCS; Alakondre Dron; and the NAKS), connecting with Fiamba and Saisa proved challenging. As someone who was outside their personal and professional networks, I had to spend several weeks pursuing information about these groups before I was able to communicate with either group's leaders or attend a rehearsal. This information circulated almost exclusively through informal networks and by word of mouth. Increasingly, however, social media and on-line resources are helping mitigate some of these challenges, allowing groups to connect with interested parties with relative ease without relying on other institutions to broker connections on their behalf.

23. Wenoeza sported a similar age demographic. Asongo noted that it was far more common for young men to continue in the group for longer durations of time, whereas "If a girl stays in the group five years, you can count yourself lucky" (pers. comm., 19 September 2009). As they reached adulthood, many of Fiamba's female members left the group owing to pregnancy or what Asongo described as jealous boyfriends who didn't want their girlfriends to dance for the enjoyment of the general public. The most senior female dancers in the period 2008–17 were typically in their late teens and early twenties.

24. Group members now rehearsed wearing kawai ankle rattles, whereas before they had used these only in performance. Greater care was taken to ensure that dancers and drummers were communicating with one another, and rehearsals included more pauses to address matters of technique—including correct footwork or pronunciation of lyrics. Many of these changes were brought about by Errel van Dijk, a particularly knowledgeable drummer who joined the group in 2007. Van Dijk had moved to the city from the village of Diitabiki—the political center of Ndyuka society and home to their gaanman, the paramount authority in the Maroon political system—where he had become an accomplished drummer and participated actively in the village's numerous rituals and ceremonies.

25. There were already a number of "gospel" groups that combined music and dance aesthetics from Maroon popular and traditional styles of song and dance (including traditional genres such as sêkêti, awasa, and songe) and popular Afro-Surinamese styles such as *kawina* and kaseko. Gadoe Talentie was a new group, but already it had a larger public presence than was typical of these groups. Herman and Minio Tojo and their mother, Irma Dabenta (all of whom had been long-standing Kifoko members) were part of the new group's leadership. If one didn't pay attention to the lyrical content of their performances or slight differences in members' apparel, Gadoe Talentie and Kikofo appeared quite similar in performance. As was the case when members of Saisa left that group for Tangiba and later Osélé, it was common for audience members to recognize performers they had associated with Kikofo and assume either that the older group had taken a different creative direction or had disbanded.

4. *Awasa*

1. Many of the interrelationships discussed here are also evident in other Surinamese Maroon dance genres. I chose to focus on awasa as it is the one genre that Kifoko, Saisa, and Fiamba shared, and because of its place of prominence in each group.

2. Among the ethnographic works that incorporate both music and dance in analysis are Hahn (2007), Gaunt (2006), Browning (1995), and Kaminsky (2014 and 2015). Although he has not incorporated dance as fully into his analyses, Kofi Agawu (1995 and 2003) has long been a strong proponent of the importance of considering dance when analyzing the musical function of African genres.

3. The tree that produces these seeds (*Thevetia nereifolia*) is also known locally as kawai.

4. Jocelyne Guilbault illustrates many pertinent challenges in defining a genre while maintaining its inherent plurality (Guilbault et al. 1993).

5. This same ensemble is standard for a number of other Eastern Maroon performance styles, including songe, mato, and susa. Furthermore, these drums and their respective roles form the basis for the core drums of the popular musical style aleke.

6. The *kwakwabangi* is generally considered a Creole instrument, related to the Maroon instrument *kwakwa*, which is a long board played with two sticks.

7. The analysis in this section is my attempt to convey the general practices of an awasa performance as I understand them and as they have been described to me. My experience watching and performing with awasa groups far outweighs my experience of the dance form as performed by the general populace in village settings, and I expect that many aspects of the dance's structure and communicative strategies have been formalized, as the pedagogical and presentational structures of the groups are necessarily more formal and unified in character.

8. This point was stressed in my interviews and conversation with André Mosis, André Pakosie, and Eddy Lante. Additionally, Mosis addresses these issues in the online essays posted on his website, www.kingbotho.com (see, for instance, "Apinti, de sprekende drum van de Marrons").

9. While these various meanings tend to be aligned, there are instances in which specificity is needed. When playing the Saamaka dance genre bandámmba, for instance, the highest pitched of the three drums in the ensemble (the pikin doon) functions as the lead (gaan doon).

10. Although in this instance names such as "doonman" or "tunman" are used within a performance role that is gendered male, the suffix "man" when used in this way can refer to a person of either sex. For instance, the words *singiman* (singer) and *boliman* (cook) can refer to either a man or woman.

11. The Creole cultural organization NAKS featured a trio of young female performers who were adept at a variety of percussion styles that are traditionally considered a male domain. It is my opinion that a Maroon group could adopt a similar model without much social resistance—both Kifoko and Fiamba discussed potential opportunities for women to learn and practice the drumming patterns for various dance genres—although at present I imagine that having a female drummer in a group featuring both sexes would be controversial. Additional restrictions would likely apply to a woman during menstruation and to the playing of drums in a spiritual context or their playing imbued with a spiritual valence. Louise Wondel recounted that she used to play the drums as a member of the cultural group Maswa, before she left to found Fiamba in 2001. While she was in Maswa, Wondel was the only woman in the group to perform on the drum.

12. In Saisa and Kifoko, the tun was played with a stick.

13. The drum strokes in the center of the drum are made with the fingers, while more of the hand is used at the rim.

14. A comparable situation in an Ewe drumming ensemble would be the relationship between the *atsimevu* and the *sogo*.

15. This transcription is excerpted from Agerkop and Mosis (1988), provided courtesy of the Department of Culture Studies. The measure markings in this example are included for reference purposes only. Metrical implications are conferred by the song, dance, and (at times) the gaan doon, and without these parts, the metrical organization is ambiguous. Since new material is interspersed between these repeated statements, this recurrence of the opening material would likely go unnoticed.

16. Although less common, some songs (as in the abbreviated chorus of "Kon go diingi labaa," discussed below in this chapter) emphasize three-beat subdivisions. In combination with such songs, there are some variations of the boli wataa dance step that further emphasize the three-beat structure. While the pikin doon is typically the most active in offsetting the implied meter, dancers are able to create a similar dynamism by switching between the regular two-beat boli wataa pattern and the less common three-beat pattern. In both cases, these shifting metrical implications create a subtle source of musical tension throughout the course of performance.

17. Here I use David Locke's definition of "The Time" (1998, 11).

18. Typically, a performance is broken into discrete units (lasting the duration of a single song), during which one or several dancers will perform. The structural uniformity of this process—the ways in which dancers navigate space during and between the units—is magnified in the performances of dance groups, yet songs structure the events in less formal performances as well.

19. In keeping track of these many functions and how they relate to the performance as a whole, readers may find it useful to refer to figure 4.9.

20. Pakosie notes that the drummer can use "Mi kaba kelle kelle" if he wishes to indicate that he is finished or "A kaba kelle kelle" if his message refers to the dancers (pers. comm., 11 May 2012).

21. The word "paata" functions as both a verb and a noun, referring to both the act of dancing in this more vigorous, demonstrative style and the movements associated with that dancing. In staged or formally presented contexts, this style of dancing has a soloistic appearance, though the concept of a solo arises in part due to the framing and circumstances of performance.

22. Water is generally made available to performers at cultural group gigs, and alcohol is available in abundance at several of the events for which awasa is performed. The cultural groups represented in this study had varying positions regarding the consumption of alcohol while performing.

23. The singer of a piki (aka koor) could be referred to as a singiman or pikiman, yet in the groups with which I worked, the term "singiman" was used most often in reference to the lead singer. I also heard the person who sang the piki referred to as the koorman. This change in word usage could be related to a changing perception of the degree of specialization required of a koor singer, as singing the response is increasingly a responsibility shared by a large group of performers. The Dutch word "koor" has obvious associations with a Christian religious context, but it may also have gained prominence through singing terminology used in primary education. I have chosen to use the term "koor" for the response phrase rather than the Okanisi term that predated it (piki) because "koor" best represents the word usage among the groups in Paramaribo during the period of my research.

24. Due to the duple organization of their footwork and their swaying bodies as they step "left, together, right, together," dancers alternate waving their left and right hands.

25. Other groups, including Tjotjo Baka Oemang of Saint-Laurent-du-Maroni, French Guiana, have designated koor singers. Most groups have multiple lead singers, in which case those who are not singing the lead for a designated piece lead the koor.

26. Notably, this group had the smallest regular membership of the three, therefore augmenting the performance responsibilities of each member.

27. This is not an exclusively urban phenomenon, as public address systems are by now common equipment at funerary rites and other major occasions taking place in villages in Suriname's interior.

28. The principles behind the interchange between lead and koor (and also to some degree the communicative dynamics between singers, drummers, and dancers) are implemented widely in Maroon song and dance, both traditional and popular. For example, the similarities between awasa and aleke are immediately apparent.

29. This is one example in which the element of repetition alters the significance of the material being sung—the incessant repetition of the song, in which both call and response are reiterating a response to an imagined request, conveys a sense that they are reacting to a relentless demand. See Monson (1999) for a relevant discussion of the functions of repetition in music.

30. The frequency of this trill or vibrato and the exact intervals in it are subject to variation (though most commonly the intervals are between neighboring pitches in a pentatonic scale). Loli is not exclusive to older genres of music; it is also implemented in popular styles from aleke to kaseko. The veteran aleke band Bigi Ting is known for its elaborate song introductions with liberal use of loli ornamentation, while Norma Sante (lead singer for the kaskawi band Naks Kaseko Loco), is an example of a singer from a younger generation who uses the same technique.

31. This audio example (audio track 3 in the supplementary materials) is taken from Pakosie 2002 in the discography, track 34. The audio was provided by the Sabanapeti Foundation.

32. An important consideration to keep in mind is that the assembled singers in Pakosie's recording were not members of a single performing group that rehearsed together regularly. In song as well as percussion and dance, having regular rehearsals of established performing groups encourages greater uniformity among their members.

33. Such moves in awasa dancing predate hip-hop and speak to a more general aesthetic continuity. That said, there have been young dancers who have explored some of these connections. In 2009, some of the young men from Kifoko collaborated with the Paramaribo-based hip-hop group Mystikal, aiming to put these styles into more overt dialogue. Mystikal is an interethnic dance group, with a number of Maroon members.

34. I use the term "fundamental step" to describe the stepping sequence most common in boli wataa and also umanpikinfutu. Although the dancing sequences of *mannengeefutu* vary more widely, the fundamental posture and step continue to inform the positions and footwork in this more improvisatory style.

35. This is a classic example of what Robert Farris Thompson refers to as an "aesthetic of the cool" (1973).

36. To clarify, dancers in an awasa dance would not go through this set of movements but rather would lower their center of gravity directly from the upright posture of the boli wataa dance move.

37. In Kifoko rehearsals in which time was devoted to singing practice, this was stated explicitly as a suggestion to help novice singers maintain rhythmic accuracy.

38. This style of waka kon or waka gwe was one that many associate with the Maroon genre songe, mentioned above.

39. I describe paata as "soloistic" in an attempt to convey the character of this move, though the notion of a solo as such does not necessarily apply—especially when awasa is being danced by a community at large as opposed to a cultural group. The movement style I refer to as umanpikinfutu is also called *umasamafutu*, which can be translated roughly as "woman foot."

40. Other examples include "gii piimisi," to beg pardon, and "gii mato," to exchange riddles. Both these examples have an interactive framework that underscores the point I make with "gii da" and "gii odi."

41. City residents often truncate these verbal exchanges, and further research is necessary to determine whether a similar process is under way in nonverbal exchanges. I contend that those exchanges between drummers and dancers that rely on kumanti'pinti are becoming abbreviated and are diminishing in their complexity, but it is more difficult to determine whether the gii futu has changed in character. Further research would be especially interesting because the patterns exchanged in the gii futu are not, to my knowledge, imbued with lexical meaning, and therefore the character of this exchange is not directly threatened by a dwindling knowledge of any particular language system.

42. These are trends that I have observed in the course of watching hundreds of dancers over a period of years. As finer points of style and as microgestures, they were seldom the topic of explicit discussion by cultural group members or Maroon audiences, but they were features that were used by dancers whose style drew comment as being particularly "*mooi* or alternatively *taanga* or *flexi*—the same words that people used to articulate the explicitly gendered ideals the dance upholds. In rehearsal and pedagogical scenarios, dancers emphasized these features in moments when they wished to draw attention to stylistic differences between umanpikinfutu and mannengeefutu.

43. A possible fourth performance role—undoubtedly an important feature of a successful performance—is the interjection of commentary and praise (physical, musical, or speech-derived) in relation to the events that transpire within the performance. All performers can play this fourth role in some form, and it is also the primary mode of participation open to onlookers. Of the performers, the saka player (if there is one), the koor, and the resting dancers are ideally situated to participate in this way.

44. A prime example of how koti manifests itself in dance is through the sharp movements of a dancer's hips in the Saamaka dance bandámmba (also termed banamba). These moves are called "koti a mindi" or just "koti mindi" (cut the middle or waist).

45. While I certainly support Agawu's general point, I find that the universality of this cognitive experience and the primacy of the feet as dancers' de facto site of articulation are both contestable points.

46. Saisa's recording sessions, discussed in chapter 3, provide one example of such a situation.

5. *Alakondre Dron*

1. In Suriname, this particular slogan was first adopted by the Vooruitstrevende Hervormingspartij (Progressive Reform Party), which is considered a predominantly Hindustani party, as it aligns well with The Hindustani politician Jaggernath Lachmon's *verbroederingspolitiek* (politics of fraternity). As Rosemarijn Hoefte notes, the phrase has gained more general acceptance in the twenty-first century (2014a, 141).

2. This distribution is largely a by-product of colonial legacies of slavery, indentured labor, and trade. Hoefte notes: "The state functioned as a recruiter of labour and a distributor of the spatial location of work and land. In colonial times, the state never acted as a neutral arbiter of interethnic relations, as the pluralists would have it, and in the postcolonial era the state remained an actor in ethnic conflict because of its varied institiutions, including schools" (ibid., 129). Pointing out that the earliest political parties in the 1940s reflected religious rather than ethnic divisions, Dew argues against treating the country's political divisions along ethnic lines as an inevitable outgrowth of long-standing

tensions between ethnic groups, which Dutch colonists had constructed and used to their political advantage (1996, 195).

3. For more on consociationalist politics, see Lijphart 1969. Dew's concept of apanjaht consociationalism drew significantly from Lijphart, according to Tjon Sie Fat's summary (2009, 11). For a further discussion of ethnopolitics, see Tjon Sie Fat (2009, 10).

4. Tjon Sie Fat explains that the word comes from "apan ('my own') and ját ('sub-caste / caste; ethnic group; race; lineage; tribe; community; nation')" (2009, 9).

5. Dew takes care to clarify that although ethnicity is firmly entrenched in the country's political logic, the multiplicity of voices representing each ethnic group (combined with a host of influential factors such as class and religion) mitigates against predetermined outcomes. He argues that "while ethnicity remains paramount in the structuring of policies of Suriname, intra-ethnic cultural and other divisions provide both the issues and resources for factionalism" (1996, 19).

6. Tjon Sie Fat sees Amerindian and Maroon efforts to lobby for land rights as a potential exception.

7. Adhin advocated "unity in diversity," from which Lachmon later conceptualized verbroederingspolitiek, as noted above. For a thorough exploration of these expressions of multicultural relations, see Marshall 2003.

8. At various points in the past, Alakondre Dron has also included Chinese and Lebanese performers, and the Creole and Maroon representatives have at times been represented by more than one group, but to function, all of Mama Sranan's five children have been represented. In the former Surinamese national flag (which featured a circle of five stars) and in Jozef Klas's *Mama Sranan* (figure 5.1), the initial groups represented were Amerindian, Afro-Surinamese, Javanese, Hindustani, white or European.

9. The cultural group Wenoeza began performing in Alakondre Dron in the 2010s. Like Fiamba, Wenoeza's membership tended to be significantly younger than that of Kifoko. In contrast to Kifoko, Wenoeza included in their regular repertoire popular forms such as aleke and loketo. Especially since Kifoko's dancers tended to be the most senior women in the group, the addition of Wenoeza was believed to give Alakondre Dron some younger Maroon representatives.

10. Tjon was cofounder and codirector of the Doe-Theater company with Thea Doelwijt. For an extended discussion, see Ockhorst 2014.

11. In Tjon Sie Fat's text, Ganga's formula relates to "state-sponsored celebrations of multiethnicity." I have changed the wording because although the state commissions Alakondre Dron to perform at an array of nationalistic events, it does not allocate resources to keep the group afloat.

12. These are tropes in the sense that they are "common or overused themes" (Merriam-Webster, "trope," accessed 8 August 2019, https://www.merriam-webster.com/dic-

tionary/trope). The wording I use to label each trope is my own, but the ubiquity of each message is thoroughly established in nationalist political texts, performance structures, and visual representations. In fact, part of my argument is that the nature of the tropes' message and meaning is performative as much as it is verbal.

13.   While the intention was to depict each group's religious practice, this did not mean that all performers occupied roles in the performance that coincided with their own spiritual beliefs. Some of the Kifoko members who were charged with depicting spirit possession were devout Christians who would not take part in such events as a part of their own spiritual practice.

14.   This initiative was headed by the strategic communication and branding bureau STAS International.

15.   René Gompers, "'Ala Kondre Dron' bevestigt Surinaamse autoriteit op Cuba," 4 July 2014, http://werkgroepcaraibischeletteren.nl/ala-kondre-dron-bevestigt-surinaamse-autoriteit-op-cuba/.

16.   Paul Beaudry, "Rhythm Road Central American Tour: 2010—Suriname," 20 October 2010, http://paulbeaudry.com/2010/10/20/rhythm-road-central-american-tour-2010-suriname/. Beaudry's comments came after a collaboration with the group on 10 October. He had come to Suriname with his jazz ensemble, Pathways, as part of the US State Department's Rhythm Road, a cultural ambassadorship program. The synergy between political and musical performance played a large part in his own creative projects.

17.   All subsequent quotes by Beaudry come from the same personal communication.

18.   Mamio quilts provide a clear example of how Creole culture and imagery can infuse a national narrative, promoting a notion of integration that underscores Creole identity while celebrating cultural intermixture. In terms of their visual organization, however, mamio quilts maintain the divisions between sources rather than an intermixture.

19.   Either explanation satisfies nationalist inclinations, the former implying a unique Surinamese character or disposition and the latter giving the impression of good fortune that these various people should converge, in place of a more sinister account of the colonial acts and interests of which this diversity is a result.

20.   For a description of a similar phenomena as the Ghana Dance Ensemble changes leadership, see Schauert (2006–7).

6. *The Avondvierdaagse*

1.   The AVD also includes a junior division for children, who start earlier in the day and complete a separate five-kilometer route for each day. Like the adult participants, the groups in the junior division represent various social groups, businesses, or other organizations from political parties to bottled water companies.

2. Prizes are awarded in "general," "business," and "cultural" classes. The general class awards prizes to the oldest participants and in regard to various subthemes, such as the most harmonious and the most disciplined. Prizes are determined by a panel of judges, with the exception of the people's choice category in each class.

3. The event was founded by the Nederlandse Bond voor Lichlamelijke Opvoeding (the Dutch League for Physical Education). The vast majority of the organization's members were military personnel ("The Complete History of the Four Days' Marches," November 2012, https://www.4daagse.nl/images/stories/files/Historische_weetjes/Geschiedenis_van_de_VierdaagseEN.pdf).

4. In addition to businesses being represented by employees walking in groups as part of the parade, major donors could establish their own media hot spots at which they could sell products and promote their services. Besides the Fernandes Company (discussed below), perennial participants and sponsors included Tele-G (an internet and mobile service provider) and Parbo Beer.

5. Note that within the NDP group, supporters (particularly those who chose to dress in an ethnically coded way) tended to walk alongside others from the same ethnic group. This calls to mind Rosemarijn Hoefte's observation that a nonaligned party's seats in parliament still tend to be parsed according to a logic of ethnic representation—the party is not so much "nonethnic" as it is subdivided among representatives of multiple ethnicities (2014a, 139).

6. This provides an interesting counterpoint with the novice members who join Kifoko but never or seldom perform with the group, as discussed in chapter 3. Together, these examples serve as a reminder that both practice and performance can motivate people to join a group, but the relationship between these facets of group activity can vary significantly, and interest in one facet of group operation does not necessarily mean a person will participate actively in the other.

7. Men developed their own fashion alternatives to the kamisa to indicate pride in and connection to their Maroon heritage. During the time of my fieldwork, it was common for men to wear a length of plaid fabric as a scarf over their everyday street attire. As a new trend and current fashion, the same material worn in a different way had the potential to seem current rather than provincial. For a further discussion of similar innovations in Maroon fashion, see S. Price 2003.

8. The praise and acceptance one receives for overt cultural affiliation on the occasion of a major event or holiday is likely to be more positive than if it is practiced on a daily basis. Cultural performance on an overt level is regulated in various ways that allow for display on the one hand, but also potentially fight off the likelihood that these practices would be normalized.

9. Sandrine said in Okanisi: "Di mi be waka Wandelmars, fotosama be piki, 'Anga a fatu fu i ya, nee I e dansi?!' Mi taiga den, 'Fatu a na noti, fatu a na nix. U a sabi san na

fatu.' Di u si fatu, fa u o kai en? Fa i de ya, i na̍e nyoni tumisi, i n'ae bigi tumisi, i n'ae fatu tumisi, i n'ae mangii, tumisi i n'ae nix. Wan sani san i lobi, toch, di i do en, leli i leli en da i o do en. . . . Nanga san Gadu gi yu, toch?"

10. Asongo couched his reflections in terms of national politics, but my presence was read as that of a foreigner. Many people assumed I was a tourist or a Peace Corps volunteer and derived significance from my participation in terms of international rather than national politics. I found myself embroiled in a representational politics that was deeply troubling to me, and knowing what I do now, I would have made different decisions about the nature of my participation. For some time afterward, I was something of a local celebrity—people frequently recognized me on the street and would greet me with references to the event or even request a picture with me. One unanticipated benefit of my participation was that at many points during the event, Maroons whom I didn't know would approach me and start conversations about their own relationships with traditional music and dance.

11. In chapter 5, I noted how the politics of participation are such that the stakes and social implications of "mee doen" depend largely on contextual and intersectional factors. I maintain that my status as a white woman and a foreigner (among other factors) facilitated my participation and shaped its social meaning.

7. *Subversive Choreographies*

1. See, for instance, Kofi Agawu's argument for characterizing musics as being "truly African" versus "uniquely African" (2016, 18; see also Agawu 2003, chapter 7).

2. See chapter 2. Additionally, Richard Price (1995) details the importance of arguing for cultural autonomy in claiming reparations for human rights violations committed during Suriname's civil war in 1986–92. For a more comprehensive treatment of Maroon resistance struggles, and the role of Maroon cultural practice therein, see R. Price (2011).

3. Eduard received some criticism from Maroon community members for spritzing his imaginary cologne below the waist. In later performances he frequently omitted this move. This decision is indicative of a broader social shift—among Maroons in the city as well as in many villages—in which sexual allusions and innuendo that have long been a source of play and humor have become increasingly restricted. Such shifts are especially evident among community members who identify themselves as Christian and who have espoused ideas of modesty and proper decorum that are derived from the church. Louise Wondel provided another example from Fiamba's repertoire. She noted the differences between the dancing in one of the group's pieces accompanied by a song, "Sampalanga," which was initially presented as a double entendre—at once imitating the back and forth motion of felling a tree with a hand saw and alluding to a sex act. She recalled how, in the earlier years of the group's operation, much fun was made of the sexual innuendo, whereas

the movement as it was performed at that time (in the late 2000s, under the direction of her nephew Clifton, a devout Christian) took a far more literal interpretation.

4. Richard and Sally Price describe having seen Saamakan sêkêti dancers incorporate the theme of preparing one's toilette into their dancing as early as the 1960s (pers. comm., 11 May 2019). Richard Price indicated that Saamaka performers touring the United States in the early 1980s used this thematic material in their public presentations abroad. My point is not that Eduard (or Benny, in the following case study) are the first to draw upon these references; rather, it is that his use and interpretation of them in the context of a series of solos demonstrates strategic and personal choices.

5. Here I draw primarily from a phone interview we had in April 2011. This interview was preceded by informal discussions of the choreography in 2009 that were similarly inconclusive.

6. The argument could be made that indoor plumbing, while it may be available in some newer buildings in camps and villages, does do some contextualizing work—if not by location alone, then by the confluence of economic status and geographic location.

7. Tangiba, the other major cultural group hailing from Santigron in 2008–9, elicited exactly the kind of crowd response Benny predicted when one of its youngest members interspersed many of Michael Jackson's signature movements throughout his solo routine. This particular solo was a consistent highlight of their performances in 2008–9, owing to the youth and undeniable talent of the performer and his ability to switch between the two styles of dance with confidence and deftness. Following news of Michael Jackson's death in 2009, this routine took on additional significance as a tribute to the pop icon.

8. It was clear that the doctor was perplexed about why I did not take care of the matter on my own, rather than visiting him. Indeed, if I had been able to diagnose myself, I would have taken care of the parasite in a manner similar to what Benny portrays in his skit. If anyone's behavior here is to be deemed weird, it is my own.

9. In subsequent performances, a few of Saisa's other accomplished female dancers would dance in Debora's stead. This piece was typically danced to the song "Te Mi Ede Go," which was also considered to be one of Debora's signature songs. In performance, for this song she often assumed the role of lead singer as opposed to featured dancer.

REFERENCES

Discography

Agerkop, Terry, and André Mosis. 1988. "Drum Rhythms of the Aukaner Maroons." Paramaribo: Suriname Department of Culture Studies. Unpublished audio recording recorded on January 24.

Bilby, Kenneth. 2011. *Music from Aluku: Maroon Sounds of Struggle, Solace, and Survival.* Washington: Smithsonian Folkways Recording.

Ducoudray, Mathieu. 2009. "Festival Awassa, Saint-Laurent du Maroni, Guyane Française, Juin 2009." 1 December. Video file. https://www.youtube.com/watch?v=-jzGdm0k078.

Ghana Junior All-Stars and Pikin fu Fiamba. 2001. *Ghana Junior All-Stars and Pikin fu Fiamba in Holland.* Amsterdam: Friends Studio.

Pakosie, André R. M. 2002. *I Greet the New Day: Classical Songs and Music of the Ndyuka Maroons of Suriname.* Recorded and annotated by André R. M. Pakosie. Utrecht, the Netherlands: Stichting Sabanapeti. CD.

Price, Richard, and Sally Price. 1977. *Music from Saramaka.* New York: Folkways Records.

Saisa. 2009. *Culturele Group Saisa Vol. 4.* Paramaribo.

Wondel, Louise. 1998. *Ten.* Paramaribo: n.p.

Print Sources

Abrahams, Roger D. 2005. *Everyday Life: A Poetics of Vernacular Practices.* Philadelphia: University of Pennsylvania Press.

Abu-Lughod, Lila. 1990. "The Romance of Resistance: Tracing Transformations of Power through Bedouin Women." *American Ethnologist* 17 (1): 41–55.

Adhin, Jñan Hansdew. 1998. "Eenheid in verscheidenheid." In *Cultuur en maatshappij: Veertig artikelen van Jnan H. Adhin.*, edited by H. R. Nehorst, 34–38. Paramaribo: Prakashan.

Agawu, Kofi. 1995. *African Rhythm: A Northern Ewe Perspective.* Cambridge: Cambridge University Press.

———. 2003. *Representing African Music: Postcolonial Notes, Queries, Positions*. New York: Routledge.

———. 2016. *The African Imagination in Music*. New York: Oxford University Press.

Agerkop, Terry. 2000. "Sekéti: Poetic and Musical Eloquence among the Saramaka Maroons from Suriname." PhD diss., University of Brasilia.

Albright, Ann Cooper. 2010. *Choreographing Difference: The Body and Identity in Contemporary Dance*. Middletown, CT: Wesleyan University Press.

Alleyne, Dillon, Michael Hendrickson, Sheldon McLean, Machel Pantin, Nyasha Skerrette, and Don Charlse. 2018. "Economic Survey of the Caribbean 2017." Santiago, Chile: United Nations.

Anderson, Benedict. 1983. *Imagined Communities: Reflections on the Growth and Spread of Nationalism*. New York: Verso.

Anzaldúa, Gloria. 2012. *Borderlands/La Frontera*. 4th ed. San Francisco, CA: Aunt Lute Books.

Appiah, Kwame Anthony. 2006. *Cosmopolitanism: Ethics in a World of Strangers*. New York: W. W. Norton.

Arnold, A. James, ed. 2001. *A History of Literature in the Caribbean*. Vol. 2, *English- and Dutch-Speaking Region*. Amsterdam: John Benjamins.

Bakboord, Carla. 2012. "Wan poku boskopu: Jonge Surinaamse musici laten hun stem horen." *Oso* 13 (1): 10–25.

Barz, Gregory, and Timothey J. Cooley, eds. 2008. *Shadows in the Field: New Perspectives for Fieldwork in Ethnomusicology*. New York: Oxford University Press.

Bauman, Zygmunt. 1991. *Modernity and Ambivalence*. Cambridge: Polity.

———. 2007. *Consuming Life*. Cambridge: Polity.

Bhabha, Homi K. 1994. *The Location of Culture*. London: Routledge.

———. 1996. "Unsatisfied: Notes on Vernacular Cosmopolitanism," In *Text and Nation: Cross-Disciplinary Essays on Cultural and National Identities*, edited by Laura García-Moreno and Peter C. Pfeiffer, 191–207. Columbia, SC: Camden House.

———, ed. 2013. *Nation and Narration*. London: Routledge.

Bilby, Kenneth M. 1990. "The Remaking of the Aluku: Culture, Politics, and Maroon Ethnicity in French South America." PhD diss., University of Michigan.

———. 1997. "Swearing by the Past, Swearing to the Future: Sacred Oaths, Alliances, and Treaties among the Guianese and Jamaican Maroons." *Ethnohistory* 44 (4): 655–89.

———. 1999. "'Roots Explosion': Indigenization and Cosmopolitanism in Contemporary Surinamese Popular Music." *Ethnomusicology* 43 (2): 256–96.

———. 2000. "Making Modernity in the Hinterlands: New Maroon Musics in the Black Atlantic." *Popular Music* 19 (3): 265–292.

———. 2001a. "Aleke: New Music and New Identities in the Guianas." *Latin American Music Review* 22 (1): 31–47.

———. 2001b. "New Sounds from a New Nation: Processes of Globalisation and Indigenisation in Surinamese Popular Music." In *Twentieth-Century Suriname. Continuities and Discontinuities in a New World Society*, edited by Rosemarijin Hoefte and Peter Meel, 296–328. Kingston, Jamaica: Ian Randle.

Bilby, Kenneth M., and Rivke Jaffe. 2018. "'Real Businengue': Guianese Maroon Music in Transition." In *Maroon Cosmopolitics: Personhood, Creativity and Incorporation*, edited by Olívia Maria Gomes da Cunha, 330–49. Leiden, the Netherlands: Brill.

Blanco-Borelli, Melissa. 2016. *She Is Cuba: A Genealogy of the Mulatta Body*. New York: Oxford University Press.

Bourdieu, Pierre. 1984. *Distinction: A Social Critique of the Judgement of Taste*. Translated by Richard Nice. Cambridge, MA: Harvard University Press.

Browning, Barbara. 1995. *Samba: Resistance in Motion*. Bloomington: Indiana University Press.

Campbell, Corinna. 2012a. "Aleke," "Bigi poku," "Kaseko," "Kawina," and "Suripop" entries. In *The Encyclopedia for Popular Musics of the World*, edited by David Horn and John Shepherd, 9:21–23, 56–58, 410–12, 412–13, and 814–16, New York: Continuum.

———. 2012b. "Personalizing Tradition: Surinamese Maroon Music and Dance in Contemporary Urban Practice." PhD diss., Harvard University.

———. 2018. "Modeling Cultural Adaptability: Maroon Cosmopolitanism and the Banamba Dance Contest." In *Maroon Cosmopolitics: Personhood, Creativity and Incorporation*, edited by Olívia Maria Gomes da Cunha, 307–29. Leiden, the Netherlands: Brill.

Carlin, Eithne B., Isabelle Léglise, Bettina Migge, and Paul B. Tjon Sie Fat. 2014. *In and out of Suriname: Language, Mobility, and Identity*. Leiden, the Netherlands: Brill.

Clifford, James, and George E. Marcus, eds. 1986. *Writing Cultures: The Poetics and Politics of Ethnography*. Berkeley: University of California Press.

Connell, Robert J. 2017. "The Political Ecology of Maroon Autonomy: Land, Resource Extraction and Political Change in 21st Century Jamaica and Suriname." PhD diss., University of California, Berkeley.

Counter, S. Allen, and David L. Evans. 1981. *I Sought My Brother: An Afro-American Reunion*. Cambridge, MA: MIT Press.

Cunha, Olívia Maria Gomes da. 2018. "Self-Fashioning and Visualization among the Cottica Ndyuka." In *Maroon Cosmopolitics: Personhood, Creativity and Incorporation*, edited by Maria Gomes da Cunha, 268–306. Leiden, the Netherlands: Brill.

Daniel, Yvonne. 2011. *Caribbean and Atlantic Diaspora Dance: Igniting Citizenship*. Urbana: University of Illinois Press.

De Bruijne, G. A. 1979. "The Lebanese in Suriname." *Boletín de estudios Latinoamericanos y del Caribe*, no. 26, 15–37.

De Certeau, Michel. 1984. *The Practice of Everyday Life*. Translated by Steven Rendall. Berkeley: University of California Press.

Dew, Edward. 1994. *The Trouble in Suriname, 1975–1993*. Westport, CT: Praeger.

———. 1996. *The Difficult Flowering of Surinam: Ethnicity and Politics in a Plural Society*. Paramaribo: Vaco N.V.

Dudley, Shannon. 2008. *Music from behind the Bridge: Steelband Aesthetics and Politics in Trinidad and Tobago*. New York: Oxford University Press.

Emanuels, Salomon. 2011. "Maroons in Suriname and National Identity: Contributing to the Construction of National Identity in Suriname." In *The African Heritage in Brazil and the Caribbean*, edited by Carlos Henrique Cardim and Rubens Gama Dias Filho, 277–94. Brasília, Brazil: Fundação Alexandre de Gusmão.

Fabian, Johannes. 1983. *Time and the Other: How Anthropology Makes Its Object*. New York: Columbia University Press.

Feld, Steven. 1984. "Communication, Music, and Speech about Music." *Yearbook for Traditional Music* 16:1–18.

———. 1988. "Aesthetics as Iconicity of Style, or 'Lift-Up-Over Sounding': Getting into the Kaluli Groove." *Yearbook for Traditional Music* 20:74–113.

Feldman, Heidi Carolyn. 2006. *Black Rhythms of Peru: Reviving African Musical Heritage in the Black Pacific*. Middletown, CT: Wesleyan University Press.

Fish, Stanley E. 1976. "Interpreting the 'Variorum.'" *Critical Inquiry* 2 (3): 465–85.

———. 1980. *Is There a Text in This Class? The Authority of Interpretive Communities*. Cambridge, MA: Harvard University Press.

Foucault, Michel. 1978. *The History of Sexuality*. Vol. 1, *An Introduction*. Translated by Robert Hurley. New York: Random House.

———. 1988. *Technologies of the Self: A Seminar with Michel Foucault*. Edited by Luther H. Martin, Huck Gutman, and Patrick H. Hutton. Amherst: University of Massachusetts Press.

Gandhi, Leela. 2006. *Affective Communities: Anticolonial Thought, Fin-de-Siècle Radicalism, and the Politics of Friendship*. Durham, NC: Duke University Press.

Ganga, Sharda. 2004. "Contemporary Theatre in Suriname; Lost in the Search for a National Culture." Paper presented at the conference "Globalisation, Diaspora and Identity Formation," University of Suriname, Paramaribo, 26–29 February.

———. 2014. "Identiteit? Bij Kid Dynamite." *De Ware Tijd*, 15 February.

Gaunt, Kyra. 2006. *The Games Black Girls Play: Learning the Ropes from Double-Dutch to Hip-Hop*. New York: New York University Press.

Geertz, Clifford. 1960. "The Javanese Kijaji: The Changing Role of a Cultural Broker." *Comparative Studies in Society and History* 2 (2): 228–49.

———. 1973. *The Interpretation of Cultures*. New York: Basic Books.

George-Graves, Nadine. 2010. *Urban Bush Women: Twenty Years of African American Dance Theater, Community Engagement, and Working It Out*. Madison: University of Wisconsin Press.

Geurts, Kathryn Linn. 2002. *Culture and the Senses: Bodily Ways of Knowing in an African Community*. Berkeley: University of California Press.

Gilbert, Will G. 1940. *Een en ander over de Negroide muziek van Suriname*. Amsterdam: Koloniaal Instituut Koninklijke Vereeniging.

Groot, Silvia W. de. 2009. *Agents of Their Own Emancipation: Topics in the History of Surinam Maroons*. Amsterdam: self-published.

Guilbault, Jocelyne, Gage Averill, Édouard Benoit, and Gregory Rabess. 1993. *Zouk: World Music in the West Indies*. Chicago: University of Chicago Press.

Guss, David M. 2000. *The Festive State: Race, Ethnicity, and Nationalism as Cultural Performance*. Berkeley: University of California Press.

Hagedorn, Katherine J. 2001. *Divine Utterances: The Performance of Afro-Cuban Santería*. Washington: Smithsonian Institution Press.

Hahn, Tomie. 2006. "Emerging Voices: Encounters with Reflexivity." *Atlantis* 30 (2): 88–99.

———. 2007. *Sensational Knowledge: Embodying Culture through Japanese Dance*. Middletown, CT: Wesleyan University Press.

Hamad, Ruby. 2018. "How White Women Use Strategic Tears to Silence Women of Colour." *Guardian*, May 7. https://www.theguardian.com/commentisfree/2018/may/08/how-white-women-use-strategic-tears-to-avoid-accountability.

Hartman, Saidiya. 2008. *Lose Your Mother: A Journey along the Atlantic Slave Route*. New York: Macmillan.

Hellier-Tinoco, Ruth. 2011. *Embodying Mexico: Tourism, Nationalism, and Performance*. New York: Oxford University Press.

Herskovits, Melville Jean. 1941. *The Myth of the Negro Past*. Boston: Beacon Press

Herskovits, Melville Jean, and Frances Shapiro Herskovits. 1934. *Rebel Destiny: Among the Bush Negroes of Dutch Guiana*. New York: Whittlesey House.

———. 1936. *Surinam Folk-Lore*. New York: Columbia University Press.

Herzfeld, Michael. 1985. *The Poetics of Manhood: Contest and Identity in a Cretan Mountain Village*. Princeton, NJ: Princeton University Press.

———. 2004. *The Body Impolitic: Artisans and Artifice in the Global Hierarchy of Value*. Chicago: University of Chicago Press.

———. 2005. *Cultural Intimacy: Social Politics in the Nation-State*. New York: Routledge.

Higman, B. W. 1999. *General History of the Caribbean*. Vol 6, *Methodology and Historiography of the Caribbean*. Hong Kong: United Nations Educational, Scientific and Cultural Organization.

Hoefte, Rosemarijn. 2014a. "Mama Sranan's Children: Ethnicity and Nation Building in Postcolonial Suriname." *Journal of Caribbean History* 48 (1–2): 128–48.

———. 2014b. *Suriname in the Long Twentieth Century: Domination, Contestation, Globalization*. New York: Palgrave Macmillan.

Hoefte, Rosemarijn, and Peter Meel, eds. 2001. *Twentieth-Century Suriname. Continuities and Discontinuities in a New World Society*. Kingston, Jamaica: Ian Randle.

Hoerburger, Felix. 1968. "Once Again: On the Concept of 'Folk Dance.'" *Journal of the International Folk Music Council* 20:30–32.

Hoogbergen, Wim. 1990. *The Boni Maroon Wars in Suriname*. Leiden, the Netherlands: Brill.

Jaffe, Rivke, and Jolien Sanderse. 2009. "Surinamese Maroons as Reggae Artistes: Music, Marginality and Urban Space." In *Ethnic and Racial Studies* 33 (9): 1561–79.

Johnson, Walter P. 2003. "On Agency." *Journal of Social History* 37 (1): 113–24.

Kambel, Ellen-Rose. 2006. "Policy Note on Indigenous Peoples and Maroons in Suriname." Washington: Inter-American Development Bank.

Kaminsky, David. 2014. "Total Rhythm in Three Dimensions: Towards a Motional Theory of Melodic Dance Rhythm in Swedish Polska Music." *Dance Research* 32 (1): 43–64.

———. 2015. "Music, Dance and the Art of Seduction." *Ethnomusicology Forum* 24 (2): 290–92.

Kedhar, Anusha. 2014. "Flexibility and Its Bodily Limits: Transnational South Asian Dancers in an Age of Neoliberalism." *Dance Research Journal* 46 (1): 23–40.

Kondo, Dorinne K. 1990. *Crafting Selves: Power, Gender, and Discourses of Identity in a Japanese Workplace*. Chicago: University of Chicago Press.

Kurin, Richard. 1997. *Reflections of a Culture Broker: A View from the Smithsonian*. Washington: Smithsonian Institution Press.

Lamur, Humphrey E. 2001. "The Evolution of Afro-Surinamese National Movements (1955–1995)." *Transforming Anthropology* 10 (1): 17–27.

Late Night with Kgomotso Matsunyane. 2011. 25 February. https://www.youtube.com/watch?v=YBkGg44h8FM.

Lijphart, Arend. 1969. "Consociational Democracy." *World Politics* 21 (2): 207–25.

Locke, David. 1998. *Drum Gahu: An Introduction to African Rhythm*. Tempe, AZ: White Cliffs Media.

Manuel, Peter, Kenneth Bilby, and Michael Largey. 1995. *Caribbean Currents: Caribbean Music from Rumba to Reggae*. Philadelphia: Temple University Press.

Marschall, Sabine. 2015. "'Homesick Tourism': Memory, Identity and (Be)longing." *Current Issues in Tourism* 18 (9): 876–92.

Marshall, Edwin Kenneth. 2003. *Ontstaan en ontwikkeling van het Surinaams nationalisme: Natievorming als opgave*. Delft, the Netherlands: Eburon.

Martinus-Guda, Trudi, and Hillary de Bruin. 2005. *Drie eeuwen banya: De geschiedenis van een Surinaamse slavendans*. Paramaribo: Ministerie van Onderwijs en Volksontwikkeling Directoraat Cultuur.

Meagher, Arnold J. 2008. *The Coolie Trade: The Traffic of Chinese Laborers to Latin America, 1847–1874*. Bloomington, IN: Xlibris.

McLeod, Cynthia, and Hannah C. Draaibar. 2007. *Paramaribo: Stad van harmonische tegenstelling*. Paramaribo: Uitgevrij Conserve.

Meel, Peter. 1998. "Towards a Typology of Suriname Nationalism." *New West Indian Guide/ Nieuwe West-Indische gids* 72 (3–4): 257–81.

Melyon-Reinette, Stéphanie, ed. 2012. *Marronage and Arts: Revolts in Bodies and Voices*. Newcastle upon Tyne, UK: Cambridge Scholars.

Mendoza, Zoila S. 1999. "Genuine but Marginal: Exploring and Reworking Social Contradictions through Ritual Dance Performance." *Journal of Latin American Anthropology* 3 (2): 86–117.

———. 2008. *Creating Our Own: Folklore, Performance, and Identity in Cuzco, Peru*. Durham, NC: Duke University Press.

Menke, Jack, and Iwan Sno. 2016. "Ras en etniciteit in volkstellingen van Suriname." In: *Mozaïek van het Surinaamse volk: Volkstellingen in demografisch, economisch en sociaal perspectief*, edited by Jack Menke, 76–95. Paramaribo: Institute for Graduate Studies and Research.

Merton, Robert King. 1976. *Sociological Ambivalence and Other Essays*. New York: Simon and Schuster.

Migge, Bettina. 2018. "Research on Maroon Languages and Language Practices among Matawai and Kwinti Maroons." In *Maroon Cosmopolitics: Personhood, Creativity and Incorporation*, edited by Olívia Maria Gomes da Cunha, 83–116. Leiden, the Netherlands: Brill.

Mintz, Sidney W., and Richard Price. 1992. *The Birth of African-American Culture*. Boston: Beacon Press.

Monson, Ingrid. 1999. "Riffs, Repetition, and Theories of Globalization." *Ethnomusicology* 43 (1): 31–65.

———. 2010. *Freedom Sounds: Civil Rights Call out to Jazz and Africa*. New York: Oxford University Press.

Mosis, André. 2012. "Apinti, de sprekende drum van de Marrons," In "Kifoko: de kleuren, de stappen, de bewegingen." Accessed 27 February 2019. www.kingbotho.com.

Mulhern, Francis. 2000. *Culture/Metaculture*. London: Routledge.

Nahachewsky, Andriy. 2001. "Once Again: On the Concept of 'Second Existence Folk Dance.'" *Yearbook for Traditional Music* 33:17–28.

Neslo, Alida. 2011. "Alakondre: A Journey to the Invisible." In *Community Art: The Politics of Trespassing*, edited by Paul De Bruyne and Pascal Gielen, 109–21. Amsterdam: Antennae.

Ockhorst, Annika. 2014. "Multicultural Encounters on Stage: The Use of Javanese Cultural Elements by the Surinamese Doe-Theatre Company." In *Verhandelingen van het Koninklijk Instituut voor Taal-, Land en Volkenkunde* edited by Rosemarijn Hoefte, 297–318. Leiden, the Netherlands: Royal Netherlands Institute of Southeast Asian and Caribbean Studies.

Oostindie, Gert J. 1996. "Ethnicity, Nationalism, and the Exodus: The Dutch Caribbean Predicament." In *Ethnicity in the Caribbean: Essays in Honor of Harry Hoetink*, edited by Gert Oostindie, 2016–31. Leiden, the Netherlands: Royal Netherlands Institute of Southeast Asian and Caribbean Studies.

Paine, Robert. 1971. "Theory of Patronage and Brokerage." In *Patrons and Brokers in the East Arctic*, edited by Robert Paine, 8–21. St. Johns, NL: Institute of Social and Economic Research Press, Memorial University.

Pakosie, André R. M. 1996. "Maroon leadership and the Surinamese State (1760–1990)." *Journal of Legal Pluralism and Unofficial Law* 28 (37–38): 263–77.

———. 1999. "Onstaan en ontwikkeling van de aleke: De popmuziek van de Marronstam der Ndyuka." *Siboga* 9 (1): 2–24.

———. 2002. "The Akan Heritage in Maroon Culture in Suriname." In *Merchants, Missionaries and Migrants: 300 Years of Dutch-Ghanaian Relations*, edited by W.M.J. van Kessel, 121–31. Amsterdam: Koninklijk Instituut voor de Tropen Publishers.

Price, Richard. 1983. *First-Time: The Historical Vision of an Afro-American People*. Baltimore: Johns Hopkins University Press.

———. 1992. "Maroons: Rebel Slaves in the Americas." http://www.folklife.si.edu/resources/maroon/educational_guide/23.htm.

———. 1995. "Executing Ethnicity: The Killings in Suriname." *Cultural Anthropology* 10 (4): 437–71.

———, ed. 1996. *Maroon Societies: Rebel Slave Communities in the Americas*. 3rd ed. Baltimore: Johns Hopkins University Press.

———. 2008. *Travels with Tooy: History, Memory, and the African American Imagination*. Chicago: University of Chicago Press.

———. 2011. *Rainforest Warriors: Human Rights on Trial*. Philadelphia: University of Pennsylvania Press.

———. 2018. "Maroons in Guyane: Getting the Numbers Right." *New West Indian Guide* 92 (3–4): 275–83.

Price, Richard, and Sally Price. 1983. *To Slay the Hydra: Dutch Colonial Perspectives on the Saramaka Wars*. Ann Arbor, MI: Karoma.

———. 1994a. *Equatoria*. New York. Routledge.

———. 1994b. *On the Mall: Presenting Maroon Tradition-Bearers at the 1992 FAF*. Vol. 4. Bloomington: Indiana University Press.

———. 2003. *The Root of Roots: Or, How Afro-American Anthropology Got Its Start*. Chicago: Prickly Paradigm Press.

Price, Sally. 1989. *Primitive Art in Civilized Places*. Chicago: University of Chicago Press.

———. 1993. *Co-Wives and Calabashes*. 2nd ed. Ann Arbor: University of Michigan Press.

————. 2003. "Always Something New: Changing Fashions in a 'Traditional Culture.'" In *Crafting Gender: Women and Folk Art in Latin America and the Caribbean*, edited by Eli Bartra, 17–34. Durham, NC: Duke University Press.

Price, Sally, and Richard Price. 1999. *Maroon Arts: Cultural Vitality in the African Diaspora*. Boston: Beacon Press.

Putcha, Rumya. 2018. "Yoga and The Maintenance of White Womanhood." Blog Post. *Namaste Nation* (blog). Accessed 31 May 2019. http://rumyaputcha.com/115–2/.

Rahaim, Matthew. 2012. *Musicking Bodies: Gesture and Voice in Hindustani Music*. Middletown, CT: Wesleyan University Press.

Roberts, Neil. 2015. *Freedom as Marronage*. Chicago: University of Chicago Press.

Roginsky, Dina. 2007. "Folklore, Folklorism, and Synchronization—Preserved-Created Folklore in Israel." *Journal of Folklore Research* 2 (1): 41–66.

Rothschild, Joseph. 1981. *Ethnopolitics: A Conceptual Framework*. New York: Columbia University Press.

Russonello, Giovanni. 2015. "Greg Tate on Burnt Sugar, Afrofuturism and Black Music's 'Maroon Spaces.'" April 30. https://www.capitalbop.com/greg-tate-on-burnt-sugar-afrofuturism-and-the-maroon-spaces-that-music-allows/.

Sarkissian, Margaret. 1998. "Tradition, Tourism, and the Cultural Show: Malaysia's Diversity on Display." *Journal of Musicological Research* 17 (2): 87–112.

Savigliano, Marta E. 1995. *Tango and the Political Economy of Passion*. Boulder, CO: Westview Press.

Schauert, Paul. 2006–7. "Performing National Archive: Power and Preservation in the Ghana Dance Ensemble." *Transactions of the Historical Society of Ghana*, n.s., no. 10: 171–81.

————. 2015. *Staging Ghana: Artistry and Nationalism in State Dance Ensembles*. Bloomington: Indiana University Press.

Schneer, Jonathan. 2001. *London 1900: The Imperial Metropolis*. New Haven, CT: Yale University Press.

Schramm, Katharina. 2000. "The Politics of Dance: Changing Representations of the Nation in Ghana." *Africa Spectrum* 35 (3): 339–58.

Scott, James C. 1990. *Domination and the Arts of Resistance: Hidden Transcripts*. New Haven, CT: Yale University Press.

Sharp, Daniel B. 2014. *Between Nostalgia and Apocalypse: Popular Music and the Staging of Brazil*. Middletown, CT: Wesleyan University Press.

Shay, Anthony. 1999. "Parallel Traditions: State Folk Dance Ensembles and Folk Dance in 'the Field.'" *Dance Research Journal* 31 (1): 29–56.

————. 2002. *Choreographic Politics: State Folk Dance Companies, Representation and Power*. Middletown, CT: Wesleyan University Press.

Shelemay, Kay Kaufman. 2011. "Musical Communities: Rethinking the Collective in Music." *Journal of the American Musicological Society* 64 (2): 349–90.

——— . 2015. *Soundscapes: Exploring Music in a Changing World*. New York: W. W. Norton.

Shiner, Larry. 1994. "'Primitive Fakes,' 'Tourist Art,' and the Ideology of Authenticity." *Journal of Aesthetics and Art Criticism* 52 (2): 225–34.

Smidchens, Guntis. 1999. "Folklorism Revisited." *Journal of Folklore Research* 36 (1): 51–70.

Smith, Anthony D. 2010. *Nationalism*. 2nd ed. Cambridge: Polity.

Sno, Iwan, and Edith J. Ritfeld. 2016. "Demografie: natuurlijke groei van de bevolking." In *Mozaïek van het Surinaamse volk: Volkstellingen in demografisch, economisch en sociaal perspectief*, edited by Jack Menke, 50–69. Paramaribo: Institute for Graduate Studies and Research.

Spivak, Gayatri Chakravorty. 1990. *The Postcolonial Critic: Interviews, Strategies, Dialogues*. Edited by Sarah Harasym. New York: Routledge.

Srinivasan, Priya. 2012. *Sweating Saris: Indian Dance as Transnational Labor*. Philadelphia: Temple University Press.

Stedman, John Gabriel, 1796. *Narrative, of a Five-years' Expedition, Against the Revolted Negroes of Surinam . . . from the year 1772, to 1777*. London: Printed for J. Johnson and J. Edwards.

——— . 1992. *Stedman's Surinam: Life in an Eighteenth-Century Slave Society: An Abridged, Modernized Edition of "Narrative of a Five Years Expedition against the Revolted Negroes of Surinam" by John Gabriel Stedman*. Edited by Richard Price and Sally Price. Baltimore: Johns Hopkins University Press.

Steiner, Christopher. 1994. *African Art in Transit*. Cambridge: Cambridge University Press.Strange, Stuart Earle. 2016. "Suspected Gods: Spirit Possession, Performance, and Social Relations in Multi-Ethnic Suriname." PhD diss., University of Michigan.

Thoden van Velzen, H.U.E. 1990. "The Maroon Insurgency: Anthropological Reflections on the Civil War in Suriname." In *Resistance and Rebellion in Suriname: Old and New*, edited by Gary Brana-Shute, 150–88. Williamsburg, VA: College of William and Mary Press.

Thoden van Velzen, H. U. E., and W. van Wetering. 2004. *In the Shadow of the Oracle: Religion as Politics in a Suriname Maroon Society*. Long Grove, IL: Waveland.

Thompson, Robert Farris. 1973. "An Aesthetic of the Cool." *African Arts* 7 (1): 41–91.

——— . 1983. *Flash of the Spirit: African and Afro-American Art and Philosophy*. New York: Vintage Books.

Titon, Jeff Todd. 2009. "Music and Sustainability: An Ecological Viewpoint." *World of Music* 51 (9): 119–37.

Tjon Sie Fat, Paul B. 2009. *Chinese New Migrants in Suriname: The Inevitability of Ethnic Performing*. Amsterdam: Amsterdam University Press.

Turino, Thomas. 1993. *Moving Away from Silence: Music of the Peruvian Altiplano and the Experience of Urban Migration*. Chicago: University of Chicago Press.

——— . 2000. *Nationalists, Cosmopolitans, and Popular Music in Zimbabwe*. Chicago: University of Chicago Press.

————. 2008. *Music as Social Life: The Politics of Participation*. Chicago: University of Chicago Press.

Van der Elst, Dirk. 2004. Introduction to H. U. E. Thoden van Velzen and W. van Wetering, 1–17. *In the Shadow of the Oracle: Religion as Politics in a Suriname Maroon Society*. Long Grove, IL: Waveland.

Van Stipriaan, Alex. 2009. "Marrons in de stad: Migratie in de Twintigste Eeuw." In *Kunst van overleven: Marronncultuur uit Suriname*, edited by Andrew Alexander van Stipriaan and Thomas Polimé, 146–55. Amsterdam: Koninklijk Instituut voor de Tropen Publishers.

Walsh, John, and Robert Gannon. 1967. *Time Is Short and the Water Rises: Operation Gwamba: The Story of the Rescue of 10,000 Animals from Certain Death in a South American Rainforest*. London: Nelson.

Waterman, Christopher A. 1990. "'Our Tradition Is a Very Modern Tradition': Popular Music and the Construction of Pan-Yoruba Identity." *Ethnomusicology* 34 (3): 367–79.

Weber, Max. 1947. *The Theory of Social and Economic Organization*. Translated by A. M. Henderson and Talcott Parsons, and edited with an introduction by Talcott Parsons. New York: Free Press.

Wekker, Gloria. 2006. *The Politics of Passion: Women's Sexual Culture in the Afro-Surinamese Diaspora*. New York: Columbia University Press.

Wetalk, Marcel. 1990. *Surinaamse muziek in Nederland en Suriname*. Utrecht, the Netherlands: Uitgeverij Kosmos.

White, Bob. 2000. "Soukous or Sell-out? Congolese Popular Dance Music as Cultural Commodity." In *Commodities and Globalization: Anthropological Perspectives*, edited by M. Priscilla Stone, Angelique Hauguerd, and Peter Little, 33–58. Lanham, MD: Rowman and Littlefield.

Wittgenstein, Ludwig. 2009. *Philosophical Investigations*. Hoboken, NJ: John Wiley and Sons. ProQuest Ebook Central.

INDEX

commoditization of traditional performance, 59–60, 65

communal performance, 56–57, 68–69

communities: engagement in *mato neti*, 91; interpretive, 57, 69–71, 94, 95; and performance, 56–60, 65; and rehearsal spaces, 94–95; as work site, 28–29

compensation for performance, 60, 90, 229n30

Connell, Robert, 47

cosmopolitanism, 16, 182, 192

cosmopolitan performance aesthetics, 15, 54, 64, 190, 233n1

Creole, 13, 151–53, 176, 243n18

Creole cultural organization (NAKS), 81, 86, 237n11

cultural groups: Alakondre Dron, 142–48, 153; ambivalence, 38–40; Avondvierdaagse, 166–71, 172, 177–78; awasa, 101, 125; the body, 25–28; changing times, 95–98; community, 28–30; and cultural difference, 182–87; differentiation, 70–71; ethnic performativity, 167–71; fieldwork, 31–33; folkloric performance, 15–18; goals, 89–93; interpretive communities, 69–71; names, 71–80; participation, 203–10; performance events, 21–25; rehearsal space, 80–89; relationships among, 68–69; song structure, 116; in Suriname, 18–21; traditional practice, 55–66; and urban Maroons, 54–55; work sites, 25–30. *See also* Fiamba; Kifoko; Maroons; Saisa

culture/cultural: affiliation, 176–79, 244n8; ambivalence, 38–40; belonging, 27–30; brokers, 15–16, 32; continuity, 2, 10, 61, 72; Creole, 243n18; culture-representational performances, 2–4, 11, 25; difference, 180–81, 182–87, 206–7; folkloric performance, 55–66; identity, 22; imagery, 200–201; intimacy, 194–95, 197; performance, 68–71, 89–93, 94, 167–71, 177, 244n8; practice, Kifoko's approach, 71–73; practice, Saisa's approach, 76–80; preservation, 27–30, 72–73; pride, 182–83; representation, 17, 167–71; shows, 58, 61, 65, 68, 71, 207–8;

tourism, 16–18, 21, 197; uniqueness, 181–82, 199–200, 201–2; work, 3, 36–37, 55, 62, 69. *See also* Maroons

Dabenta, Irma, 54, 120

dance, awasa, 25–27, 122–23

dancing body, 25–28, 69, 129, 195

Da Tipa Tojo, 85

de Bruijne, G. A., 42

Deel, Mano, 53, 175–78

Denku, 18–19

Dew, Edward, 45, 138–39, 241n2, 242n5

Dewinie, Saiwinie "Maria," 1–3, 24, 25–26, 29–30, 97, 120, 205

dictatorial period, 45–46

difference, 180–81, 182–87, 206–7

domination, 186–87

drumming, 102–13; in Alakondre Dron, 146–48; aleke, 22; apinti doon, 103; call and response, 114–15, 128, 132, 134–35; First-Time, 9; gaan doon, 102–3, *107,* 107–13, *115,* 134; and the performing body, 26; pikin doon, 102–7, *105, 106,* 132; postures, *104*; and rehearsal space, 83–84; spiritual practice, 234n17; tun, 102–4, 132, 134–35

Ducoudray, Michel, 63–64

Dudley, Shannon, 162

Emanuels, Saloman, 46

emotional or affective ambivalence, 39

ethnicity: affiliation, 82, 139–40, 160, 167–71; Alakondre Dron, 142–45; clientelism, 159–60; diversity in Suriname, 11–13; identity/identification, 139–42, 156, 169, 182–84; legibility, 175, 177; multiethnic discourse, 137–42, 242n5; in Paramaribo, 14–15; performativity, 138–39, 155–56, 167–71, 172, 175; political divisions, 46–48, 241n2; representation, 153, 162–63, 244n5; social tensions, 51–54

"The Execution of Breaking on the Rack" (Blake), 5

exercise, awasa's basic posture, 123

integration, 140–41

intellectual or cognitive ambivalence, 39

Inter-American Court of Human Rights, 47–48

intercultural relations, 140–42, 154–56

international performance, 89–91

interpretive communities, 57, 69–71, 94, 95

interpretive moves, 199

Irma Dabenta Performing Informally in a Hotel Room in Georgetown, Guyana, 120

"*Jang joe njang*" ("*Eat Your Food*"), 116–18; transcription, *117–18*

Johnson, Walter, 17, 38, 39

Jungle Commando, 45–46

Kaluli performance, 60–62

Kambel, Ellen-Rose, 45, 47–48

kaskawi music, 75

kawai ankle rattles, 127, *127*, 236n24

Kifoko: Alakondre Dron, 89, 143, 153; aleke, 22; audio track, 120; Carifesta, 235n19; communities, 28; comparative tables, 211–14; as cultural group, 3–4; cultural performance, 68–69; cultural preservation, 29–30; differentiation, 70–71; founding, 84–85; gaansamapee, 24; goals, 89–91; membership, 87–88, 97, 244n6; names, 71–73, 94; overview, 18–21; rehearsals, 67–68; singing practice, 240n37; songs, 115; space for rehearsals, 81, 84–87, 96–97; specialized knowledge, 88–89; spiritual practice, 243n13; and Tojo's bigi yali, 204–6; tuka, 24; waka kon, waka gwe, 125

Kifoko Garden, 85

Klas, Jozef, *143*

Kondo, Dorinne, 173–74

"*Kon go diingi labaa*," 120

Koninkrijkspelen, 164

koor singers, 113–21, 132, 134, 239n23, 239n25, 239n28

koti, 241n44

Kourou, French Guiana, 89

kumanti (war spirits), in Saisa repertoire, 78

kwakwa/kwakwabangi, 102, *102*, 113, 237n6

Kwinti Maroons, 4–6

Lachmon, Jaggernath, 140–42, 241n1, 242n7

Lante, Eddy, 9, 18, 24, 72, 90, 97, 234n11, 234n17

Lazo, George, 52, 78

learning new moves, 195–99

Locke, David, 135, 238n17

loketo, 22–23, 74, 193, 234n9

loli technique, 239n30

Mama Sranan (Klas), *143*

mamio quilt trope, 151–53, *152*, *157*, 158, 243n18

mannengeefutu (man foot), 125–26, *126*, 126–27, 129–30, 134–35, 240n34

Maranjaw, 63

Maroon Arts (Price), 183

Maroons: about, 4–11; Aluku (Boni), 4–6; ambivalence, 38–40; awasa, 100–101, 129; call and response, 118–20, 239n28; choreographies, 189–99, 245n3; communities, 28–30; cultural affiliations, 175–78; cultural difference, 182–87; culture-representational performance, 2–4; diaspora, 55; drums, 103; ethnic performativity, 171; fashion, 244n7; and Fiamba, 172, 234n9; fieldwork, 30–33; folkloric performance, 15–18, 55–65; gii futu, 128; interpretive communities, 67–71; interpretive work, 27–28; and Kifoko, 76, 88, 97, 143; Kwinti, 4–6; Matawai, 4–6; Ndyuka (Okanisi), 4–6, 76, 79, 100, 232n16; Pamaka, 4–6; and Paramaribo, 2, 14–15, 49–55, 232nn13–14; participation, 208–10; performance culture, 205–6; performance events, 21–25, 199–201; performance goals, 89–93; political affiliations, 168; populations, 8, *8*, 142, 228n23; Rastafarians, 232n17; religious structure, 227n13; Saamaka, 4–6, 48–49, 226n8; and Santigron, 76–80; spaces, 81–83, 85; spiritual practice, 9–10, 234n17;

"Uman Daguwe," 205
umanpikinfutu (woman child foot), *126,*
126–27, 129–30, 134, 240n34
"U n'á gaanwan" (Sikanar), 73–74
urban Maroons, 3, 14, 39, 48–55, 58–59, 73, 76,
81, 186–87

van Stipriaan, Alex, 51
Vierdaagse (four-days walks), 163–64
voluntary or conative ambivalence, 39

waka kon, waka gwe, 124, 125–26, *126,* 133, 187,
240n38
Wandelmars. *See* Avondvierdaagse
Waterberg, Dansi, 82–84, 196–97
Weber, Max, 70
weirdness, 180–88, 195, 201
Wenoeza, 20–21, 95–96, 236n23, 242n9

women: Afro-Surinamese, 227n17; and awasa,
100–101; call-and-response framework,
115; drumming, 103, 147, 237n11; in Fiamba,
27, 74, 96, 236n23; folkloric performance,
78; gendered foot positions, 126; gendered
movement, 129–30; gendered names,
237n10; in Kifoko, 87, 97; Maroons, 227n17
Wondel, Louise, 22–23, 74–76, 82–84, 237n11,
245n3
wooden bench *(kwakwa/kwakwabangi),* 102,
102, 113, 237n6
work, 1–3; function of, 15; "working out," 3, 15
work sites, 25–30
World Kinderfestival, 74–75

youth affiliation, in Fiamba, 20, 74–76, 96

Zus en Zo (restaurant), 206–8

MUSIC / CULTURE

A series from Wesleyan University Press
Edited by Deborah Wong, Sherrie Tucker, and Jeremy Wallach
Originating editors: George Lipsitz, Susan McClary, and Robert Walser

Marié Abe
*Resonances of Chindon-ya:
Sounding Space and Sociality in
Contemporary Japan*

Frances Aparicio
*Listening to Salsa: Gender, Latin Popular
Music, and Puerto Rican Cultures*

Paul Austerlitz
*Jazz Consciousness: Music, Race,
and Humanity*

Harris M. Berger
*Metal, Rock, and Jazz: Perception and the
Phenomenology of Musical Experience*

Harris M. Berger
*Stance: Ideas about Emotion, Style,
and Meaning for the Study
of Expressive Culture*

Harris M. Berger and
Giovanna P. Del Negro
*Identity and Everyday Life: Essays
in the Study of Folklore, Music,
and Popular Culture*

Franya J. Berkman
*Monument Eternal: The Music
of Alice Coltrane*

Dick Blau, Angeliki Vellou Keil,
and Charles Keil
*Bright Balkan Morning: Romani Lives and
the Power of Music in Greek Macedonia*

Susan Boynton and Roe-Min Kok, editors
*Musical Childhoods and the
Cultures of Youth*

James Buhler, Caryl Flinn,
and David Neumeyer, editors
Music and Cinema

Patrick Burkart
Music and Cyberliberties

Thomas Burkhalter, Kay Dickinson,
and Benjamin J. Harbert, editors
*The Arab Avant-Garde: Music,
Politics, Modernity*

Tomie Hahn
*Sensational Knowledge: Embodying
Culture through Japanese Dance*

Edward Herbst
*Voices in Bali: Energies and Perceptions
in Vocal Music and Dance Theater*

Deborah Kapchan
*Traveling Spirit Masters:
Moroccan Gnawa Trance and Music
in the Global Marketplace*

Deborah Kapchan, editor
Theorizing Sound Writing

Max Katz
*Lineage of Loss: Counternarratives
of North Indian Music*

Raymond Knapp
*Symphonic Metamorphoses:
Subjectivity and Alienation in Mahler's
Re-Cycled Songs*

Victoria Lindsay Levine and
Dylan Robinson, editors
*Music and Modernity among
First Peoples of North America*

Laura Lohman
*Umm Kulthūm: Artistic Agency and the
Shaping of an Arab Legend, 1967–2007*

Preston Love
*A Thousand Honey Creeks Later:
My Life in Music from Basie to Motown—
and Beyond*

René T. A. Lysloff and
Leslie C. Gay Jr., editors
Music and Technoculture

Ian MacMillen
*Playing It Dangerously: Tambura Bands,
Race, and Affective Block in Croatia
and Its Intimates*

Allan Marett
*Songs, Dreamings, and Ghosts:
The Wangga of North Australia*

Ian Maxwell
*Phat Beats, Dope Rhymes:
Hip Hop Down Under Comin' Upper*

Kristin A. McGee
*Some Liked It Hot: Jazz Women in Film
and Television, 1928–1959*

Tracy McMullen
*Haunthenticity: Musical Replay
and the Fear of the Real*

Rebecca S. Miller
*Carriacou String Band Serenade:
Performing Identity in the
Eastern Caribbean*

Tony Mitchell, editor
*Global Noise: Rap and Hip-Hop
Outside the USA*

Christopher Moore and
Philip Purvis, editors
Music and Camp

Rachel Mundy
*Animal Musicalities: Birds, Beasts,
and Evolutionary Listening*

Keith Negus
Popular Music in Theory: An Introduction

Johnny Otis
*Upside Your Head: Rhythm and Blues
on Central Avenue*

Kip Pegley
*Coming to You Wherever You Are:
MuchMusic, MTV, and Youth Identities*

Jonathan Pieslak
*Radicalism and Music: An Introduction
to the Music Cultures of al-Qa'ida, Racist
Skinheads, Christian-Affiliated Radicals,
and Eco-Animal Rights Militants*

Lorraine Plourde
*Tokyo Listening: Sound and Sense
in a Contemporary City*

Matthew Rahaim
*Musicking Bodies: Gesture and
Voice in Hindustani Music*

John Richardson
*Singing Archaeology:
Philip Glass's Akhnaten*

Tricia Rose
*Black Noise: Rap Music and Black Culture
in Contemporary America*

David Rothenberg and
Marta Ulvaeus, editors

*The Book of Music and Nature:
An Anthology of Sounds, Words, Thoughts*

Nichole Rustin-Paschal
*The Kind of Man I Am: Jazzmasculinity
and the World of Charles Mingus Jr.*

Marta Elena Savigliano
*Angora Matta: Fatal Acts of
North-South Translation*

Joseph G. Schloss
*Making Beats: The Art of
Sample-Based Hip-Hop*

Barry Shank
*Dissonant Identities: The Rock 'n'
Roll Scene in Austin, Texas*

Jonathan Holt Shannon
*Among the Jasmine Trees: Music and
Modernity in Contemporary Syria*

Daniel B. Sharp
*Between Nostalgia and Apocalypse:
Popular Music and the Staging of Brazil*

Helena Simonett
*Banda: Mexican Musical Life
across Borders*

Mark Slobin
*Subcultural Sounds: Micromusics
of the West*

Mark Slobin, editor
*Global Soundtracks: Worlds
of Film Music*

ABOUT THE AUTHOR

Corinna Campbell is an associate professor of music at Williams College. She received her PhD from Harvard University in 2012. Her research has been funded by a number of institutions, among them the Fulbright Program, Harvard University's David Rockefeller Center for Latin American Studies, and the Andrew W. Mellon Foundation.